ROUTLEDGE LIBRARY EDITIONS:
ADULT EDUCATION

Volume 15

ADULT EDUCATION AND
CULTURAL DEVELOPMENT

T0394106

ADULT EDUCATION AND CULTURAL DEVELOPMENT

DAVID JONES

Routledge
Taylor & Francis Group

LONDON AND NEW YORK

First published in 1988 by Routledge

This edition first published in 2019
by Routledge
2 Park Square, Milton Park, Abingdon, Oxon OX14 4RN

and by Routledge
52 Vanderbilt Avenue, New York, NY 10017

Routledge is an imprint of the Taylor & Francis Group, an informa business

British Library Cataloguing in Publication Data
A catalogue record for this book is available from the British Library

ISBN: 978-1-138-32224-0 (Set)
ISBN: 978-0-429-43000-8 (Set) (ebk)
ISBN: 978-1-138-36831-6 (Volume 15) (hbk)
ISBN: 978-1-138-36836-1 (Volume 15) (pbk)
ISBN: 978-0-429-42933-0 (Volume 15) (ebk)

Publisher's Note
The publisher has gone to great lengths to ensure the quality of this reprint but points out that some imperfections in the original copies may be apparent.

Disclaimer
The publisher has made every effort to trace copyright holders and would welcome correspondence from those they have been unable to trace.

ADULT EDUCATION AND CULTURAL DEVELOPMENT

DAVID JONES

ROUTLEDGE
London and New York

First published in 1988 by
Routledge
11 New Fetter Lane, London EC4P 4EE
29 West 35th Street, New York NY 10001

Printed and bound in Great Britain by
Biddles Ltd, Guildford and King's Lynn

British Library Cataloguing in Publication Data
Jones, David
    Adult education and cultural development.
    — (International perspectives on adult
and continuing education).
    1. Adult education. Curriculum subjects.
Arts
I. Title II. Series
700'.7'15
    ISBN 0-415-00553-1

Library of Congress Cataloging-in-Publication Data
Jones, David, 1944 Sept. 2-
    Adult education and cultural development / David Jones.
       p.   cm. — (International perspectives on adult and
continuing education)
      Bibliography: p.
      Includes index.
      ISBN 0-415-00553-1
  1. Adult education. 2. Affective education. 3. Arts. I. Title.
II. Series: International perspectives on adult and continuing
education (Routledge (Firm))
LC5219.J65   1988
374—dc19   88-26337

    ISBN 0-415-00553-1

CONTENTS

For Matthew

PREFACE

In recent years much has been written about adult education which fails to take into account those learning activities which are not cognitive in nature. It is as though writers are not aware that a great deal of what goes on in adult education is not concerned with the acquisition and application of knowledge but rather with the development of skills and abilities and with the education of the senses. The world of the feelings and of emotions appears to be similarly excluded from the educational world which these writers inhabit.

I offer this book as an attempt to redress the balance, to speak out for the arts in adult education and to provide a theoretical framework within which those involved in the arts in adult education can work. The arts are more than leisure time recreational activities; they are the measure of civilisation. The creative spirit makes a mark in the history books which becomes the manifestation of that culture which engendered it. The great civilisations of the world are remembered as much by their artefacts as by their achievements in politics or commerce. The smallest community is remembered by its songs and folk tales rather than by its industry.

This book is written in the belief that, should we choose to, we can all work creatively and in so doing make our contribution to the way in which our culture might be remembered. We can also learn to respect and enjoy the arts of our own culture, whether they be high art or folk art, the arts of past civilisations as well as the arts of cultures other than our own. Students of the symphony and students of dressmaking, students of Shakespeare and students of woodwork, students of ballet and students of ballroom dancing can all make their contribution. Adult educators are in a position to help adult students to enrich both their own lives and the culture in which they live and work. It is hoped that this book will assist and encourage them to do so.

David J. Jones
Tobermory

ACKNOWLEDGEMENTS

I wish to thank my colleagues at the University of Nottingham for making it possible for me to allocate time to the writing of this book and record my debt to Matthew Doyle for checking my manuscript and to Barbara Jones and Christine Wright for checking the proofs. My thanks also go to the series editor, Peter Jarvis, for his encouragement and help. Most of all, though, my thanks go to my students who, over the years, have forced me to question and rethink my approach to the teaching of art. It is from the seeds of their questioning and their honest enquiry that this book has grown.

Chapter One

INTRODUCTION

This book is about the arts in adult education. It is intended for those involved in adult education as either teachers, policy makers or theorists. It is not aimed at regular adult education students, though some of them may find it interesting and useful, but rather at the student of adult education. It aims to offer a means whereby practitioners can locate their work in relation to a theory of cultural development. It is argued that whenever people become involved in the arts in the context of adult education they can either preserve the dominant cultural value system or they can develop it. Development can take place when the participants in the educational activity are involved in creative or appreciative work. The preservation of cultural values can take place in a creative class just as much as in an appreciation class.

It is not suggested that one form of activity is of greater value than the other, indeed, it is argued that it is as important to engage with the arts of the past and the value systems they embody as it is to develop new art forms and new value systems. It is suggested, however, that current practice in developed countries is biased towards the preservation of a largely European cultural tradition and there may be a case for adult educators to redress this balance by becoming more involved in cultural development.

Before this can be done, however, it is necessary to have a means of identifying whether or not a given arts activity in adult education is concerned with cultural conservation or cultural development. In order to do this the book sets the arts in adult education in a wider cultural context and provides a means to analyse the value and

1

conceptual systems which underpin that culture. It also offers a means whereby adult educators can identify the way in which their learning activity is oriented to the cultural context in which they are working; a means of deciding whether a particular approach to the arts in adult education preserves or develops the cultural tradition.

In writing this book it is my intention to relate theory to practice and I attempt, throughout, to make clear the practical implications of the theories under discussion. I try to avoid jargon but this is not always possible. It is especially difficult where the works of other writers are being discussed. However, it is hoped that I can avoid some of the worst excesses of language. Above all, I would like the book to be accessible to the reader who has a background in the arts or crafts but who does not have a specialist knowledge of those aspects of psychology, sociology and philosophy to which I refer.

The theoretical framework which informs much of the writing in the following chapters derives from critical theory, that philosophical tradition which had its origins in the work of the Frankfurt School. Horkheimer (1972 and 1974), Adorno (1941, 1967 and 1972), and Marcuse (1956 and 1964) were associated with the Institute of Social Research founded in 1923 at the University of Frankfurt. It was here that the ideas which we now refer to as critical theory were first developed. These theories have been further developed by Habermas (1970 and 1974) and, more recently and in the field of education, Gibson (1986). This last writer explains the essence of critical theory like this:

> Critical theory argues that in human affairs all "facts" are socially constructed, humanly determined and interpreted, and hence subject to change through human means.
>
> (Gibson 1986:4)

Gibson suggests that critical theory can be both enlightening and emancipatory by enabling individuals to become aware of the conflicting interests which shape their understanding and their lives. He suggests that critical theory sees 'art as an inherently emancipatory activity, but one which is frequently used to serve other interests' (1986:12). He goes on:

> Critical theory, therefore, seeks to locate artistic work

2

in its social context, to consider author and audience in
the light of history, to seek the social shaping of
criteria for aesthetic evaluation and to identify the
social purposes and interests served ...
... Not only are the arts important for the emancipatory
images they provide for society, but their potential for
individual liberation is great.

(Gibson 1986:12-13)

This view coincides with my own intention in writing this
book. All my professional life as an adult educator I have
endeavoured to make the arts more widely accessible and
my writing here draws, to a large extent, on that
professional experience. My own background is in the visual
arts and my first qualifications in higher education were in
the fields of pottery and painting. The experience from
which I draw my illustrations and examples will reflect this
initial education and there may be a bias towards the visual.
I will try, however, to refer to all art forms and, indeed, to
allow for the possibility of extending our concept of the arts
to include activities which we currently do not consider to
be arts. A critical approach will allow an examination of
how a concept of the arts is socially determined.

In a similar way, critical theory allows a much broader
view of education and learning than is often the case in
writing on the subject. In reviewing the work of Bourdieu
(1974, 1977a and 1977b) Gibson makes the following point:

Learning, for Bourdieu, thus becomes far more than
merely a cognitive activity. As the process and
outcome of cultural activity it is deeply embedded in
all aspects of an individual's being; mind, feeling, body.

(Gibson 1986:57)

Such a broad view of the nature of learning permits a
discussion of those activities in the arts which are not
cognitive but concerned with creative process and aesthetic
response. Education is not seen as being solely about the
acquisition of knowledge. It is seen, rather, as involving a
realisation of a far broader conception of human potential.
Engaging with the arts involves a range of skills and abilities
which do not fit neatly into a narrow cognitive view of
educational activity.

I do, though, acknowledge a debt to what Sanford
(1987:xi) refers to as the new 'discipline of cognitive science

3

which is an interdisciplinary subject using insights from linguistics, philosophy, computing science and engineering, as well as from psychology'. In writing about the arts, particularly the non-literary arts, one becomes aware of the inadequacies of language and the way in which our thoughts on a given topic can become trapped in an inappropriate conceptual framework.

> But our main point is that the metaphors people use set the tracks along which thoughts and beliefs will tend to run. Language restricts thoughts just as thoughts manifest in language.
>
> (Sanford 1987:59)

I am only too aware that the analysis which I offer occasionally retreats into language which is rooted in much earlier conceptual systems. The references to Jungian psychology in the section on appreciation are an example. They seem curiously out of date in the context of late 20th century Britain. My guiding principle has been a pragmatic one. If a particular system of metaphors offers an explanation for events or experiences which seems to me, the writer, to· be appropriate, then I have valued it as worthy of consideration. All that I can offer is what I feel is the best explanation to date of the topics under discussion.

The social and political context within which these discussions take place is one where the value of the arts in society is increasingly being questioned. Debates about the content of school curricula are taking an increasingly utilitarian turn. Subjects are evaluated according to their usefulness in what is perceived as a predominantly scientific age. It appears that the practices and the values of the arts are not currently congruent with the direction in which society is thought to be moving. There are many explanations for this and all of them are complex. Williams offers the following list of what he terms socially based factors:

> ... (i) the crisis, for many artists, of the transition from patronage to the market; (ii) the crisis, in certain arts, of the transition from handwork to machine production; (iii) crises within both patronage and the market, in a period of intense and general social conflict; (iv) the attachment of certain groups to a pre-capitalist and/or pre-democratic social order, in which some arts had

been accorded privilege within a general privilege; (v) the attachment of other groups to the democratisation of the social order, as part of the process of general liberation and human enrichment to which the arts, if they were allowed, could contribute; (vi) a more general opposition, often overlapping and even seeming to unite these diverse political views, to the practices and values of a 'commercial' and 'mechanical' civilisation, from which the practice and values of the arts could be distinguished.

(Williams 1986:72)

It is within this context that the role of adult education in relation to the arts is examined. The values which are both implicit and explicit in educational and in artistic activity are analysed so that those involved in adult education can better understand the contribution they are making to the cultural environment in which they work.

It is hoped that this book makes a contribution to the theory of adult education. The evidence which is brought to bear on the arguments which I develop comes from a wide range of sources; there are references to material from psychology and sociology as well as to the work of educationalists and philosophers, artists and critics. My assumption is that individual readers, in approaching this book, will pick their way to the sections which are of most immediate interest to them. Readers who may not wish to become involved in a philosophical discussion of the nature of culture can turn straight to the section on adult education which is of a more practical nature. In order to facilitate this I offer a brief guide to the structure of the book.

Following this introductory chapter the book begins with a discussion around the concept of culture. According to Gibson (1986:9) 'four major aspects of culture have significance for critical theory'. He identifies these as 'High culture, popular culture, youth culture and culture and nature'. This formulation is too restrictive for my purposes. The critical theory philosophers, who were members of the educated elite of Frankfurt society, related to a concept of high culture which was born of their experience. But this is not the experience of the majority of people. Consequently, I have attempted to develop an alternative formulation and in Chapter 2 offer a typology of culture which may better serve both my purposes and the needs of adult educators.

The central thesis of Chapter 2 is that a culture is better thought of as being quite modest in size. It is difficult to identify the major characteristics of a macro-culture, say European or Western culture, but the concept becomes manageable if we think in terms of micro-cultures, say, the working class youth culture of Birmingham in the 1960s. It is at this level that adult educators can identify the cultural context in which they work and begin to have an impact upon it.

Chapter 3 is concerned with the arts. In an attempt to clarify and understand what is meant by the term 'arts', the different ways in which the term is used are analysed. The ways in which we distinguish the arts from other human activities are discussed in order to demonstrate that our concept of the arts is a social construct. This resort to linguistic analysis serves to show that our concept of the arts is relative; what is included in a concept of the arts depends on the cultural context in which the term is being used. I do not want to propose that the different views of the nature of the arts should be valued in a hierarchical sense, one conception being superior to another. The suggestion is that equal weight is afforded to the many differing views of the arts and that they should be seen in their cultural and historical context. The historical record supports this view of what Lawson refers to as a 'normative relativism' in relation to the arts and to values in the arts. He discusses three sorts of relativism which he terms 'descriptive', 'methodological' and 'normative'. Of the latter he says:

> A normative relativism can then be introduced which claims that because there are examples of people who do make different value judgements, and because there are no criteria for testing their various points of view, then what is thought to be right or good for one person or group is right or good for them, but is not right or good for some other group. Put slightly differently, the actual differences between people on matters relating to values ought to exist.
>
> (Lawson 1982:13)

It is, then, not only the concept of the arts which is shown to be relative but also the value systems which such concepts embrace. Chapter 3 demonstrates that values in the arts are not constant, that even within a given cultural context values can change over time. The chapter identifies three different ways in which the arts are valued and demonstrates that they are all relative. The arts and any notion of what constitutes 'good art' are both shown to be social constructs.

Chapter 4 is perhaps the most important to the educational theme of the book. It is about the different ways in which we engage with the arts as either appreciators, creators, or participants. Each mode of engaging is analysed in order to identify what skills or abilities are involved and what difficulties or constraints might operate to the disadvantage of an adult student. The appropriate mode of attending to the task in hand, be it appreciation, creation or participation, and the appropriate form of consciousness for each mode of engaging with the arts is identified and analysed.

It is proposed that there is a need for high levels of perceptual acuity for involvement in artistic activity and the nature of perception is discussed in relation to the arts. There is a great deal of evidence from psychology to demonstrate that perception is culturally determined and this evidence is reviewed and the implications for the arts in adult education are outlined. The nature of the creative process is analysed so that those involved in adult education can better understand the nature of the educational undertaking.

In order to provide a framework for the discussions in Chapter 4, I acknowledge the concept of the arts which is currently accepted. What is included in this concept of the arts is described in the chapter. Much of what is said, however, will be applicable to other forms of creative activity which we currently do not associate with the arts. It should be remembered that what we conceive of as the arts at the moment may change in the future, but in order to discuss ways of engaging with the arts it is necessary to fix an idea of what we mean by the arts.

Chapter 5 is about access to the arts and principally demonstrates that the majority of opportunities available for an adult to engage with the arts are opportunities to engage as an appreciator. Opportunities for participative involvement are rare and opportunities for creative involvement even rarer. The chapter also touches on those factors which inhibit people from becoming involved in the arts. These are economic, social, psychological and educational. The general picture painted in this chapter is of a vast undertaking with the state, the private sector, the media, education and voluntary agencies all involved in one way or another in providing a means for us to engage with the arts.

The final chapter examines current thinking on the definition and the purposes of adult education before going on to discuss adult learning in relation to the arts. There follows a section on facilitating adult learning where the concept of andragogy is examined in relation to adult education and the arts.

The next section in Chapter 6 deals in detail with teaching and learning and evaluation in the arts in adult education. Conventional ways of identifying educational aims are rejected and an alternative way of thinking about individual development in adult education is offered. This section does not deal with specific teaching or learning plans but rather identifies those factors which teachers and learners should take into consideration when organising their educational work. The section on evaluation suggests ways of identifying criteria for the evaluation of education in the arts and identifies sources of evidence necessary to decide if these criteria have been met.

The final section is about adult education and cultural development. It pulls together the themes which have been running throughout the book and suggests ways in which participants in the arts in adult education can identify whether they are involved in cultural development or whether they are preserving existing cultural values. Both approaches are acknowledged as valid and important, and adult education organisers are encouraged to examine the balance of their programmes in this respect. Participants in adult education have choices about the ways in which they engage with the arts. The suggestion is that they analyse their current activity to identify their current orientation to the arts so that they can make more informed choices in the future.

Throughout the book it is proposed that what we currently consider to be the arts is relative. Educators can, if they wish, extend this concept. Much of what we consider to be the crafts does not really differ from that which we choose to call artistic activity. The intention is to provide opportunities for adults to become involved in appreciation, creation, or participation in a way that either acknowledges the contemporary cultural climate or in a way that extends it.

REFERENCES

Adorno, T.W., 1941, 'On Popular Music', Studies in
    Philosophy and Social Science, 9, New York, Institute of
    Social Research
Adorno, T.W., 1967, Prisms: Cultural Criticism and Society,
    London, Neville Spearman
Adorno, T.W. and Horkheimer, M., 1972, Dialectic of
    Enlightenment, New York, Herder and Herder
Bourdieu, P., 1974, 'The School as a Conservative Force', in
    Eggleston, J., Contemporary Research in the Sociology
    of Education, London, Methuen
Bourdieu, P., 1977a, 'Cultural Reproduction and Social
    Reproduction', in Karabel, J. and Halsey, A.H., Power
    and Ideology in Education, New York, Oxford University
    Press, pp. 487-511
Bourdieu, P., 1977b, Outline of a Theory of Practice,
    Cambridge, Cambridge University Press
Gibson, R., 1986, Critical Theory and Education, London,
    Sydney, etc., Hodder and Stoughton
Habermas, J., 1970, Toward a Rational Society: Student
    Protest, Science and Politics, Boston MA, Beacon Press
Habermas, J., 1974, Theory and Practice, London,
    Heinemann
Horkheimer, M., 1972, Critical Theory: Selected Essays,
    New York, Herder and Herder
Horkheimer, M., 1974, Critique of Instrumental Reason,
    New York, Seabury Press
Lawson, K.H., 1982, Analysis and Ideology: Conceptual
    Essays on the Education of Adults, Nottingham,
    Department of Adult Education, University of
    Nottingham
Marcuse, H., 1956, Eros and Civilisation, London, Routledge
    and Kegan Paul
Marcuse, H., 1964, One-Dimensional Man, Boston MA,
    Beacon Press
Sanford, A.J., 1987, The Mind of Man - Models of Human
    Understanding, Brighton, The Harvester Press
Williams, R., 1986, Culture, London, Fontana

Chapter Two

CULTURE

Commonly, when the term 'culture' is used in conversation, there is a tendency to confuse ideas related to it with those connected with the idea of 'the arts'. Indeed, when we begin to examine the way in which the word is used it becomes clear that it can have several different and distinct meanings. This chapter explores the idea of culture and establishes how the world of the arts relates to it. The next chapter will focus more clearly on the arts but it is first necessary to establish what we mean by the term 'culture' and clarify the way in which it will be used in this publication. There follows an attempt to identify ways in which we define or delimit a culture and ways in which we can categorise the characteristics of a culture.

Raymond Williams (1983:87) has claimed that 'culture' is one of the three most complicated words in the English language. In his book, 'Keywords', he describes the many uses of the term and gives an account of its etymology. For our purposes we will confine the discussion to two particular uses of the term, the anthropological and the artistic. 'Culture' is used, in one sense, to describe the beliefs and values, indeed, the whole way of life of a social group; this is what Williams (1986:111) calls the anthropological use of the term.

When using the term in this sense we talk about working class culture or primitive cultures and in Sociology refer to a sub-culture. Just how big or how small the social group needs to be to comprise an identifiable culture is a matter of debate. One can accept that a quite small teenage gang shares common beliefs, assumptions and behaviour patterns which could fairly be described as a sub-culture. Describing the group in this way assumes that there is another over-arching set of values and behaviours which comprise the dominant culture of which this sub-culture forms only a part. Such a dominant culture can be defined in terms of a geographical area or by a set of values or other attributes which distinguishes one particular group from another group. Thus, in the first instance we can discuss British culture or even European culture and in the second case we can refer to teenage culture or middle class culture. The difficulties arise when one tries to identify the values and behaviours which characterise the dominant culture.

Whether or not there is any value in using the term to refer to large geographical groupings is questionable. It is difficult enough to identify just what values are common to the many different lifestyles and belief systems represented in a 'multi-cultural' society like Britain. Even so, we still hear people referring to British culture as though it were a clearly identifiable entity. To identify a European culture becomes even more complex. Yet there are serious attempts, not only to identify a European culture, but to promote one. In 1984 European Ministers responsible for Cultural Affairs under the auspices of the Council of Europe (1984:xvii) signed a Declaration which set out to 'promote an awareness of the importance of cultural values and a cultural identity common to all Europeans'. It went on to invite member states to 'initiate and support action to develop creativity and the European cultural heritage, ensuring its protection, enhancement and enrichment, and improving access to it'. There is, implicit in this declaration, an assumption that the nature and characteristics of a culture are open to change through normal political processes. We will return to this theme later. For the moment I want to do no more than suggest that there is an extent to which cultures are deliberately fashioned; they do not always simply arise.

No doubt some people believe that they could identify a European tradition in, say, the arts which binds together the countries of Europe. Though even here they would probably have to distinguish between a separate Northern and a Southern European tradition. Whether or not there are values and belief systems shared by all the people of Europe is a very different question. It is unlikely that we could identify beliefs, values or behaviours which were common throughout the continent; common to both an Italian aristocrat and a German mineworker, a Norwegian fisherman and a Spanish dancer. The idea of 'culture' as the way of life of a large group or nation is consequently problematic. Whilst one might understand what is meant, in a general sense, by the term 'European Culture', it becomes impossible to be specific about the nature and characteristics of a culture unless the numbers of people or the geographical area involved is quite small. The value and usefulness of the concept seems to be in inverse proportion to the size of the culture under consideration.

At this point it will be useful to give some attention to the second usage of the term 'culture' to which Williams (1986:11) refers. In this sense it is used to refer to the arts of literature, music, painting and sculpture (Fine Art), theatre, film, dance and, increasingly, photography. The word relates to a range of art forms which comprise what we sometimes think of as high culture. We also use it to describe the person or group which is interested or knowledgeable in these art forms. Thus we speak of a cultured person or a cultured society. Additionally, the word is used to describe the activities and processes engaged in by people involved in the arts; thus we speak of cultural interests or cultural activities.

What is included in any definition of culture as 'the arts' is not constant. Williams (1983:90) refers to only music, literature, painting and sculpture, theatre and film. He does include certain intellectual activities as being associated with the idea of the cultured person but includes only the above art forms. These, together with opera and ballet are what we commonly think of as the high arts which constitute our cultural heritage. Thus, in his report, 'Support for the Arts in England and Wales' Lord Redcliffe-Maud argues,

> By 'cultural' activities I mean all that involve any of the performing, visual, or literary arts and crafts mentioned above. Gardening, walking, riding, fishing and many other forms of sport and recreation are in some sense cultural activities but for my purpose I must concentrate on 'arts'.
>
> (Lord Redcliffe-Maud 1976:14)

Increasingly, however, this narrow definition of culture is being challenged and some writers and cultural activists are tending towards the wider anthropological definition. Thus, Simpson argues,

> Culture itself is no longer fully definable, or rather it has become blurred by a multitude of definitions ... it means the behavioural norms and mores and values and attitudes and rules and taboos which make the framework of life in any given society. In this sense of the word, a refrigerator, or skittles in a pub, or a "No admission" sign, is as cultural as a Parthenon frieze, or an opera, or a performance of Phedre. Culture, then, is something which covers a much broader spectrum of human activity than the leisure pursuits of a cultivated minority.
>
> (Simpson 1976:29)

This is a very wide view of the concept and some of the problems associated with it have been outlined above; its very breadth limits its usefulness. What seems to have happened in the last decade is that writers like Horne (1986), Jor (1976), Kelly (1984) and Martin (1981) have tried to identify a sort of mid-point between the anthropological and the artistic uses of the word. The anthropological concept proves unworkable for those who are primarily interested in the arts. It is too wide and there are problems associated with describing a specific culture. Whilst accepting that there is a sense in which, say, a washing machine or a jet aeroplane could be as much of a cultural product as a painting or a piece of music, there are difficulties in elevating these consumer durables to the status of 'art'. But those concerned with the arts are also dissatisfied with the narrow 'high art' use of the term. A definition which omits, for instance, much popular music and a great deal of television drama is clearly inadequate. The list of art forms is felt to be too short and too exclusive.

Such writers seek to develop a pluralistic definition of the term and have begun to identify and unravel the social and conceptual structures which have contributed to this exclusive list of art forms. At the same time that Simpson (1976:passim) turns to a wide anthropological definition Finn Jor, in his book The Demystification of Culture, attempts to clarify the concept by drawing a distinction between 'elite' and 'popular' culture:

> We have already suggested that, broadly speaking, 'elite culture', as opposed to 'popular culture', is a historically and socially conditioned description. Thus, the struggle

against the concept of an elite culture is in no small part an offshoot of the political struggle in this century. We must therefore go behind this frontier in order to find out what this culture really is, and what the concept encompasses.

From time immemorial, cultural life has been thought of as a process in which professionals (characteristically enough, 'creative artists') produce the cultural products, institutions and - in our time the electronic media - disseminate them, while the public receives them. This pattern turns ordinary people into 'consumers' of culture, and important questions are left unanswered.

(Jor 1976:29)

Elite culture is seen here as an aspect of a consumer society. It is something produced by experts for consumption by ordinary people. Creative artists are seen as those who produce artistic goods or entertainment for the benefit of the population at large. But is this really true? Whilst one can go some way to seeing some artists as producers of cultural consumables, it takes a leap of the imagination to accept that these are received by 'ordinary people'. Writers like Simpson (1976:30), Pearson (1982:101), Horne (1986:54) and Jor himself (1976:55) have pointed out that the great mass of the population do not interest themselves at all in high culture. In discussing artists in residence schemes Su Braden put it like this:

Concern for the separation of art and artists from the rest of society, expressed by a growing concentration on new ways of putting art and artists back into social contexts, may be seen as the stamp of this decade.

(Braden 1978:3)

In a sense the idea that there are only two sorts of culture, elite and popular, is in itself an over-simplification. It is too easy to try to relate culture to a simplistic analysis of society based on a notion of social class. It is, however, an analysis used by a number of writers. Kelly in his book, 'Community, Art and the State: storming the Citadels' attempts to demonstrate that 'culture' has been appropriated by a powerful ruling class.

What had happened was that the interests of one group

within society, that powerful group which ruled the Empire abroad and the factories and land at home, had come to set the standards of what it meant to be a cultured person. The tastes of this group were connected to what, in a previous era, had been the court arts; and they were located here for a variety of reasons, some of which were to do with education, and some of which were to do with aspirations of a newly ascendant group to legitimise itself socially. The tastes of the working classes, as a class, were largely drawn from what had previously been the folk arts.

(Kelly 1984:88)

Nicholas Pearson (1982:109) also takes this line of argument and suggests that 'the visual arts have traditionally and historically reflected the interests and tastes of small and powerful sections of society'. He further suggests that these elite sections of society have 'universalised' their idea of culture so that it is seen as the culture of society as a whole. The fact that the majority of the population do not get involved in these cultural activities is usually explained away by reference to their lack of education or intelligence. Unfortunately few of these writers attempt to identify just what artistic activities do interest the mass of the population.

Such analyses, however, ignore the great popular appeal of, say, Elizabethan drama; Shakespeare's plays were enjoyed not by a ruling elite but by the ordinary people of London. Similarly, much visual art, particularly in medieval churches, was enjoyed by the population as a whole. Nowadays, the patrons of the theatres and the concert halls are not a ruling elite but are drawn from the massed ranks of the middle class. This point is made and expanded by Donald Horne:

'High culture', overall, is not the culture of the rulers. Some rulers may appropriate parts of it: in both capitalist and Communist societies the lavishness of the opera, for example, can attract them. In capitalist societies the costliness of paintings by celebrated artists can appeal to the rich. But rulers can now see many aspects of 'high culture' as, simply, beyond their intellectual power, perhaps as challenging their social prestige, perhaps as challenging their social order.

(Horne 1986:185-6)

15

In trying to come to terms with a concept of culture it is necessary to go beyond attempts to define the concept in class terms. There is no doubt that socio-economic class is a factor in determining in what cultural activities a person will or will not become involved. But there are other factors which play an equally if not more important part.

The concept of culture is not, as suggested by some of the writers above, two dimensional, 'elite' or 'popular'. It is, rather, multi-dimensional; many factors play a part in determining the cultural identity of a social group. Social class is one of these but additionally we must consider ethnic or racial background and geography. We have already mentioned age as a determining factor when talking about youth culture and it is clear that different age groups can develop distinct and different forms of cultural activity.

It is also worth remembering that the distinctive nature of a culture is not constant; it changes over time. In identifying a culture for study or analysis it is important to locate it temporally. There is a cultural dynamic which allows choices to be made about the direction and nature of cultural activities and which allows us to explore the idea of cultural development.

Let us spend some time in looking at the ethnic dimension of culture. In 1976 Naseem Khan published a book entitled The Arts Britain Ignores - The Arts of Ethnic Minorities in Britain. This report alerted us to the fact that there were a great number of artistic and cultural activities taking place in Britain which were not recognised as part of our national cultural output. These activities tended not to be funded by the national or regional arts funding organisations and were little known outside the immediate social and ethnic group which arranged them. In the book, the author was able to devote a chapter each to the artistic output of Bangladeshis, Chinese, Cypriots, East and Central Europeans, Indians, Pakistanis and West Indians. It was clear that the concept of British culture needed close and urgent re-examination. As a nation we were host to a great number of cultural activities of which the majority of us had no knowledge. Not only did we have little knowledge of these activities but we were ill-equipped to enjoy or make judgements about them.

Naseem Khan made an interesting point about the way in which immigrant cultures impinge upon the consciousness of the dominant host culture. In doing so she is using the word 'culture' in the wide anthropological sense.

> ... the beneficial results of immigration can be seen at an immediate level in the streets of virtually any town in Britain. Food is an effective ambassador. Since the last war, Asian, Chinese and Cypriot restaurants have increased enormously. Moreover there are indications that what began as merely cheap food of variable quality is now being regarded with more discrimination. Food columns in the newspapers and restaurant guides now make some attempt to understand different methods and assess the products critically .... In the arts, a similar process of acceptance and discernment has yet to take place.
>
> (Khan 1976:6)

The underlying assumption here is that the desired end is not a levelling out whereby we end up with a common culture which is a hybrid of the various constituent parts. The philosophy is rather one of cultural plurality; a range of very different cultures existing side by side in the same location. Such a notion makes it very difficult to identify what one might call a national British culture. This is something the Welsh, Irish and Scottish nationalists have been telling us for a long time. The term multi-cultural has been used to describe this situation. What this concept does is bestow on the immigrant cultures a status equal to that of the host culture. The immigrant cultures are not therefore seen as sub-cultures existing within a dominant white British culture but rather as the constituent parts of the cultural tapestry of the nation.

Khan's book led to a move by the arts funding bodies in Britain to examine ways in which they could help the arts of ethnic minorities to develop. The Arts Council of Great Britain and the Regional Arts Associations all developed policies for the promotion of ethnic minority arts. This led to further problems of definition.

The arts funding bodies in Britain, by and large, do not fund amateur arts activities nor do they aid what has been referred to as the folk culture. But immigrant groups brought with them a classical tradition, sometimes more than one, as well as a wealth of folk traditions from their country of origin. Just as the host community had developed a historic legacy of what could be described as high culture which existed side by side with a folk tradition, both of which were developing and changing with the production of new contemporary works, so the immigrant cultures brought

17

with them the same cultural mix. What is more, many of the art forms were not produced by professional artists and performers but by amateurs anxious to keep their cultural traditions alive. Ways had to be found to preserve and develop these traditions:

> Although developments only come from a sure traditional base, the object should not be to preserve that alone. Since cultural expressions spring out of social conditions, they should change with conditions, otherwise merely the effect is preserved without the cause. For instance, several of our ethnic arts come from rural roots; they are village songs and dances celebrating harvest or rainfall and so on. When, however, farmers become Midlands charge-hands or even more important the children of charge-hands (possibly accountants or teachers), the picture changes; the links to the situation behind the song become tenuous. Preserved culture has, like dried fruits, a certain limited attractiveness.
>
> (Khan 1976:8)

Of course, any immigrant culture will have an effect on the cultural output of the host community. In the same way that Impressionist painters were influenced by Japanese prints, exposure to the art of an immigrant culture will inevitably have its effect. Artists cannot predict or control the way in which their work will respond to a new range of stimuli. What is certain is that they will not be able to deny their exposure to new forms of cultural expression and will accommodate these perceptual experiences in their personalities and in their work.

What I hope that I have been able to demonstrate in these last few paragraphs is that the characteristics of a given culture, whether in the anthropological or the artistic sense of the term, are determined by something more than social class or age group. The particular traditions of immigrant groups will contribute to the development of a national culture as well as existing in their own right as an alternative to the culture of the host community. The social status of the members of an ethnic grouping will in turn affect the nature of cultural development within that ethnic group. There are, in effect, a number of factors which are active in determining the way in which we identify or delimit a given culture. So far we have mentioned ethnic background, social class and age. Let us now turn our attention to the geographical area which can in some cases help to define the boundaries of a culture.

One of the weaknesses of Naseem Khan's book was the assumption that, say, the Polish community in Leeds was interested in the same sort of activities and shared the same sort of beliefs and values as say, the Polish community in Leicester. They may indeed share the same sort of cultural norms but it would be a mistake to assume that this was always going to be the case.

Much has been made about the north/south divide in the United Kingdom. It is often suggested that not only is there an economic divide between the wealthy south and the disadvantaged north but there is a also a cultural difference. This is sometimes caricatured as a south populated by commuting, golf-playing, stock-brokers and a north inhabited by beer-swilling, chip-eating manual workers. Whilst this is only a caricature there is no doubt that different value systems, different interests and different forms of cultural expression can predominate in different parts of the country. Even if all other factors coincide, the very geographical location (and with it, of course, the local cultural history) of an area will affect the cultural characteristics of the communities inhabiting it. Therefore the Polish community in Leeds, because it is developing in a different cultural context, may indeed develop differently from that in Leicester.

Culture, then, is to be seen as dynamic. It is in a state of constant change and development. The factors which define the form of a particular culture, which determine its characteristics, which distinguish it from other cultures can be any combination of age, social class, ethnic or racial background, and geographical location. This is true whether or not we use the term culture in its anthropological or in its artistic sense. And within any culture we are likely to find a range of creative activity, a variety of cultural expressions. In societies with a long history of cultural development there is likely to be an historical tradition of high culture. Its forms will be precise, immutable and rooted in the history of a ruling elite. Alongside this classical culture there will usually be a folk tradition. This will comprise the art and cultural expressions of the ordinary people. It is likely that it will reflect their everyday concerns; their work, their pleasures and their religion. Consequently, any analysis or discussion of a culture must locate it in history and identify the particular traditions which are to be discussed.

In any culture one can adopt two perspectives. One can be interested in the arts of the past, whether in the high art or folk tradition, and one can be interested in the creation of the new forms of cultural expression which move the tradition forward. Bearing this in mind it is possible to draw up a typology of culture. A culture is defined in terms of one or more of the following dimensions:

1. Social Class. Thus we speak of working class culture, or the culture of a ruling elite or aristocratic culture.
2. Ethnic or Racial background. Here we can refer to West Indian Culture, or Asian culture or an all embracing black culture.
3. Age. The most common reference here is to youth culture, or teenage culture.
4. Geographical location. In this instance we can quote examples like British culture, or European culture.

Any culture that we wish to discuss or analyse will be defined or delimited in some or all of these terms as well as being located in time. Thus we can focus on, say, the culture of the contemporary working class Indian community in Birmingham; or we can concentrate on nineteenth century teenage culture in Britain or in Scotland; or on working class culture in South Wales. It is in this way that we can identify the culture under discussion.

In order to describe its particular characteristics we need to first of all decide whether or not we are concerned with culture in the anthropological or the artistic sense. If we are interested in the former then we must concentrate on the whole way of life of the community in question. If we are concerned with the artistic output of the culture then we can expect to identify both a 'high culture' and a folk tradition and to observe participation in both the maintenance and the development of both these traditions. Diagram 1.1 may help to illustrate this point.

Clearly, in analysing a culture, the more localised one can focus the more precise one can be. This book is concerned both with policy on a national level and also with local initiatives. Which perspective is being used in any particular instance will be clear from the context.

Diagram 1.1

Descriptors		
	Time/Historical period	
Dimension for defining a culture	High Culture tradition	Folk tradition
Social class Ethnic or racial background Age Geographical location	Participation in either the maintenance or development of either or both traditions	

Now I want to go on to examine the mechanisms by which cultural values are transmitted from generation to generation and to analyse the forces which contribute to cultural development. I should make it clear that, at this stage, I am not concerned to describe any particular culture, I only wish to identify some of the ways in which a culture maintains its distinctive identity and at the same time develops. I intend to explore the ways in which a new generation learn about the culture into which they are born; how they acquire the particular set of beliefs, the particular perspective that is the hallmark of a given cultural grouping. Additionally I want to make suggestions about those factors which determine the ways in which a culture, particularly the artistic output of a culture, grows and develops into new forms of artistic expression.

The beliefs and value systems, the forms of expression and traditions which allow us to describe a particular culture are transmitted in both formal and informal ways.

Many of the assumptions on which a particular culture is founded are picked up almost unconsciously by living and growing up in a particular society. Just as we refer to the hidden curriculum in schools there is a hidden curriculum in the ways in which families bring up their children. I am using the word 'families' fairly loosely here to denote parents, relatives and friends who may be influential in the development of a child. Thus moral codes of behaviour, manners, customs and taboos can be learned in a subliminal way.

Dominant religions do, of course, spell out the moral and ethical basis of a culture but this need not always be the case. It could be argued that, today, in a largely atheist Britain, the media, particularly the press, have taken on the role of moral watchdog which used to be that of the church. Parents, however, seem to pass on a moral framework in informal rather than formal ways. It is done more by hint and innuendo than by structured teaching. Alongside this there is, in developed countries, a formal education system which will also embody and teach the prevailing values.

When one begins to examine the value and belief systems embodied in the processes of a formal education structure then it is legitimate to ask questions about what aspects of cultural activity are included in the formal curriculum and how decisions about their inclusion are arrived at. After all, it is not long ago that the arts curriculum in schools concentrated almost solely on white 'European' culture, even where large proportions of the children in school were from Asian or Afro-Caribbean backgrounds.

The reasons for this state of affairs is not difficult to discover. It lies in the structures which constitute our educational system. One can raise the spectre of a political conspiracy to ensure the pre-eminence of the European tradition, but I think that the evidence for this would be slight. I do not believe that the issue was originally on this level of consciousness. It is my belief that for quite a long time it simply did not occur to anyone that the school art curriculum no longer reflected the culture in which numbers of school pupils were living. Examination boards still concentrate on the Western European tradition but at least, nowadays, in schools where there are large immigrant populations, cultural studies are more broadly conceived.

Educational institutions are often very conservative in their thinking. There is a long way to go before the school curriculum fully reflects the cultural diversity of the country. Responsibility must in some part lie with those within the school who decide upon the non-examination syllabus as well as with those external agencies which set examination papers. There is, of course, greater flexibility and greater potential for engaging in cultural development in the non-examined, non-compulsory sector of adult education.

There are important questions about which artistic culture, the curriculum and the examination syllabus reflect. Are they, for example, concerned with the classical or with the folk tradition? Earlier in this chapter I introduced the views of those who felt that a ruling elite perpetuated what we came to think of as 'high culture' at the expense of the folk tradition. If this were true then we need to look no further than the education system to discover one of the mechanisms by which this was done.

There is a set of values, preferences and personal tastes shared by many of those in control of deciding upon the content of our educational provision. Course content, particularly in arts subjects, is often decided upon by those white middle class educationalists who themselves are the products of the same education system they now wish to perpetuate. A cultural hegemony exists within the compulsory sector of the education service, and maybe in the country at large, which perpetuates a set of values rooted in what we have come to call high culture. As Donald Horne points out:

> The culture that dominates the public scene is not a ruling-class culture of triumphal display, but a fabricated 'public culture' that purports to be the culture not just of the rulers but of all the people.
> (Horne 1986:184)

Despite these efforts the majority of people who come through the British education system feel alienated from this high culture. In a perverse way they are persuaded it is of value, even though they themselves derive no pleasure from it. They are persuaded that their lack of sympathy stems from their own educational inadequacy. High culture is still believed to be superior, even though the majority of the population feel no sympathy for it. Nicholas Pearson argues that this lack of interest is partly social and partly arising from unfamiliarity with the content.

23

> The exclusion of the mass of society from high culture is usually partly social, and partly to do with the iconography, content or meanings inherent in the work of art. The social exclusion is usually the most powerful. The style and feel and atmosphere of an art gallery, along with the tones of voice, forms of dress and ways of behaving of a gallery audience, can be more excluding and incomprehensible to someone not brought up to visit galleries than the work on the wall.
>
> (Pearson 1982:101)

There are, of course, those educationalists with vision who wish to broaden curricular content. And there are those who quite simply believe that the European tradition is best and is what every British child should know about. Such educators adopt these particular philosophical positions for their own personal reasons. I do not wish to pass comment on such positions. My concern here is only to identify one of the ways in which a set of values is passed on from one generation to the next; one of the ways in which the predominance of a particular culture can be institutionalised.

There are other ways in which cultural values are transmitted. It sometimes happens that these values are in conflict with the values promoted by those who have an interest in maintaining a cultural hegemony. The media, press, film, radio and television play an important role as cultural transmitters. Whether a so-called 'popular' newspaper is debunking the latest acquisition of the Tate Gallery or a 'serious' newspaper is extolling the latest production of Aida there will be a set of cultural values implicit in the writing. Similarly, the hushed tones of a Radio Three announcer are instrumental in persuading the audience that the work they are about to hear has to be taken seriously.

Again I do not wish to get sidetracked into a discussion of artistic values. This will come later. For the moment it is sufficient to identify the media as another route by which cultural values are transmitted. Just who, in the radio station or the newspaper office, decides upon the particular perspective from which an item will be recorded is always a matter for conjecture. It is most likely that there is a house style and programme producers or news editors do it that way because they have always done it that way. Again we see that the mechanisms of cultural transmission may be fairly well institutionalised and consequently difficult to modify.

The final sort of cultural transmission I want to mention is the culture industry itself. To explain what I mean by 'culture industry' I refer again to Donald Horne.

> In the liberal-democratic capitalist societies the culture and information industries are usually either big business or a part of government. In the communist societies they are likely to be accepted as one of the most significant parts of the regime. This high centralisation of the information and culture bureaucracies helps explain the survival of modern industrial nation-states.
>
> (Horne 1986:32)

Horne goes on to assert that it is in the interests of states to promote or control the culture industries in order to both define the world in terms of certain realities and to diffuse new kinds of instructions about what matters and about how people should behave.

Such messages can be intrinsic to both the form and the content of a work of art. Not only can Britain be seen as a nation which enjoys radio and television soap operas, the content of soap operas themselves is seen as reflecting the reality of contemporary Britain.

It is at this point that I want to focus more narrowly on the arts; to begin to shift the emphasis from an anthropological definition of culture to a more artistic one. Since the next chapter will be concerned solely with the arts it is necessary to begin to refine our concept of culture. For the moment we will continue to concentrate on what Horne (1986) referred to above as the culture industries.

In Britain there is a state culture industry which is funded for the most part through a range of state agencies. One can immediately identify the Arts Council of Great Britain, The Crafts Council, and the British Film Institute. These organisations can clearly take their place in the pantheon of cultural providers, though one may have to raise questions about the last two organisations if they are to be included in a concept of the arts; film and the crafts are not always considered as art forms. The Design Council is more problematic. It exists to promote what it believes to be good design. In that sense it exercises an important influence over the visual appearance of the utilitarian products of a culture. But again, we may later have to question its role in a non-utilitarian concept of the arts.

The British Broadcasting Corporation I include as part of the state culture industry because, whilst it is an independent organisation, it does receive its monies from income collected by the government in licence fees. Since the BBC's income can be identified in terms of a licence fee - that is, a notional amount paid by customers for a service - it is slightly different from the other organisations, but nonetheless I include it in this list of state providers.

Finally of course there is a large private sector. Here one can include independent television and radio, commercial cinema and theatre, publishing and a whole range of galleries and art houses.

I have not included in this list those agencies which maintain and promote historic buildings and sites, what are sometimes referred to as the 'heritage' services. Often those who wish to promote the idea of a government Ministry of Culture include these interests within the general remit of such a ministry. They certainly form part of our cultural heritage in the wider sense of the word. But I exclude them here because I do not wish to include architecture in a definition of the arts. The creative activity involved in designing a building is of a different order to that involved in creation in the other arts. I acknowledge that this point is arguable and hope that the distinction that I am making will become clear in the following two chapters. I mention it here in order to make it clear that architecture has not been forgotten, it has been deliberately excluded. I acknowledge that many historic houses contain great works of painting and sculpture and this fact will again be referred to when we come to examine access to the arts. But, for the moment, I wish to exclude the owners and promotors of the buildings themselves from our analysis of the culture industries.

What all the above agencies have in common is that they can set the cultural agenda, they can influence what we do or do not consider to be art. They can assert what is to be considered as high art and what is to be relegated to the status of folk art. They can be instrumental in popularising either sort of art. They can bring new works to the notice of the general public and to the notice of the influential public, that group which set themselves up as arbiters of cultural tastes. They can turn a popular or folk movement into a commercial enterprise, as has happened with some folk music and pop music. Most importantly, perhaps, they can ignore those new art forms in which they see no commercial value or simply which they do not like. This is true in the worlds of music, publishing, the visual arts and the performing arts. The workings of these agencies constitute a powerful means of transmitting and maintaining cultural values. They also provide an important means of directing cultural development.

What I hope that the foregoing illustrates is that the characteristics of a given culture are as they are from choice. Within the history of that culture choices have been made to retain this sort of art form or to forget another sort of art form, to allow this new development or to curtail another new development. The choices are made both individually and corporately. They are rarely made by the people as a whole. They affect the arts as well as other areas of cultural life. Implicit in the choices are value systems which are rarely articulated. In the next chapter I will discuss the concept of 'the arts' but more importantly examine some of the ways in which values in the arts are established, maintained and occasionally changed.

REFERENCES

Braden, S., 1978, Artists and People, London, Henley, etc., Routledge and Kegan Paul

Council of Europe, 1984, 'Berlin: Ministers adopt Declaration on Cultural Objectives', in Forum 2/84, Strasbourg, Council of Europe

Horne, D., 1986, The Public Culture - the Triumph of Industrialism, London, Sydney, etc., Pluto Press

Jor, F., 1976, The Demystification of Culture, Strasbourg, Council of Europe

Kelly, O., 1984, Community, Art, and The State: Storming the Citadels, London, Comedia Publishing Group

Khan, N., 1976, The Arts Britain Ignores - The Arts of Ethnic Minorities in Britain, London, Community Relations Commission

Martin, B., 1981, A Sociology of Contemporary Cultural Change, Oxford, Basil Blackwell

Pearson, N., 1982, The State and the Visual Arts, Milton Keynes, The Open University Press

Redcliffe-Maud, Lord, 1976, Support for the Arts in England and Wales, London, Calouste Gulbenkian Foundation

Culture

Simpson, J.A., 1976, Towards Cultural Democracy,
    Strasbourg, Council of Europe
Williams, R., 1983, Keywords, London, Fontana
Williams, R., 1986, Culture, London, Fontana

Chapter Three

THE ARTS

This chapter is about the arts. It begins by exploring the idea of 'the arts' as a social construct and looks at the various rather unsatisfactory ways in which attempts have been made to distinguish the arts from other sorts of creative activity. There follows a section about values in the arts which distinguishes between commercial, artistic and subjective value and concludes that values, like the concept of art itself, are relative and specific to a particular time and place.

When we speak of 'the arts' we usually have in mind a range of activities similar to those identified in the previous chapter. In attempting to identify 'the arts' Williams (1983:90) refers to music, literature, painting and sculpture, theatre and film. But many would think that this list was too short and too exclusive. Dance and opera should surely be added and increasingly photography and video are being seen as independent art forms. Performance Art, that hybrid that seems to lie somewhere between Fine Art and Theatre, is also gaining increasing recognition.

One could stop here and simply assert that this is what art is, but this would be too simplistic. Art is a social construct and as such should be examined within a social context. Appleyard points out that:

> The word (art) was created in its modern context at the time of the industrial revolution; just as we enter the so-called post-industrial society, it is becoming defunct.
>
> (Appleyard 1984:122)

There are areas of debate about what we now mean when we speak of the arts. Some forms of theatrical presentation are thought to be art but not others. The term is used legitimately to refer to, say, a play by Chekov but not to a variety performance; grand opera is legitimate art but there are question marks about the musical comedy. And what of the distinction which is drawn between 'art' and 'craft'? Why is it that some forms of creative activity are excluded from the category 'art' and relegated to the lower status category of craft? Are all those who produce artefacts operating as creative artists or just some of them? This chapter will address these questions and discuss some of the issues which inform and form our ideas about the arts.

Art is one of those concepts which is in general use but about which there is little agreement. Many philosophers writing on aesthetics begin by taking the term 'art' as denoting a fairly obvious range of activities, then they pursue intricate discussions in an attempt to ascertain what these activities have in common. Thus, for instance, Williams (1983:90) presents us with the list referred to above; Hegel (1979:87-8) refers to architecture, sculpture, painting, music and poetry; and Wollheim (1968) avoids offering a list but at various times refers to a range of art forms. These sorts of philosophical discourses seem to spring from a certain knowledge of what the arts are, a knowledge, however, that is specific to a particular time and culture. Philosophers tend to regard the arts as those activities which have gained status and credibility for the educated patron. This is a little too restricting for our purpose.

One could attempt to define the term by adopting Wittgenstein's (1953 para.312) procedure of including activities which have a 'family resemblance'. The idea is that the activities included in a concept like 'the arts' resemble each other in the same way as members of a family. Some members will share some characteristics with other members but not with all, and these others will share different characteristics with yet more members of the family. No members of the family will be exactly alike but they will be sufficiently related to be identifiable as a family.

If the arts are thought of in this way one could easily accommodate activities such as radio and TV documentary, ice dancing, pop concerts and much popular theatre. But we know that in everyday practical terms this is not done. The above examples are excluded from a concept of the arts by writers, philosophers, teachers and administrators. And in any event, the problem with Wittgenstein's model is that it becomes difficult to know where to stop. Does one include competitive ice skating, for instance, because it has a lot in common with ice dancing, which in turn shares many of the characteristics of ballet? This procedure, whilst allowing us to extend the range of activities included in a concept of the arts becomes less helpful when we have to decide which activities to exclude.

What all the activities alluded to above have in common is that they all involve, at a stage in their development, some sort of creative activity. The term 'art', or its derivations, is used to describe the person creating the work, the artist; the work itself, a work of art; and the process of creation, as in the term 'art lessons' where one learns to do Art. Pearson explores the way in which he believes the word has shifted its allegiance from describing a work of art to describing a person.

> However, as the painter and sculptor became 'artist', the qualities ascribed to 'art' (creative, imaginative, special, and expressive of human as opposed to utilitarian values) were increasingly also ascribed to the artist. The specialness of the work became in part a function of the specialness of the person.
>
> This shift in emphasis from the person being defined by the activity (a painter is somebody who paints) to the activity being defined by the person ('art' is something created by 'artists') is discernible in the Romantic movement and before.
>
> (Pearson, 1982:6)

I am not convinced, as Pearson asserts above, that we have reached a stage where the activity, 'art', is defined only in terms of the person engaged in the activity, 'the artist'. Certainly if one achieves the status of being a recognised artist then it is easier to convince an often sceptical public that what one produces is art. But we still define certain processes, like painting or composing, as art. Indeed we still refer to certain objects as works of art. Those aspiring to the status of artist must first demonstrate that they can produce art. Reference to the process by which art is produced and reference to the work itself, the artefact, are

31

both still legitimate usages of the term. The position is not at all clear, not as simple as Pearson would have us believe.

WAYS OF DISTINGUISHING THE ARTS FROM OTHER ACTIVITIES

What we can say is that there is a range of human activities which we choose to include in a category of experience and behaviour to which we attach the word 'art'. It may help to clarify the position by exploring the ways in which attempts have been made to distinguish between art activities and other similar human activities. For our purposes it may be better to identify the ways in which we discriminate between different arts-type activities in order to categorise them. By the term 'arts-type activities' I mean those behaviours which in common sense terms might be thought to have a legitimate claim to be included in a definition of the arts. It would appear that such distinctions have been made in four different ways; art has been defined by reference to either (A) the medium in use, (B) the usefulness (or non-usefulness) of the product, (C) the uniqueness of the product or (D) the seriousness of the product.

(A) **The medium**

Those activities which we choose to call art are sometimes distinguished on the basis of the medium in use. It is by reference to the medium that distinctions have been drawn between art and craft. Almost irrespective of what is produced, we tend to refer to those professionals who work in paint or in stone as artists. The painter and the sculptor are accorded this status because of the medium in which they choose to work. On the other hand much work in clay or, say, in yarn or precious metals is usually referred to as craftwork. (Though I must acknowledge that some sculptors work in clay). Thus the potter, the weaver and the silversmith are referred to as craftsmen or, more recently, craftspersons.

Wollheim outlines what he calls the Ideal theory of art and describes as follows the ways in which the theory distinguishes the crafts from art.

The contrast between art and craft, which is central to

Collingwood's 'Principles of Art', would appear to rest upon three distinctive characteristics of craft. First, every craft involves the notion of a means to an end, each distinctly conceived, the end being definitive of the particular craft, and the means whatever is employed to meet that end; secondly, every craft involves the distinction between planning and execution, where planning consists in foreknowledge of the desired result and calculation as to how best to achieve this, and the execution is the carrying out of this plan; finally, every craft presupposes a material upon which it is exercised and which it thereby transforms into something different. None of these characteristics, the theory argues, pertains to art.

(Wollheim 1968:33)

The reference to 'a material' is puzzling; it seems to assume that paint and the media used in sculpture are not 'materials' in the same sense that the materials of so-called crafts (clay, fabric, yarns, etc.) are materials. One is not clear on what basis this distinction is made and is left in considerable doubt about the way in which art is distinguished from craft.

But this theory goes beyond simply using the medium as the basis for distinguishing art from craft and includes reference to the nature of the creative process, arguing that it is different in art from the process in craft. The final assertion that none of these characteristics pertains to art is simply not demonstrable or not true. There are those working in traditional craft methods and materials who are involved in the same sort of creative work as the painter or the sculptor, they are working as creative artists. The painter and sculptor as well as the potter can be involved in 'planning and execution', can see their work as a 'means to an end' and can transform a material into something different. Consequently there are no serious grounds for focussing on the medium in use nor the nature of the creative process as a means of distinguishing between art and crafts and no reasons for excluding what we call the crafts from the category of activity which we call art. Wollheim himself goes on to point out the inadequacies of the Ideal Theory of art by making similar references to the processes of creation in both art and craft activities.

(B) **The usefulness of the product**

It is sometimes claimed that the distinction between art and other forms of production is made on the basis of whether or not the end product has any utilitarian value. Craftspersons are thought to make utilitarian items such as pots, fabric or metal objects for use in the house, whilst artists produce non-utilitarian objects like paintings and sculptures. A similar distinction can be made in writing where the non-utilitarian novel or poem are seen as art whilst most of what we refer to as non-fiction is seen as useful.

Increasingly, however, with the advent of mass industrial production, the independent craftsperson is seen to be doing something more than simply making utilitarian objects for use around the house. The work of the independent potter or weaver is not the same as the mass produced factory-made article. Thus terms like 'craftsman potter' and 'handloom weaver' have been used to distinguish these workers from those involved in mass production. Indeed, many of those involved in the crafts consider themselves to be artists and describe themselves as such using terms like 'artist potter' or 'graphic artists' for those involved in the production of advertisements and posters. It would be difficult to sustain an argument which stated that simply because some people produce artefacts which have a use they could not be categorised as artists.

(C) **The uniqueness of the product**

Distinctions were further drawn between the creative artist who made unique one-off objects and the craftsperson who was involved in the repetition of the making process to obtain sets of pots or lengths of fabric. Thus, the craftsperson, because of this involvement in a repetitive process was thought to be more of an artisan than an artist. But this would mean that Dürer woodcuts or Hockney prints would have to be considered as some sort of inferior art form. In any event, there is no basis on which one could argue that because there is more than one edition of an artefact it somehow devalues its status as a work of art.

(D) **The seriousness of the work**

I want now to turn to the idea of 'seriousness' in art. Art is not, as discussed above, simply about making useful objects. It is about loftier aims. Art is supposed to make a statement about life. Implicit in our notion of the arts is a belief that a work of art conveys a message, communicates meaning across space and time. It seems that some categories of creative activity are excluded from the category 'art' because it is difficult to translate their meaning into words. Serious art makes important statements. It may make them in an amusing or light-hearted way but they are, nonetheless, considered to be important comments about the world and about the human condition.

In the novel or the play, where the theme of a particular piece can often be articulate in words, we can describe what it is about. One can also cite examples from representational art where the content can be discussed in literary terms. It is also clear that the potter and the embroiderer, the silversmith and the calligrapher can make statements of significance, but it is often a great deal more difficult to translate these statements into words, particularly if the work under consideration is non-representational. How can one, in all seriousness, verbally articulate the meaning of a Sung bowl or an Egyptian scarab broach. Yet it is clear that these artefacts held, and perhaps still hold, meaning for those who made and enjoyed them. A description of a pot is only a pale shadow of the experience of the pot. Indeed, some would argue that any description of any work of art must of necessity fail to convey the experience of that work. But it does seem that if we are to ask what a particular work of art is about, it is easier to answer for the literary arts and for representational art than for what we call the crafts and other non-representational and visual art forms. The visual arts, like music, transmit meaning in a much more non-verbal, non-literary way. This should not be taken to imply that they are devoid of meaning, only that they convey meaning differently, and they are no less serious as works of art because of this.

A more difficult situation arises in the performing arts when one tries to distinguish between serious art and what for the moment we might call entertainment. A performance of Don Giovanni is considered art, yet a performance of Cats is entertainment. A concert of music by Beethoven is considered art, a rock concert is entertainment. It is not simply a question of the more popular forms of performance being excluded from the category 'art', though there does seem to be some truth in the observation. It is, as suggested above, something to do with the idea of seriousness; the more popular art forms are, almost automatically, thought of as somehow less serious.

These, then, are some of the ways in which we, in so-called developed societies, attempt to distinguish activities as relating to a concept of the arts. None of them, it would seem, are entirely satisfactory. It is clearly necessary to explore the problem further.

Hegel provides a fairly simple if wide explanation of what might constitute a work of art as follows:

> What we are acquainted with, at the start, as a familiar idea of the work of art, falls under the three following heads:
> (i) The work of art is no natural product; it is brought about by human activity;
> (ii) it is essentially made for man's apprehension by the senses;
> (iii) it has an end and aim in itself.
>
> (Hegel 1979:25)

Whilst this is a fairly wide explanation of the concept it has the merit of allowing us to include many of the activities mentioned above which are normally considered to be crafts. This is in contrast to Williams (1983:40-3), however, who excludes the so-called crafts from his definition, even though many of those working with clay or with fabric and yarns or precious metals are today involved in the same category of activity as the painter and the sculptor. The old distinctions and divisions still exist. There is clearly a case for re-defining our concept of the arts to more accurately reflect the creative activity which is taking place.

In practical terms this whole issue would not matter so much were it not for the fact that these distinctions have become institutionalised. Thus, state financial aid to those involved in creative work is disbursed via The Arts Council of Great Britain, The Crafts Council and The British Film Institute. Such an organisational structure perpetuates what might be an unhelpful conceptual framework. One could suggest that this is not a particular useful division of interest and, as an anachronistic relic of the past, it should be abandoned. For the moment I want to come back to this notion of seriousness in the context of a general discussion about values in the arts.

VALUES IN THE ARTS

We are persuaded that opera and what is commonly called classical music are serious concerns, whilst the musical and pop music are somehow of lesser import. The basis on which such judgements are made is confused, rarely articulated and does not stand up to critical examination. It is as though there were a conspiracy of silence surrounding the criteria used for assertions about artistic value. Values are shared amongst groups of cognoscenti but they are rarely identified or justified. What, then, <u>are</u> the processes by which judgements are made and values established in the arts?

Kelly sees the very way in which we define the term art as being instrumental in maintaining a certain value system:

> Art is an ideological construction; a generalisation which has a complex history through which its meaning has both shifted and narrowed. In its current usage its chief purpose is to bestow an apparently inherent value on to certain activities and the products resulting from these activities, while withholding this value from certain other similar activities. In this respect the term 'art' functions as one of a series of categories whose purpose is to assist in the construction and maintenance of a hierarchy of values which, having been constructed, can be made to appear as both natural and inevitable.
>
> (Kelly 1984:54)

Kelly goes on to outline a theory which attributes a narrow definition of art to a ruling metropolitan elite who are bent on pursuing their own interests at the expense of others. He argues that there is nothing intrinsically different between sculpting in bronze and making model railways, yet the former is accorded the status of art whilst the latter is relegated to the category of hobby.

Whilst he makes some persuasive points there are parts of his argument which do not hold up to examination. He fails, for instance, to identify just who benefits from this narrow definition of art, who comprise this ruling

37

metropolitan elite. To a certain extent he implies that artists themselves will benefit. But artists are not the ones who have thus defined art and who are exercising power to maintain a given definition. He appears to believe that the arts funding agencies are the tools of this powerful metropolitan elite and define art on behalf of the members of this elite in order to ensure that they can continue to enjoy their chosen art forms of opera and ballet. Whilst it may be possible to find some evidence to support such an argument there is equal evidence to negate it. The fact that the term 'art' enjoyed its current meaning and was in use well before the Arts Council, (or its forerunner C.E.M.A.), came into existence seems to point up the inadequacy of this approach. In order to better understand the situation it is necessary to analyse the ways in which values in the arts are established.

Values in the arts operate at three levels. First, there is, on perhaps the simplest level, the idea of commercial value; what a work of art is worth in hard currency. Whilst this is not the main concern here it is important to acknowledge its existence. Second, on another and more complex level one can explore the artistic value, the value of the artefact as a work of art. This is sometimes referred to as the aesthetic value. This is a problematic area where it is difficult to attribute (objectively) any qualitative measure of excellence. Third, there is what I shall call subjective value, the value of a work to an individual. This may be, and often is, at odds with any financial or artistic assessment of its worth arrived at by experts.

Commercial value

It is clear that certain definitions of the term 'art' will serve certain financial interests better than others. Even though our concern is not strictly with the financial, it may be as well to begin by discussing that sort of value which is the concern of the international art market. Back in 1968 Sir Herbert Read, in an article intended to warn of the problems of this development, saw it like this:

In the past fifty years two developments have taken place that have as their aim the promotion of an international style in the arts. In the capitalist world the motive is economic: art has become an international commodity and works of art now rival gold as a medium of exchange. Art dealers, like bankers, now have their branches or agents in every great city in the Western World. To meet the demands of an international market art is now subject to international methods of promotion and distribution. Various mass-media of communication - the press, art books, illustrated magazines and television - give hot news to artists, their dealers and the public of any change in fashion or reputation.

The motive behind a similar phenomenon in the communist countries is political. Art is conceived as a powerful instrument of propaganda; The State requires artists to serve the supreme revolutionary purpose, spreading a clearly defined programme of education and idealism by means of a style known as 'socialist realism'.

(Read 1968:1)

Whether one likes it or not one has to acknowledge that there is an international trade in works of art. Commodities in that market are thought of and treated in the same way as any other commodity. New artists are promoted like any other consumer product. A visit to the opening of any exhibition in the well-established London galleries will provide ample evidence of the way in which the market works. Gallery owners are promoting their latest product in much the same way that manufacturing industry will promote washing powder. A premium is placed on publicity, on attracting the interest of influential critics and collectors. Once artists are well-established the supply of their work can be controlled in order to maintain a high price. In a sense, works of art are thought of rather like gold or precious stones; intrinsically they have little value, they can be quite decorative, and their supply on to the market can be controlled to maintain their value. Once artists are dead and their output finite then the price of their works is a function of, amongst other things, their rarity value. When other forms of investment are felt to be risky speculators will often play the fine art market.

Similar points could be made about other art forms. Publishers and theatre owners are out to make a profit just like gallery owners. They have a feel for the market and will publish what they think will sell. One might argue that there is nothing wrong in that. The point at issue is whether or not the value of a work of art is established solely by such commercial criteria. The history of art demonstrates that new art forms have difficulty in gaining acceptance. Their commercial value is only established after a long period during which potential audiences can learn to appreciate these new forms. The market value of a work fluctuates with the tastes of the art-buying public. There are fashions in the arts. The fortunes of particular works rise and fall with the popularity of their creators.

Sandy Nairne (1987:58-87) in State of the Art provides a fascinating insight into the workings of the market and the ways in which values are established. He considers five places in which the validation and valuation of works of art occurs and identifies them as the private gallery, the private collection, the public museum, the art magazine, and the public site. He hastens to point out that these are not the only places where such validation occurs.

> The teaching institutions, art schools and colleges, local and state subsidies to the arts, artist-run galleries and art centres, art history books, international public exhibitions, Documenta and the biennales, all affect the current assessment of qualities and ideas about art.
>
> (Nairne 1987:58)

Artistic value

It is in the way outlined above that the commercial value of a work or an artist is promoted and established. What, one might ask, about the second level of value in the arts, the artistic value of a work? I am deliberately not using the term 'aesthetic' here, though some readers will recognise that I am referring to what they understand as aesthetic value. The term 'aesthetic' has become ambiguous and there is little agreement about its meaning, consequently I will refer to the 'artistic' value of a work.

If new art forms displayed any sort of artistic merit, why was it not recognised from the start and reflected in the market value? Why was the value of so many works only established after the death of the artist. I am using the term value here in both the commercial and the artistic sense. Part of the answer to this question is to do with the rarity value of an artist's oeuvre once the artist is dead. But beyond this, part of the answer is to do with the way in which artistic values are established.

The ways in which we identify or attribute the artistic value of a work of art are notoriously difficult to analyse. Often there is little agreement about works, even amongst experts, and the general public, by and large, is indifferent. There is disagreement between those who believe that it is possible to identify objectively the intrinsic artistic merit of a work of art and those who believe that artistic value is attributed entirely subjectively. Yet the fact remains that there are some works which are almost universally accepted as masterpieces and some artists who are considered to be 'Old Masters'. Richard Hoggart has been much exercised by this point. In the following extract we can see him demonstrate a faith in artistic value but offer no arguments to silence his detractors who claim that artistic value can not be objectively identified or empirically demonstrated.

> Yet to be concerned at all about this argument you have to believe that some works of art are better than others, that some music is better than other music, some novels better than others and some paintings better than others. Even if such a view can never be incontrovertibly proved, there is no refuge in the 'good of its kind' fog which invites you to settle for saying that a best-selling crime novel is <u>in its own way</u> as good as Middlemarch, and the Beatles in their own way as good as Beethoven. One has to recognise, against all todays force of levelling, that some products of the human imagination deserve to be called 'high art', or to be given some other description which indicates that they have qualities which lift them way above the rest.
>
> (Hoggart 1985:13)

This is a credo. Like many who argue in this way no evidence is offered, no criteria suggested, no explanation of how 'high art' is defined or recognised. What we are left with is a belief, a belief that a person who has been educated to enjoy the high arts has some sort of right or ability to make judgements about the value of works of art generally. When Hoggart asserts that certain works of art are better than others he is making a value judgement. He is making a qualitative statement about their worth as works of art, a judgement about their artistic merit. Is it not reasonable to ask those who make such judgements to identify the criteria they use and, further, to identify the evidence they require to decide whether or not those criteria have been met? This never seems to be done.

The history of art provides ample evidence that values in the arts are not constant. They are dynamic, changing from one century to the next, from one country to the next. There are many examples of new works being rejected by the prevailing tastes of the day. Artists like Turner and many of the Impressionists were not immediately acknowledged by the Academy or the Salon, the official arbiters of taste, let alone by the public at large.

It is tempting to argue that if it were possible to identify objectively the artistic value of a work of art then this should never have happened. How could these experts have got it so wrong when there were, supposedly, criteria which one could apply to determine the merit of these works? It should have been immediately possible to identify their value. What is now clear is that criteria change. Just as human societies evolve, so forms of art evolve, as both a reflection and an expression of that society. As forms of art evolve, so artistic values evolve within the context of a developing culture. Similarly, I would argue, as a culture evolves, so our concept of art evolves, and we come to include in that concept activities which were previously not considered to be art.

Those who believe in the objective nature of artistic value explain away the idiosyncrasies of expert opinion by calling into question the expertise of those giving an opinion. In attempting to explain why the works of Van Gogh and Gauguin were not valued by contemporary expert opinion, Child proposes the following rationale:

> An example is provided by paintings of Gauguin and Van Gogh, where we recognise that their high evaluation today disagrees with their evaluation by some experts at the time they were painted. The experts of that period may have been poorly prepared by their culture for adopting an esthetic attitude toward anything unconventional, and while believing they were giving an esthetic evaluation, they may instead have been principally rating the unconventionality of paintings.
>
> (Child 1970:399)

One is tempted to ask, 'what price expertise?' Such explanations really will not do. There are many other examples in the history of art where experts got it wrong.

There is no reason to believe that experts today will be any better than experts from previous eras. There are those like Child who believe in the objectivity of esthetic value and seek ways to demonstrate this. One applauds these efforts. But even Child is forced to admit that:

> And for the present, at any event, agreement of experts is the only basis for objectifying esthetic evaluation. It is the basis, I think, from which any further inquiry needs to start.
>
> (Child 1970:396)

But unfortunately experts, even some of those taking part in research cited by Child, stubbornly refused to agree.

There is inevitably a time lag between an artist developing a new vision of the world or a new form of expression and the experts, art critics and the general public, developing a means of perception and appreciation which allow them to engage with the work. Artists seem to develop their own vision, what Gregory (1970:106-22) calls their own perceptual hypotheses. These perceptual hypotheses allow them to make sense of the image which falls on the retina. He argues that observers need to share the perceptual hypotheses of the artists for communication to occur. Hence it takes time for any artist presenting a personal and unique vision of the world to educate a potential audience. The world represented by the artist is not the perceived world but a sort of stored vision of the world.

> It is tempting to regard artists' pictures as representing not so much the world as they see it at any one time, but rather compositions of stored object-hypotheses ... there must be shared perceptual hypotheses for communication to occur.
>
> (Gregory 1970:120)

What seems to happen is that certain artists succeed in promoting their work to a degree where they become eminent or famous. The processes by which this occurs are societal processes. They have little or nothing to do with artistic value. With this eminence their work becomes available to a wider public. Familiarity with the work, with the new vision, together with educational input in schools and colleges eventually lead to, first of all, a growing ability on the part of the general public to perceive the work and, eventually, to make value judgements about it. When such eminence has been achieved the artists concerned are regarded as legitimate and their work acquires both status and value. Such commercial value and eminence or fame seem to become confused with artistic value. To refer to a painting as an 'Old Master' is to make a comment about its eminence, the degree to which it is known, rather than about its artistic quality. Indeed, there are serious doubts about whether or not it is possible to identify the artistic value of a work of art. It is claimed that such judgements are entirely subjective and have no validity outside that to the person making the judgement.

It is also important to remember that value systems in the arts tend to be culturally specific. It is likely that the set of artistic values espoused by any given culture will differ from those espoused by other cultures. Thus members of youth cultures will not necessarily share the same values as adult cultures, eastern cultures will not necessarily share the same values as western cultures, working class cultures will not necessarily share the same values as middle class cultures, and Afro-Caribbean cultures will not necessarily share the same values as Asian cultures.

As I hinted above, it is becoming clear that tastes and their attendant value systems change over time. What is accorded high status in the last quarter of the twentieth century was not necessarily accorded the same status in the last quarter of the nineteenth century. What was valued in the sixties is not necessarily the same as what is valued in the eighties. I use 'necessarily' to condition all these statements because one has to allow for circumstances where values have remained the same. Values may both change or remain constant over a given period of time. In twentieth century Britain change seems to characterise values in the artistic world. One has to remember, however, that in, say, ancient Egypt artistic values, and to a large extent modes of artistic expression remained the same for centuries. This was, of course, because in ancient Egypt art was so closely linked to the dominant religion which itself remained fairly constant. Thus, modes of expression and values in the arts are seen to be a social construct; to in some way reflect the prevailing social order. They are specific to a particular time and place. John Pick makes the point:

If we had created an Arts Council at the end of the Eighteenth century, it would have turned its attention to preserving the approved arts of gardening, sword fighting, needlework and dancing while letting such commonplace arts as novel-writing and drama fend for themselves on the commercial market. In like manner we might notice that the art of juggling is state-supported as high art in the Chinese People's Republic, and the arts of circus are state-supported as high arts in the USSR. In Britain we support neither.

(Pick 1986:11)

Members of the women's movement have been instrumental in demonstrating that western values in the arts have been socially constructed; constructed moreover in a way which excludes women. Reacting to the fact that there seemed to be no women 'Old Masters', Greer (1979), Parker and Pollock (1981), Fletcher (1982), Hunt (1982) and Nunn (1982) had a fresh look at the artistic record to discover that there were, indeed, women artists throughout the ages but they had somehow been missed out of the official histories. They discovered that the history of art had been written largely by men for men about men. Many customs and practices in the art world specifically excluded women. It is only in recent years that the record is beginning to be put straight.

I quote the instance of women artists to demonstrate how not only the history of art, what is recorded, is a matter of choice but also to demonstrate how values are similarly constructed. Who does the choosing, who decides on the value system is clearly an influential factor in determining the nature of that system. Anyone reading art historical texts twenty years ago would be forgiven for thinking that women were no good at art; the fact that there were no, or at best few, recorded women artists could be explained by reference to an inability of women to produce good works of art. We now know that such a value system is built upon a false premise. Masculine vested interest was a more significant determinant than supposed artistic merit.

A similar fate has befallen the history of black African art. In this case much of the artistic tradition of the African continent has been appropriated by Europe or the Near East. Kwesi Owusu makes the point as follows:

An idea that sustains much of racist mythology in popular consciousness is the lie that black people have barely made any contribution to the process of world civilisation. In European historiography, this has been maintained by a persistent attribution of African achievement to outside inventors. When Carl Mauch, the German geologist, stumbled over the ruins of Great Zimbabwe in southern Africa, he claimed that he had discovered the legendary land of Ophir from which sandlewood was taken for the temple of King Solomon of Israel ...

The case of Egypt is perhaps the most celebrated, for even today few Europeans know that it was an African civilisation. In education and in the cultural media generally, Egypt is lifted out of African history and added to Mediterranean or near-Asian history ... If the philosophers of the European renaissance succeeded in establishing Greece and Rome as the original basis of Western Civilisation, they did so by poignantly ignoring the source of much of that wisdom in the land of the African pharaohs.

(Owusu 1986:45)

So, the idea of artistic merit is a problematic one. It seems that values are constantly changing, as is the idea of what comprises 'the arts'. Whilst at any given time it may be possible to identify the prevailing value system, it would be wrong to think that this was immutable, fixed for all time and true for all places. The answer to the question 'what is good art?' is not a constant. In an illuminating article Munro (1963) points out:

The methods of the artist, the styles of art and the standards of value by which it is judged are all products of cultural evolution and subject to change; they have no absolute authority, but express changing culture-patterns of various groups.

(Munro 1963:39)

Similarly, Wollheim argues:

I hope it is clear that I have said nothing to cast doubt on the fact that what counts as a representation of what, or how we represent things, is a culturally determined matter. (Wollheim 1968:18)

This should not be surprising. After all, art is concerned with creative activity and, by definition, creating is concerned with the production of new artistic objects and with the development of new means of expression, and these will inevitably reflect the cultural context in which they exist.

It is true that some artists cease to be creative, that they become self repetitive, and this raises questions about their status as creative artists. It is not unreasonable to suggest that when painters or sculptors, composers or writers begin to become predictable and repetitive then they are in some way forfeiting their right to be designated as artists.

Before I go on to consider the third level of value, what I called above 'subjective value' in the arts, I want, for a moment, to turn my attention to the idea of craftsmanship (I acknowledge the sexism implicit in the term but can find no substitute to convey my meaning). It seems to me that this is an area where it is possible to make value judgements.

When we refer to craftsmanship we are usually referring to the degree of skill or expertise either exhibited by a craftsperson or observable in a work of art. Where the method of production is complex and the artefact displays a high level of proficiency in this method then we can say that the object displays a high level of craftsmanship. The term is usually used to refer to the degree of sophistication of the method of production, the control which the artist displays over the medium. What is being acknowledged is the degree of skill and expertise which has gone into the making of the object.

This is not to say that the object is artistically better or worse than something which does not display a high level of craftsmanship. The judgement is solely about the degree of skill related to the method of production, not about the value of the object as a work of art. Thus because a Ming vase displays a higher degree of control by the artist than, say, a primitive earthenware pot, we can not say that the vase is somehow better as a work of art. There are no criteria by which we can make such judgements. There is no sense in which complexity or sophistication of method can be equated with artistic merit. To make such a simplistic link would be to create an indefensible set of values whereby the most complicated work of art would be accorded the value of best. Such a position would be untenable.

So far we have used the term 'craftsmanship' only in relation to the visual arts and crafts. But the term is also used in other art forms. Critics speak of novels or plays being well crafted. The sense here shifts somewhat from the way the term is used in the visual arts. It is more to do with structure and form than with method of production. The judgement here seems to be an artistic one rather than one related to manual skills. It is to do with whether or not the structure of a work conforms to a preconceived notion of what a good piece of literature should be. As such the judgement is subject to the changes in fashion and taste which we have already noted. The idea of what constitutes a 'good' work in literature is, as with the visual arts, not constant.

One has also to ask questions about whether or not it matters whether something is or is not well made. Certainly if one was buying a useful object one would want to be sure that it was not going to fall apart immediately one used it. But even in circumstances where the object was obviously not well made one might still value it because of its appearance. In such cases judgements are made on the basis of something other than craftsmanship. They are based on the appeal of the appearance of the object to an individual. This is a very subjective form of judgement. What one person finds appealing or stimulating may leave another person totally unmoved. This sort of value in the arts is what I have referred to earlier as the subjective value, the value to the observer.

Subjective value in the arts

The reasons why we tend to prefer some sorts of art to others is not fully understood. There is probably a cultural dimension; it would be reasonable to suggest that we relate more easily to the art forms which are predominant in our own culture. This is not to say that we cannot move beyond this stage and begin to understand and enjoy art works from other cultures. It is merely to suggest that the way in which we perceive works of art is, initially at any rate, more likely to favour those works rooted in the culture of which we are a part. One can of course develop one's perceptual acuity to the level where it can cope with art forms from other cultures; but this takes time as well as an effort of will.

Responses to works of art operate on a number of levels. First of all there is the initial emotional response. One is struck by a painting or a piece of music. The work seems to demand our attention. Our reaction may be one of sympathy or antipathy; some works can fascinate us but may, at the same time, repel us. No matter what the response is, there is an initial emotional reaction.

This reaction may lead us to another level of engagement with the work where we want to find out more about it, to embark on an analysis of its form and content, to seek meaning in it. Such an analysis may require research, may require familiarising oneself with a particular musical form or genre in painting. One may, at this stage seek out other works by the same artist in order to make comparisons or to see if there is any development between one work and the next.

The search for meaning may lead to another, more intellectual or academic level of activity. We may embark upon a study of the artist or composer in order to place the work we first admired in an historical setting. This would involve a study of the life and times of the artist, of the age in which it was produced in order to try to understand whether or not the work somehow reflected the interaction between its creator and the times in which he or she lived. This may lead us to look at the work of other artists of the same period or at artists from different periods doing similar sorts of work. In any event, the possibility exists that from an initial emotional response to a work one may end up embarking upon a complex academic study which can serve to heighten one's enjoyment and understanding of the work.

There are those who feel that such a study detracts from the initial experience of the work, that the first emotional response cannot be heightened by further study. This is certainly true for some people and for some works. The levels of engagement with works of art which I have described above in no sense constitute a recommended progression. Different people will cease engaging with works of art at different points in the sequence of events I have postulated. No value judgements are implied or intended in the progression. My aim is simply to identify the ways in which observers and audiences react to works of art.

The difficulty in this area arises from the fact that, within the artistic output of any culture, some people will like and gain satisfaction from certain works and not others.

I am, for the moment, excluding from the argument considerations related to the degree of difficulty involved in understanding a work. To understand a Shakespeare play requires a familiarity with Shakespearean language which must be learned. To perceive any work of art requires a level of perceptual development which we tend not to require in ordinary everyday life, hence one may have to apply oneself to the appreciation of a work of art. But even when this is done, when levels of perception are adequate and sufficient time is spent in engaging with the work, the fact remains that certain people are sympathetic to and derive satisfaction from certain works of art rather than others. Why should this be so?

Evidence for the answers to such questions comes from the realms of theory rather than empirical research. As far as I am aware there has been no successful empirical research in this area. There have been attempts to relate creative output to personality type, most notably by Herbert Read (1961), but hitherto there have been no attempts to identify the factors, whether in terms of personality type or in other terms, which dictate individual preference for particular works of art.

Theory in this area is mainly psychological and derives from the work of Jung and his followers. Jung, like Freud before him, postulated that the creation of a work of art was similar in process to dream formation. The images which are to be found in works of art are seen as being derived from the same source as those experienced in dreams. These images are seen as what Jung calls archetypal symbols or primordial images. They are expressions of inner psychological states which reflect the collective experience of the species. Jung explains it as follows:

> Just as the human body represents a whole museum of organs, each with a long evolutionary history behind it, so we should expect to find that the mind is organised in a similar way. It can no more be a product without history than is the body in which it exists. By 'history' I do not mean the fact that the mind builds itself up by conscious reference to the past through language and other cultural traditions. I am referring to the biological, prehistoric and unconscious development of the mind in archaic man, whose psyche was still close to that of the animal. (Jung 1964:67)

Jung referred to the images which constitute the 'history' of the mind as 'archaic remnants' which he calls 'archetypes' or 'primordial images'. He arrived at his conclusions by comparing myths and legends, stories and visual representations, and rites and rituals from a range of different cultures. He found that these creative outputs bore a striking similarity to each other, even though the cultures concerned had never interacted. He was convinced that the images in these stories could not have been passed on as part of an oral tradition and subsequently adapted to a new cultural environment. He concluded that the themes of these artworks must reflect different states of the human psyche, that they were external manifestations of inner states of mind. The artist or creator of these images somehow externalised the inner self and in so doing made a statement about the human experience which was expressed as a primordial image.

An observer of these archetypal symbols responds when his or her own psychological profile is in sympathy with that of the creator at the time when the work was produced. Thus, certain symbols are appropriate to certain stages of psychological development. If a particular image was generated by an adolescent male then it is likely that it will appeal to other adolescent males. Jung (1964:110) demonstrates how throughout the world and throughout history young males have been drawn to hero myths. He quotes as examples the Greek hero Achilles, King Arthur, the Scandinavian hero Sigurd, the ancient Babylonian epic hero Gilgamesh, the American comic strip hero Superman, the biblical hero Samson, and the Persian hero Rustam. He demonstrates that even though all these myths vary in detail they are all structurally very similar. His observation is as follows:

> they (the myths) were developed by groups or individuals without any direct cultural contact with each other - by, for instance, tribes of Africans or North American Indians, or the Greeks, or the Incas of Peru. Over and over again one hears a tale describing a hero's miraculous but humble birth, his early proof of superhuman strength, his rapid rise to prominence or power, his triumphant struggle with the forces of evil, his fallibility to the sin of pride (hybris), and his fall through betrayal or a 'heroic' sacrifice that ends in his death. (Jung 1964:110)

51

Jung goes on to show how this particular myth is relevant to the psychological development of adolescent boys and provides a similar analysis of the story of 'Beauty and the Beast' and its relevance to adolescent girls.

What this thesis leads to is a tentative explanation of why, at certain stages in our lives, we are drawn to certain images rather than others; why, throughout our lives, our tastes change; and why, quite simply, we cannot expect everyone to like everything all of the time. According to Jung an observer can find himself in sympathy with the creator of a work of art, even though that creator lived many centuries earlier and perhaps in a different culture. Such sympathy with the work, it is suggested, will evoke response. The nature of the response will establish the value or worth of the work to the individual.

Jung's theory is the nearest we can get to explaining why we might react to particular works of art in the way we do. It has its flaws. It concentrates on the psychology of the individual and ignores the social context. It is difficult to decide how far these archetypes really are cross-cultural and trans-temporal. It is difficult to answer adequately the accusation that the hero myths only took the form they did because they were the product of male dominated societies. This may be true. And maybe, in order to understand what is going on, one needs to separate an emotional from an intellectual response to the symbolism. It is possible, after all, for one to respond to something emotionally whilst intellectually despising it; one responds, as it were, in spite of oneself. If our emotional response to art and to archetypes are conditioned by the prevailing social and cultural norms, then any initiatives in the area of cultural development will have to address the question of how to deal with a cultural history, embedded in emotionally powerful archetypal symbols, which may be at odds with the emerging cultural value systems. Raising levels of consciousness about these symbols and about why they exert such a powerful influence may be the only way to neutralise their emotional appeal. For this reason alone it is important for any efforts in the area of cultural development to pay attention to the subjective value we attribute to the art of the past as well as to generate new developments.

CONCLUSION

This chapter began by looking at the nature of the concept 'art' and rejected any unitary definition. Art and the 'Arts' are seen as a social construct which changes over time and can be different in different places. Indeed, as Horne points out, there can be societies with no concept of art at all:

> In societies where participating performing culture survived, such as that of the Australian Aborigines, the people, in dance and song, in instrumental music, drama and recitation, and in painting, themselves perpetuated the meaning they gave the world. The people themselves made their own 'art' (although to them there was no distinction between 'art' and the rest of their life).
>
> (Horne 1986:5)

Any definition of the arts is seen as being culturally and temporally specific, as are value systems in the arts. What is required for inclusion in the category of activity which we call the arts is that, at some stage, creative activity has taken place. Creativity is the sine qua non for inclusion in a concept of the arts. The idea of creativity will be explored in detail in the next chapter.

Values in the arts are relative. This chapter has explored these value systems and identified three ways in which worth is attributed; these are concerned with commercial or financial value, with artistic value, and with subjective value, the value or worth of a work of art to an individual who is engaging with that work. The next chapter will examine in detail the differing ways in which individuals engage with the arts.

REFERENCES

Appleyard, B., 1984, The Culture Club, London, Boston, Faber and Faber

Child, I.L., 1970, 'The Problem of Objectivity in Esthetic Value', in Pappas, G., Concepts in Art and Education, New York, Macmillan

Fletcher, J.M., 1982, '"The Glory of the Female Sex", Women Artists c.1500-1800', in Women's Art Show 1550-1970, Nottingham, Nottingham Castle Museum

The Arts

Greer, G., 1979, The Obstacle Race, London, Picador
Gregory, R.L., 1970, The Intelligent Eye, London, Weidenfeld and Nicolson
Hegel, G.W.F., 1979, Introduction to Aesthetics, translated by T.M. Knox with an Interpretative Essay by Charles Karelis, Oxford, Clarendon Press
Hoggart, R., 1985, 'False Populisms, False Elitisms', in Arts Express no. 12. Feb. 1985, London, Arts Express Publishing Ltd
Horne, D., 1986, The Public Culture - The Triumph of Industrialism, London, Sydney, etc., Pluto Press
Hunt, J., 1982, 'Art with a Capital "A", Woman With a Capital "W"', in Women's Art Show 1550-1970, Nottingham, Nottingham Castle Museum
Jung, C.G., 1964, Man and His Symbols, London, Aldus Books
Kelly, O., 1984, Community, Art and the State: Storming the Citadels, London, Comedia
Munro, T., 1963, 'The Psychology of Art: Past, Present, Future', in Hogg, J. (ed.), 1969, Psychology and the Visual Arts, Harmondsworth, Penguin
Nairne, S., 1987, State of the Art, Ideas and Images in the 1980s, London, Chatto and Windus in collaboration with Channel Four Television
Nunn, P.G., 1982, 'Women Artists in the Nineteenth Century', in Women's Art Show 1550-1970, Nottingham, Nottingham Castle Museum
Owusu, K., 1986, The Struggle for Black Arts in Britain - What can we consider better than freedom, London, Comedia
Parker, R. and Pollock, G., 1981, Old Mistresses: Women, Art and Ideology, London, Routledge and Kegan Paul
Pearson, N., 1982, The State and the Visual Arts, Milton Keynes, Open University
Pick, J., 1986, Managing the Arts? The British Experience, London, Rhinegold
Read, Sir H., 1968, 'The Problem of Internationalism in Art', The Magazine, Oct 68, no. 7, London, Institute of Contemporary Arts
Read, H., 1961, Education Through Art, London, Faber and Faber
Williams, R., 1983, Keywords, London, Fontana
Wittgenstein, L., 1953, Philosophical Investigations, translated by Anscombe, G.E.M., Oxford, Basil Blackwell
Wollheim, R., 1968, Art and its Objects - An Introduction to

54

The Arts

Aesthetics, New York, Evanston, etc., Harper and Row

Chapter Four

ENGAGING WITH THE ARTS

The last chapter discussed a range of ideas related to the arts. It looked at the way in which the arts are culturally defined and examined some of the ways in which the arts are perceived. It examined values in the arts and demonstrated that these were a social construct. Finally the chapter looked at the ways in which meaning is communicated in the arts and addressed the question of why people like and gain satisfaction from certain works rather than others. In this chapter I want to examine the different ways in which people participate in or relate to the arts. It is necessary to do this before going on to analyse the role of adult education in promoting participation in the arts and, at the same time, promoting or developing a particular idea of culture.

People relate to the arts in one of three ways; they relate as either appreciator, creator or participant. Before expanding on them I will briefly explain these terms. I am using the term appreciator to denote those people who are the audience in the arts. They are the ones who go to concerts or exhibitions, read novels or poetry or simply watch a play on television. I would not wish to categorise their relationship to the arts as passive, since many art forms can be quite demanding, but their engagement with the arts is not active in the same way as the engagement of a creative artist or a performer. Appreciators are the consumers of the art world.

The term creator is fairly self-explanatory. It refers to those people who are creative artists. This does not mean that they necessarily make a living from arts; it simply means that, whether professional or amateur, they spend some of their time working as creative artists.

The last category, that of participant, refers to those people who are either directors or performers in the arts. I want to distinguish here between first, the activity engaged in by a dramatist or composer; second, that engaged in by the director of a play or the conductor of an orchestra; and third, that in which the actors and instrumentalists participate. It seems to me that in the performing arts the creative source of any work is the composer or playwright. The conductor and director are responsible for interpreting the work but there is no sense in which they could be said to be working on the same creative level as the prime originator of the work. They may be original and inventive in their interpretation, but the essence of a work, its theme or its message, belongs to the original creator. When, later, I discuss the nature of creativity it will be clear that the director and the conductor are engaged in something other than the integrated creativity of the composer or playwright.

Actors and musicians may be even further removed from the creative source of a work. It is acknowledged that in some forms of music, like jazz for instance, the musician is operating as both creator and performer. Similarly in some form of improvised drama the actor is also the creator. The point I wish to make is that the orchestral players and their instruments are the artistic medium through which the conductor interprets the work of the composer. Similarly, in a play, the actors, together with the sets, the costumes and the lighting, are the medium through which the director interprets the work of the playwright. This way of relating to the arts is neither creation nor appreciation, hence I have called it participation. It requires knowledge, skill, sympathy and its own form of discipline.

I have defined the three categories above as though they were a characteristic of individuals, as though some people were creators, others appreciators and yet others participants. This, of course, gives a false impression of the reality. Any individual may operate in all three ways. The terms are more appropriately used to describe the way in which an individual is operating in relation to the arts. They describe the process, the nature of the activity, rather than the person. A painter will sometimes operate as a creative artist but at other times will be an observer at an exhibition or part of an audience at a concert. Similarly a composer may also play an instrument in a string quartet as well as attend recitals as a listener. Henceforth I will use the terms to refer to process rather than people. By doing this I hope to demonstrate that activities like acting, which are normally thought of as participative, can, in effect, be highly creative.

APPRECIATION

Appreciation in the arts involves a range of activities. As indicated in the previous chapter, appreciators relate to the arts in a number of ways and it is possible for an individual to develop from an initial enjoyment of a work of art to a full scale academic enquiry of the work of a particular artist or genre. The skills required for these different sorts of engagement with the arts vary considerably.

Clearly, in order to appreciate a work of art it is necessary to approach it with as open a mind as is possible. It is, of course, impossible to divest oneself entirely of the layers of cultural conditioning which one brings to a work of art. One cannot deny one's previous experience, one's preferences and tastes. Yet it is important, if one wishes to interact with a work, to approach it with a certain innocence.

Some art forms appear to be more demanding than others. A piece of music heard on the radio can create an immediate impression, evoke an immediate emotional response. A painting may call forth an immediate reaction and increase its attraction the longer one looks at it. In contrast to this we often take only one opportunity to sit through a production of a play and base all our judgements on that experience. A novel, on the other hand, takes more time to read; it is consequently much more demanding of our attention.

The idea of 'attention' is well established in psychology. It is known that we are able to direct our perceptual senses in order to focus on certain configurations of stimuli rather than others. Underwood puts it like this:

> ... attention also serves to determine which configurations should be processed. Whilst engrossed in a novel the reader is unlikely to be sampling continuously stimuli from his surroundings, unless for some specific purpose. We have the ability to attend to one source of stimulation to the exclusion of others,

and this has obvious biological advantages.
(Underwood 1976:210)

Attention is seen as being potentially a means of selecting what is to be perceived. Though, as Wilding (1982:102-32) acknowledges, it is possible to perceive without paying attention and it is possible to perceive subliminally. Wilding notes two aspects of attention:

the notion of attention, which has commonly been used in two main senses:
1. selective attention, the mechanisms which reject some information and take in other (whether the latter enter awareness or not);
2. capacity, an ill-defined reference to the idea that the amount of processing that can be carried out on incoming information has some upper limit.
(Wilding 1982:102)

The reference to capacity acknowledges that people can do two or more, often quite complex things, at once. I will return to this point in the section on creation. Bartley (1980:19), rather than talking about attending to a task or activity prefers to characterise what he calls 'three modes of personal existence'. As will be seen from the quotation below, these 'modes' are ways of attending to a task or to an activity.

The first is the appreciative mode, which is the general state that characterises the individual at a symphony or at an opera or at an art gallery. The various patterns of impingement (of stimuli upon the senses) are reacted to with a disposition of extracting pleasure and appreciation. The organism is in a state of searching for understanding and pleasure.
A second mode is called the motoric mode, this is exemplified by players in a game of football. The major responses to all that affect eyes and ears are motor. The players run, pause, pivot, avoid other players, and so forth. These motor responses are perceptual responses.
The third mode is the meditative, the individual is preoccupied with thoughts, memories, and so forth. In this state, one does not respond to what reaches the sense organs in the same way as in other modes. It is as

> though one does not hear nor see what is going on around him or her.
>
> (Bartley 1980:19)

It is obviously important for an appreciator to adopt an appropriate mode of attention, or in Bartley's terms, an appropriate mode of personal existence. This would appear to be the starting point for any sort of appreciative activity.

Appreciation in the arts takes time and skill. If one is to move beyond the first emotional response it also takes a certain amount of perceptual, analytic and intellectual ability. These skills, together with the appropriate skills of attending must be learned.

In order to become involved in appreciation in the arts it becomes important to develop more acute levels of perception. It is known that in everyday life we operate at minimal levels of perceptual activity; we see as little as we need to see in order to survive. If it is important to distinguish between different colours in very close tonal arrangements or to be attuned enough to enjoy the variety in a narrow range of harmonic sounds, then levels of visual and auditory perception need to be fairly highly developed.

After attending to a work of art, perceiving represents another mental activity necessary for appreciation; yet the idea of perception is a concept which is still not fully understood.

> To complicate matters further, the term 'perception' has been employed to refer to several quite different processes. Moreover, while some writers intend that the term be interpreted quite literally, (i.e. as perceiving in the sense of seeing, hearing and otherwise detecting or discriminating some aspect of environment), others have employed the term almost metaphorically to designate a world view, an outlook on life, or some other very general cognitive product.
>
> (Segall, Campbell, Herskovits, 1966:24)

Additionally there is little agreement amongst researchers about the way in which perception works. There are, currently, two theories which may not be as mutually irreconcilable as their advocates would have us believe.

In the previous chapter I referred briefly to a reference from Gregory (1970:106-22) about the idea of perceptual hypotheses. This concept belongs to the traditional theory of perception which suggests that the image on the retina is matched against possible and hypothetical interpretations until its meaning can be ascertained. Bruce and Green (1985:322) suggest that according to traditional theory we must reconstruct the world around us by piecing together more primitive elements such as edges or blobs. In order to do this we need knowledge of the world, such as the knowledge of the sizes of objects in order to detect their distance from the observer. By matching these visual images against previous experience we construct our image of the world around us.

> Traditional perceptual theory holds that perception is indirect and mediated by higher cognitive processes. We do not "just see" the world but actively construct it from fragmentary perceptual data.
>
> (Bruce and Green 1985:203)

Contrary to this is a theory of perception developed by J.J. Gibson, (1979), which explores an ecological approach to seeing. It would be wrong of me to suggest that these two approaches to understanding perception totally contradict each other. Bruce and Green (1985:189) suggest that the two approaches should be regarded as complementary, though it is doubtful that Gibson would accept this compromise.

According to Gibson's theory perception is seen as being direct and not mediated by higher cognitive processes which involve inference and problem solving. His starting point is not the image on the retina but the total optic array which an observer samples. The term 'optic array' is explained as follows:

> When ambient light, at a point of observation, is structured it is an ambient optic array. The point of observation may be stationary or moving. The point of observation may be unoccupied or occupied by an observer.
>
> (Gibson 1979:92)

The starting point for understanding perception is for Gibson, not the image on the retina, but this ambient optic array in which light waves are structured by the objects which exist in that array, the tables and chairs and other objects in a room for instance. Bruce and Green explain other aspects of the theory as follows:

61

Gibson maintains that it is flow and disturbances in the structure of the total optic array, rather than bars, blobs or forms in an 'image', which provide the information for perception, which unambiguously informs the observer both about the world and about him or herself simultaneously. In this ecological approach, perception and action are seen as tightly interlocked and mutually constraining. More controversially, Gibson's is a 'direct' theory of perception, in which he maintains that information is 'picked up' rather than processed.

(Bruce and Green 1985:190)

The idea of a direct theory of perception is somewhat complex and difficult to grasp if one has been used to thinking of perception as the process by which one makes sense of the retinal image. This is how Gibson himself explains it:

Direct perception is what one gets from seeing Niagara Falls, say, as distinguished from seeing a picture of it. The latter kind of perception is mediated. So when I assert that perception of the environment is direct, I mean that it is not mediated by retinal pictures, neural pictures, or mental pictures. Direct perception is the activity of getting information from the ambient array of light. I call this a process of information pickup that involves the exploratory activity of looking around, getting around and looking at things. This is quite different from the supposed activity of getting information from the inputs of the optic nerves, whatever they may prove to be.

(Gibson 1979:147)

According to Gibson it is the relationship between textured surfaces in the total optic array which structure the light entering the eye and provide the information for perception to take place. He criticised many perceptual experiments for using figures without backgrounds and argued that in the real world the relationship between figure and ground provides crucial information for perception to take place. Gibson also suggests that in the real world we do not see objects as stationary and from a fixed point of view, as in many experiments. On the contrary, we walk up to an object, walk round it and handle it in order to acquire enough sensory information to perceive it. Vision provides us with information about the environment but also with information about ourselves and our relationship to the environment. Perception, then, is as Bartley (1980:24) defines it, the 'name for the immediate interaction of the organism with its physical surrounds'.

Both Gibson (1966) and Bartley (1980) see the senses as perceptual systems which collect information from a range of sensory inputs. Thus, distance may not be perceived by comparing knowledge about the expected size of an object with the perceived size so that we conclude that the smaller an object is, the further away it must be. Distance may be perceived by seeing an object in relation to other objects, by moving the head and noting the relative changes in position of object and background, by sensing the different position of the eyes in their sockets when focussed on a near rather than a distant object, or by sensing the degree of parallax between the images on the two retinas when using binocular vision (the degree to which the image on the retina of the right eye is different to that on the left).

It used to be thought that there were the five senses of sight, hearing, touch, taste and smell. This rather simplistic view of the way in which we interact with the world has been replaced by a paradigm which allows six perceptual systems. The paradigm was developed by Gibson (1966) and the six systems described by Bartley (1980:8-9) as the visual, the auditory, the savor, the haptic, the basic orientation, and the homoeostatic systems.

The visual system involves looking in order to detect light waves. We thus gain information about size, shape, location, distance, colour, texture, hardness and softness. We do this using the eyes and the ocular muscles.

The auditory system involves us in listening to detect air vibrations which provide information about the nature and location of acoustic sources. We do this using the cochlea and the middle ear.

The savor system involves the two actions of tasting and smelling. In smelling we use the nose to detect the chemical composition of inspired air in order to gain information about the characteristics of volatile sources. In tasting we detect the chemical composition and thermal state of ingested material in order to acquire information about the palatable attributes of ingested material and to detect noxious substances. Both the nose and the mouth can also be involved in the perception of pain.

63

The haptic system involves us in not just touching but also in handling, pushing, pulling, lifting, kicking etc. In doing this we detect the deformation of tissue, the actions and positions of the joints, the stretching of muscles, and thermal and painful stimuli. We thus gain information about our contact with the ground or floor, mechanical encounters, object shapes and material states such as softness, hardness, wetness, dryness, coldness and hotness. We do this by perceiving sensory input from the skin, muscles, joints, ligaments and tendons.

The basic orientation system enables us to detect static gravity and acceleration in order to gain information about pushes and pulls and the direction of gravity. This perceptual system involves us in posturing and locomotion and we acquire sensory input through vestibular organs, kinesthetic receptors and visual sense organs.

Finally the homoeostatic system provides us with information about comfort and well-being and allows us to avoid overheating and chilling. The system allows us to detect temperature, pressure and CO_2. We receive sensory information via the carotid sinus receptors, depressor sensory endings in walls of intra-pericardial vessels and pulmonary veins, pressor sensory cells in the vestibular nuclei, thermal-sensitive neurons in hypothalamus and receptors in the tracheo-bronchial tree.

I have offered this brief description of the six perceptual systems because they represent an important development in thinking in this area. For our purposes we are principally concerned with those perceptual systems which are important to the arts. Which systems are important depends on the nature of one's engagement with the arts as well as the nature of the art form with which one is engaging. In appreciation the visual, auditory and haptic systems will be the most important, though it is not inconceivable that some art forms may impinge on the savor system. Most art forms require the use of the visual system. Music and other performed arts also rely on the auditory system. Sculpture and other arts or crafts which exploit tactile qualities will require the use of the haptic system. Participation requires all these systems as well as, in dance or theatre, the basic orientation system. Similarly, creation in the arts will demand the development and use of the appropriate perceptual systems. Any educational activity designed to enable engagement with the arts needs to take account of the possible varying levels of perceptual acuity within these systems.

A further development in the area of perception concerns the mounting evidence which seems to demonstrate that perception is culturally determined. The term 'culture' is used here in the anthropological rather than the artistic sense. The thesis is that we need to learn to perceive the world and in so doing are influenced by the prevailing cultural mode of perception as well as the visual environment. Thus, someone brought up in an urban environment of straight streets and tall buildings would see converging straight lines as parallel lines receding into the distance. Someone brought up in, say, a desert environment would not interpret converging lines in this way. In many experiments subjects have been tested to find out if they interpret linear perspective as indicating distance. People from different cultures are tested to find out if they interpret converging lines and a series of optical illusions in the same way. Gregory describes some results as follows:

> The people who stand out as living in a non-perspective world are the Zulus. Their world has been described as a 'circular culture' - their huts are round, and have round doors; they do not plough their land in straight furrows but in curves; and few of their possessions have corners or straight lines. They are thus ideal subjects for our purpose. It is found that they do experience the arrow illusion to a small extent, but that they are hardly affected at all by other illusion figures.
>
> Studies of people living in dense forest have been made. Such people are interesting, in that they do not experience distant objects, because there are only small clearances in the forest. When they are taken out of their forest, and shown distant objects, they see these not as distant, but as small.
>
> (Gregory 1973:160-1)

Wilding cautions against complete acceptance of these findings by suggesting that the results may be equally due to the fact that the subjects were not accustomed to looking at two dimensional representations.

> However, part of the explanation for these reduced effects could lie in differences in perception of two-dimensional representations in general which have no particular implications for three-dimensional

perception.

(Wilding 1982:234)

Whilst Wilding's caution may dismiss the results as inconsequential in terms of everyday living in a three-dimensional world, they reinforce our interest in the phenomenon. In the visual arts it is precisely the perception of two-dimensional pictures that concerns us.

A theory like this depends on our being able to demonstrate that perception is learned. There is an impressive amount of evidence, both old and relatively new, which suggests that this might be the case.

It has been known for a long time that, in an age when they were a reasonably new phenomenon, black, and white photographs could not be understood by many primitive tribes. Herskovits (1948:381 and 1959:56) reports that members of these primitive social groupings simply could not make sense of the images on the paper. It appeared as though they had to learn to 'read' the images. Other evidence from Thouless (1933), Beveridge (1935 and 1939), Hudson (1960) and Dennis (1960) indicated that the way in which a person learned to read these images might be culturally determined.

Latta (1904), Senden (1932), Hebb (1949), London (1960) and Gregory and Wallace (1963) all provide evidence from cases where a subject was born blind or near blind and subsequently gained their sight after a surgical operation. In each case the patient could not make sense of the visual stimuli and had to learn to interpret the images on the retina, or in Gibson's terms, to interact with the optic array.

The most convincing evidence comes from Segall, Campbell and Herskovits (1966) who used empirical tests and statistical techniques to show that people from different environments, (urban American, rural African, etc.), scored significantly differently on a range of perceptual tests for the researchers to conclude that their perception was determined by the culture in which they learned to see. They were able to demonstrate that this difference in perception was not due to inherited factors but depended on culturally determined differences in learned perceptual behaviour.

The implications for this for both adult education and the arts in a multi-cultural society have hardly begun to be explored by either teachers or academic researchers. It seems that our perception of colour, form, texture, location and distance will be dependent on our cultural environment. Clearly art forms relating to a particular culture will require a different mode of perception from those relating to another culture. In order to appreciate works of art from cultures other than our own it becomes necessary to develop new ways of seeing and hearing and to increase our levels of perceptual acuity.

There is some evidence from the field of health education that it is important not to assume that everyone perceives in the same sort of way. Alan C. Holmes describes the problems encountered in developing visual aids for health education programmes in developing countries. He sees the natives as having, not a different form of perceiving the world but as having an 'inferior form of visual understanding'.

> On the other hand, when a picture or a model larger than life, even though it may be of a familiar object, is shown to an audience with low levels of visual understanding, it often produces confusion. For example, when a scaled-down picture or model of a house, a tree, a goat, a cow or some other familiar object is used, understanding is usually immediate and complete; but when an object such as a fly or mosquito, equally familiar in their life size, is made larger either in picture or model form, then it at once becomes unfamiliar and is not recognised. When testing a drawing or a model of a fly made much larger than life, the reply received by the author was courteous but firm, 'It can't be, we don't have flies that size in Kenya.
> (Holmes 1964:65)

It is reasonable to suggest that such failures of communication are not to do with one mode of perception being either inferior or superior to another but caused by a failure on the part of the teacher to realise that perception is culturally determined and that this needs to be taken into account when preparing visual teaching materials.

What most writers seem to agree on is that levels of perception can be improved through learning. Bruce and Green point out:

> Finally, there is agreement (between traditional and ecological theorists) that perceptual experience can be influenced by learning. (Bruce and Green 1985:322)

Engaging with the Arts

Hochberg discusses the effect of practice in the following terms:

> One effect of practice and experience is to increase our power of differentiation in what we perceive - that is, to enable us to see distinguishing characteristics and distinctive features by which we can respond differently to stimuli that previously looked alike.
> Indeed, the general trends that appear in the course of perceptual learning are increasing differentiation, increasingly efficient direction of attention, and increasing economy of picking up information.
>
> (Hochberg 1978:100)

The knowledge that perceptual systems can be improved through exercise and practice is important for educators. Anyone who has been involved in the visual arts will know from experience that this is true. People simply see more when they have learned to direct their attention and concentrate on the optic array. Practice in looking is an important yet neglected educational activity.

Having directed our attention to a work of art and ensured that we can perceive it adequately, it is necessary to turn to questions of aesthetics to begin to understand how we might derive satisfaction from art. It is difficult enough to understand why we might gain satisfaction from representational art forms, where the content can be perceived as representing something in the real world, but it is even more difficult to understand why we gain satisfaction from entirely abstract art forms.

Both Williams (1983:31) and Redfern (1986:16) attribute the first use of the word 'aesthetic' to Alexander Baumgarten who held that beauty was a property of things, of objects or scenes, and it was apprehended through the senses. This idea that beauty or ugliness resided in things was challenged by Immanuel Kant (1933) who argued that it is the activity of the human mind which establishes beauty or ugliness. Redfern (1986:15) suggests that the idea gradually emerged that some thing or activity could be appreciated not only for its efficiency or its craftsmanship but as a source of intrinsic satisfaction, something to be prized for its own sake. Redfern goes on as follows:

> But aesthetic qualities, Kant further argued (in the

'Critique of Judgement'), are to be thought of as constituted in a way which contrasts with that of ordinary everyday perception - one in which our powers of imagination and feeling function differently.

On this view, now quite widely accepted in broad outline but with some variations in detail, there are no distinctively aesthetic features such as beauty or ugliness that are perceivable and recognizable as are, say, loudness, hardness, or angularity. Rather, an object of ordinary perception is regarded from a special standpoint ('under a particular description' in contemporary philosophical language); and this involves a certain freedom of judgement and discrimination, an active personal response that has a markedly affective, as well as intellectual, dimension.

(Redfern 1986:18-19)

Redfern (1986:19) concludes that aesthetic awareness is a matter of how we attend rather than what we attend to, and suggests that the aesthetic appreciation of the structured form of a work of art may not involve a critical judgement of its content. Aesthetic awareness then is subjective in nature; it is a form of seeing which invites an individual to exercise a sort of skilful perception. Redfern goes on to suggest that:

aesthetic awareness involves an imaginative apprehension of some object encountered at first hand, whose form thus perceived yields a certain satisfaction or dissatisfaction: interest is in something regarded as if it existed purely for being looked at, or listened to, or (as in the case of literature) in some other way imaginatively contemplated.

(Redfern 1986:21)

If aesthetic awareness is subjective in this way then it is not unreasonable to suggest that aesthetic judgements are also subjective. The satisfaction gained from a given work of art should be considered as being unique to the individual. It may be that other observers experience a similar satisfaction, but the experience of each individual personality and imagination interacting with a work of art must be unique to that individual. No-one else can bring the same personality and personal history to bear on the work. As mentioned above, the concern so far has been with the form of the work of art, not the content. An appreciation of the content of a work requires a different form of critical judgement, more intellectual and cognitive in nature. It may be that whilst one acquires satisfaction from contemplating the form of a work, one may disagree violently with its content. It is possible to admire a portrait of Napoleon without agreeing with the regime over which he presided.

It could be argued that some art forms are entirely non-representational. Music is the most obvious example. Satisfaction here can be obtained without reference to any content that relates to the world in which we live. One can think of abstract painting and sculpture in the same sort of way. What these works do embody is a philosophy, an approach to the arts, and this can be articulated and appraised. The judgement here is not about the content of the work of art but about what the work stands for, about the statement implicit in the work about the nature of art. This involves going beyond the immediate aesthetic satisfaction to be gained from the work and approaching it more in the role of a critic. In this role it becomes possible to share one's perception of the work. Redfern explains it like this:

> The citing of particular details is precisely what is often found in the critical literature of the various arts, crafts and sometimes in sports journalism; critics and reviewers characteristically provide descriptions of works and performances which may support their interpretations and valuations. And the successful outcome is that on testing these interpretations against the publicly perceptible features of a play, a necklace, a ski-jump etc., another person is brought not to believe the truth of a proposition but to share the critics imaginative perception and, with that, his response.
>
> (Redfern 1986:62)

This is, of course, one of the ways in which value systems in the arts are established. There is a danger that certain value systems will acquire a dominant status at the expense of others which have not been so energetically promoted. The critic and the teacher-as-critic can play a central role in the maintenance of cultural hegemonies. The danger is that they persuade us to approach works of art with a predetermined mode of perception; a perception which favours one form of expression rather than another. It is surely better to open our eyes and ears to different forms of cultural expression and to develop perceptual and cognitive skills so that we can appreciate the cultural artefacts of different societies and different ages. Developing levels of perception in this way has implications for the way in which we understand the world. Perceiving and knowing are closely interrelated.

If one accepts Gibson's ecological theory of perception then there are implications for our understanding of the nature of cognition; perception becomes a way of knowing.

> Perceiving is the simplest and best kind of knowing. But there are other kinds of which three were suggested. Knowing by means of instruments extends perceiving into the realm of the very distant and the very small; it also allows of metric knowledge. Knowing by means of language makes knowing explicit instead of tacit. Language permits descriptions and pools the accumulated observations of our ancestors. Knowing by means of pictures also extends perceiving and consolidates the gains of perceiving.
>
> The awareness of imagining entities and events might be ascribed to the operation of the perceptual system with a suspension of reality testing.
>
> Imagination, as well as knowledge and perception, can be aroused by another person who uses language or makes pictures.
>
> (Gibson 1979:263)

It seems to be increasingly accepted that perception is a form of cognition. Both psychologists and aesthetic philosophers are tending to this view. The analysis of a work of art usually demands a resort to language. The term language is used here to include musical and other notation systems and mathematical symbols as well as words. Whether or not Gibson's assertion that language 'makes knowing explicit instead of tacit' is a matter of debate. There is an alternative argument which suggests that language restricts our view of the world. The suggestion is that we can only conceive of those things for which we have words. This restricts the nature of our knowledge of the world to a particular language in a particular time and place. There are obvious questions about whether language can convey the meaning, the knowledge, which derives from the aesthetic appreciation of a work of art. The case is perhaps best put by Louis Arnaud Reid. He is discussing the feelings aroused from looking at a work of art:

> What I am saying here, that feeling's immediate awareness is cognitive, is in contradiction to the current propositional view that one cannot be said to know anything unless one can state it under a named category or concept. I am merely implying, once again, that this is a too limited view of knowing and knowledge. The content of what we are immediately aware is unlimited, whilst the range of our categorical language is extremely limited. A few of the contents of our feelings can be named but only in a general way. Many are not, and some cannot be. The content of our cognitive feeling for art, for instance, can never be translated adequately into words or symbols other than those of art itself.
>
> (Reid 1985:119)

Whether or not resorting to language to discuss or otherwise communicate the meaning of a work of art is a useful or helpful practice is open to debate. It is a practice engaged in by critics, philosophers and art historians. Whether or not it enhances the degree to which one can aesthetically appreciate a work of art has not been proven. For some people, increased knowledge about the structure of a work and the context in which it was created will increase the level of satisfaction to be gained from the work; the content of the work, whether it is representational or not, can be studied as well as the form enjoyed. And it may be that the formal qualities which an observer enjoys enhance the appreciation of the content. For other people the need to acquire such knowledge will detract from their enjoyment of the work. It is difficult, if not impossible, to demonstrate that increased knowledge about a work increases enjoyment of a work in any measurable sense, yet much educational activity is directed to this end, indeed, large university departments are founded and exist for this purpose.

The above paragraphs have described and analysed the skills and abilities necessary for the appreciation of the arts. It may seem odd to discuss appreciation before creation since, chronologically, a work must be created before it can be appreciated. I have chosen to tackle the job this way round because the skills required for appreciation are also required for creation. The act of creation, however, requires additional abilities.

CREATION

I have written elsewhere about creativity (Jones 1978, 1981 and 1985) and for a fuller account of creative activity in adult education the reader should refer to these texts. My purpose here is to provide an overview of the different ways in which creativity has been and is understood so that, in a later chapter, discussion can focus on the teaching of creativity in adult education as a contribution to cultural development. I will draw on evidence from both old and new studies to show how our understanding of the concept of creativity has been developed.

Research in the area of creativity has not seen the concept as relating solely to the arts, indeed many studies have been carried out on creative scientists and creative military personnel. Research and writing on creativity can be categorised in terms of the way in which creativity is thought to manifest itself. It is seen as either a quality of a work of art, an aspect of personality or as a psychological process. Writing, therefore, concentrates on either the product, the work of art, the personality or the process.

There is a school of thought which asserts that creativity is identified in the product of creative activity, in the work of art, rather than in the mental process which formed that work of art or in the personality of its creator. Colin Symes puts it like this:

> Thus, to talk of creativity solely in dispositional terms, without reference to some emergent product, smacks of the spurious. Private though the process might be, the only way it can be judged 'creative' is by the significance of what is engendered.
>
> As J.P. White rightly points out, 'creative' is a medal that is pinned on public products, not the processes which supposedly led to them. That being the case, the whole matter of what properly constitutes creativity is a question of aesthetics as much as psychology.
>
> (Symes 1983:85)

The idea that creativity manifests itself in the work of

art, that we can say that a particular piece is or is not creative depends, according to this argument, on our being able to identify objectively the aesthetic value of a work. Earlier I referred to Child's work which attempts to demonstrate the existence of aesthetic value, though, it has to be said, with little success. He (Child 1970:390-404) tries to show that objective aesthetic value exists by measuring agreement amongst individuals in aesthetic preference. Unfortunately his findings are inconclusive and fail to demonstrate that either aesthetic value or creativity can be established as qualities inherent in works of art.

It is difficult to see how this line of enquiry might develop. Whilst it has so far proved impossible to demonstrate the existence of objectively identifiable aesthetic value, it has to be acknowledged that many respected academics believe in the existence of such value. This belief forms the basis of Hoggart's position outlined in the previous chapter (Hoggart 1985:13). But, as I said earlier, such a position remains at the level of speculation since no evidence is ever identified to support it.

It is as though writers like Hoggart are attempting to support an academic tradition which, concerned as it is with analysis, categorisation and periodisation rather than with creation, generates and maintains a value system which justifies the existence of the tradition. The basis of this value system is rarely challenged and artists themselves sometimes collude in its maintenance by seeking the approval of influential critics. One cannot see how these writings can be taken seriously until the criteria used for establishing worth have been identified. For our purposes this area of enquiry does not look promising.

On the face of it, it looks as though research into the creative personality might be more useful to our enquiry. A difficulty with this research is that one can never be sure that researchers are all looking at the same thing when they assert that they are trying to identify creativity. I will come back to this problem later. For the moment the reader should be aware of the potential difficulties arising from different researchers having different concepts of the nature of creativity.

In this area of research, creativity is usually seen as a problem solving operation. What is tested is the ability to find novel or original solutions to problems set by the researcher. In this way an attempt is made to measure creative ability so that its level can be correlated with

74

scores on other personality tests. The intention is to identify the personality correlates of creative ability, to show that creative people are likely to have a particular sort of personality and behavioural characteristics. Both Barron (1955:478-85) and MacKinnon (1962a:11-39) adopt this approach and come out with similar results. They see the creative individual as being independent, able to tolerate disorder or chaos, occasionally rebellious and energetically committed.

There have been other attempts to establish a correlation between creative ability and intelligence as measured on standard IQ tests. These studies have been inconclusive. Their results have been summarised as follows:

> in the study of creativity and intelligence results have been conflicting owing partly to the presuppositions of the investigators and partly to the misunderstandings about the strengths and limitations of techniques ... Actual research results have more commonly revealed high correlations between tests of intelligence, low correlations between tests of creativity, and correlations between the two kinds of test that have varied from zero to high.
>
> (Freeman, Butcher and Christie 1968:9)

One of the problems here is that there is little agreement about the nature of intelligence tests. There is a belief amongst some researchers that intelligence tests do no more than measure one's ability to do intelligence tests. It certainly seems to be the case that people can learn to do intelligence tests; that, with practice, they can get better results without being, in any real sense, more intelligent.

Despite problems with regard to tests attempting to correlate creative ability with intelligence, work in the area of personality produces results which are remarkably similar. Thus, writers like Rogers (1961:349), Hudson (1966) and Ross (1978:1) all make similar statements and come to conclusions similar to those of Barron (1955 and 1958) and MacKinnon (1962a, 1962b and 1965) about the nature of the creative personality. But it is difficult to see where this line of enquiry takes us. Certainly it identifies attitudes and behaviours which, in, say, an educational setting, might at first glance seem inappropriate but which may have to be tolerated if creative activity is to take place. At a time when the concept of personality itself is being questioned one has to treat this research with caution.

There is no clear way in which this research can be seen to be useful. In adult education it may be helpful as a pointer to what we are trying to achieve, adults who are able to behave in a certain (creative) way which can be identified by reference to personality correlates. But we do not really work like this in education. If one accepted the value of such tests one could administer a personality test at the beginning and end of a course to see how far participants had developed towards a model of the creative personality. But such procedures are not felt to be appropriate for adult education students. At best this line of enquiry can be instrumental in persuading teachers that if they are to foster creativity then they may need to tolerate a certain amount of rebellious, individualistic and unconventional behaviour.

Before going on to look at research which concentrates on the creative process I want to return to the problem of what we mean by the term 'creative'. When referring to the writings on the creative personality I pointed out that not all researchers mean the same thing by the term. In an attempt to clarify the various usages of the concept I want to draw attention to a model of creative activity developed by Maslow as long ago as 1968. Here he distinguishes three types of creative activity which he relates to what he calls the self-actualising phase of his hierarchy of human needs. He calls these three types of creativity, primary, secondary and integrated creativity. These terms are derived from the Freudian idea of primary and secondary thought processes. These processes are described by Wollheim as follows:

> In the Interpretation of Dreams, Freud was driven to conclude that two fundamentally different types of psychical process can be discriminated in the formation of dreams. One of these, which also accounts for our ordinary thinking, issues in rational trains of thought. The other process, which is the survival of our earliest mental apparatus, seizes hold of this train of thought and operates upon it in certain characteristic ways: the ways in which Freud singled out for scrutiny are condensation, displacement, and the casting of thought into a visually representable form. The more primitive of the two processes, Freud called the primary process: the other, the process of rationality, he called the secondary process. (Wollheim 1968:109)

Thus the primary process is seen as primitive and the mechanism by which dreams are produced. It functions at the level of the unconscious. The secondary process is a more conscious affair. It relates more to the telling or narrating of dreams, in Freudian terms, than to the act of dreaming. It relates to the contributions of the teller of a story to the story told. It often involves the design of form or structure to convey the content of the dream, the story or the image.

This distinction between two different types of mental functioning was mainly a theoretical construct until 1976 when Colin Martindale did tests to establish that the different forms of mental functioning were characterised by different sorts of brain-wave activity. He measured the degree of cortical arousal in the brain with an electroencephalogram (EEG) of brain-wave frequency. He summarises his results as follows:

> Secondary thought, then, rests on medium levels of cortical arousal ... Primary process thought may occur both with very high and very low levels of arousal. From dream states at one end to emotional highs at the other, the irrational stuff of new ideas surges into the mind on brain-waves too high or too low for calculated planning.
>
> (Martindale 1976:16-19)

It was this distinction between primary and secondary processes which Maslow (1968:135-45) used as the basis for identifying three different types of creativity.

Primary creativity is seen as 'that which proceeds from and uses the primary process much more than the secondary process'.

Secondary creativity is 'based in the secondary thought processes and includes a large proportion of production-in-the-world, the bridges, the houses, the new automobiles, even many scientific experiments and much literary work'.

Finally 'that creativity which uses both types of process easily and well, in good fusion or in good succession, I shall call integrated creativity. It is from this kind that comes the great work of art or philosophy or science'.

From these descriptions it will be seen that primary creativity is concerned with processes akin to dream formation; it is concerned with the generation of symbolic images, with myth, legend, ritual, and fantasy. It is more concerned with content than form, with metaphor rather than structure.

Secondary creativity is concerned more with structure, with the solving of design problems. It is an altogether more conscious attempt to develop original solutions to problems. It concerns designing rather than dreaming.

Where these two processes come together, where the metaphorical images derived from primary process functioning are structured through secondary process activity one can expect the outcome to aspire to the condition of art as a product of integrated creativity.

I have explained these categories at some length because they will inform the analysis of creative process which follows. The review of research into product and personality undertaken above was somewhat inconclusive. I acknowledge that I have not given a proper indication of the range and extent of the work in this area. In the field of creative personality studies there is a vast literature. My intention was to include enough to demonstrate that, for the purpose of this book, this line of enquiry, whilst justifiable and interesting in its own terms, is not really helpful; it is difficult to see how one could apply such studies to adult education practice. It is in the area of the creative process that the most pertinent writing has been carried out.

One of the difficulties is that readers are never quite sure which type of creativity, in Maslow's terms, writers are focussing on. One can only try to ascertain from the context which form of creativity is being considered. Not all writers are concerned with the arts and one has to glean what useful material one can from studies of engineers, scientists, medics, etc.

Much of the writing in this area is speculative. Some of the work is concerned with artists but not by any means all. There are few references to the creative work of non-professional adults, the ordinary man-in-the-street, other than those concerned with the mentally ill. A substantial body of the writing relates to the creative work of children. In attempting to explain the nature of the creative process I intend to draw on all these sources.

Before going on it is important to point out that in reviewing the literature relating to an area of enquiry one is obliged to use the same conceptual frameworks as the writers under discussion. This is not always helpful but, in a sense, unavoidable. I make this point because much of the writing on creativity assumes a paradigm based on Freudian psychology. Thus, the various explanations of creative activity seek to explain it in terms of conscious and unconscious processes. But it may be that the concept of conscious and unconscious mental activity is in itself flawed. Only two levels of activity are postulated and there is the suggestion of a hierarchical relationship between them. It is possible that resort to a different model of mental functioning might prove more fruitful but as yet there has been no work in this area. The idea of 'parallel distributed processing' as developed by Rumelhart, McClelland and the P.D.P. Research Group (1986:passim) looks promising but as yet they have not directed their attention to the study of creativity. For the moment it is necessary to accept the Freudian model.

Most writers acknowledge the importance of unconscious primary process activity to the creative process. Both Freud and Jung recognised the centrality of the unconscious to creative activity. This reliance on the idea of unconscious primary processes to explain the phenomenon of creation has persisted to the present day.

Ehrenzweig (1968:102) attempts to explain how images arise from these unconscious processes by suggesting that the artist works, as it were, in collusion with the work in hand. He suggests that 'any work of art functions like another person, having independent life of its own'. The work appears to tell the creator what to do next. The creator, the artist, needs to be open to suggestions from the work and should not try to dominate or consciously control the work. This, it is thought, would inhibit the generation of image.

It is suggested that the work, operating as though it were another person, speaks for the artist's unconscious in a dialogue with the conscious which is attempting to control and structure the primary process activity. The work of art is born out of this conflict between the primitive primary processes of the unconscious and the structuring formal and rational secondary processes of the conscious. A pre-requisite for fruitful dialogue between conscious and unconscious is that the conscious must be willing to abandon the natural tendency to structure and direct the work and allow the primary processes of the unconscious to operate.

This account of the creative process corresponds with many reports from artists that, when they are working, they are not really in control of what is going on. Novelists sometimes express the feeling that during the writing of a novel the characters of the story 'take over' the plot. It is as though the denouement was not controlled by the writer but by forces outside the writer's control. Similarly painters will recount that whilst they are painting they are not really conscious of what they are doing. Their work turns out in unexpected ways and they are often surprised to see what they have painted. This anecdotal evidence lends credence to the view that an important part of creative ability lies in the willingness and skill required to give up the conscious control of the work in hand and trust in intuitive unconscious processes.

Ehrenzweig goes on to suggest that the painter begins by projecting fragmented split-off parts of the personality onto the canvas. These are seen as the apparently uncontrolled and accidental aspects of the work, the unintentional and unstructured marks and blobs of paint which seem to characterise a work in its early stages. The next stage is when the creator orders these fragmented marks into some sort of structure. Central to this ordering process is what Ehrenzweig refers to as a process of unconscious scanning. The suggestion is that the artist is unable to decide consciously where to put the next mark or the composer the next musical note, the possibilities being almost infinite. There are no criteria for the creator to use in order to make a conscious decision. What happens is that the artist unconsciously scans the possible variations of line, tone, hue, position, size and direction of mark and makes a decision of which he has no conscious knowledge until it is made. The choice appears to the artist to have been intuitive, no conscious thought having been involved, and there is often a feeling of rightness or appropriateness about the decision.

Again it is important for the creator to have confidence in the ability of the unconscious to operate in this sort of way. It is necessary to give up conscious control in order to allow these unconscious primary processes to operate.

Finally, according to Ehrenzweig, when the fragmented parts have been ordered, the now integrated structure is taken back, 're-introjected', into the artist's ego and contributes to the easier accommodation of the previous split off aspects of the personality.

What begins to emerge from the writings of Ehrenzweig and others is that creative activity demands an ability

(a) to tolerate a fragmentation of aspects of the

personality,
(b) to withstand a degree of creative chaos, born out of uncertainty, and
(c) willingly to abdicate control of the activity to unconscious processes.

May (1975:92) refers to this as creative courage and points out that 'artists love to immerse themselves in chaos in order to put it into form'. He goes on:

> I need not remind you ... of the 'fear and trembling' of artists and creative people in their moments of creative encounter ... Creative people, as I see them, are distinguished by the fact that they can live with anxiety.
>
> (May 1975:92)

The capacity to tolerate anxiety, then, is seen as an important aspect of creative ability. Other research in the area has looked at creativity and mental illness where involvement in creative work can act as both a diagnostic and a therapeutic tool. Creative activity has often been associated with mental disorder or mental instability but there is no evidence to suggest that this must necessarily be the case. Cohen examines the empirical research in creativity and lists his findings as follows (my notes in brackets):

> Creativity is a function of the brain and its beginnings can probably be traced to our evolutionary heritage. (This from experimental work with primates)
> Highly creative people are rarely mad and may in fact enjoy better mental and physical health than the general run of the population.
> The highly creative, however, either are or are allowed to be somewhat more adventurous or eccentric.
> High creativity and high intelligence are not necessarily the same.
> Some degree of creativity seems to be present in all of us.
> Creativity cannot flourish in a vacuum. Social conditions must allow, and preferably encourage, creative activity.
> That most mysterious element of creativity, intuition or inspiration, may arise in the right

hemisphere of our brain.

(Cohen 1977:148)

Several psychologists interested in the psychology of perception have speculated on just what the artist (usually the visual artist) is doing when involved in creative activity. As might be expected, their speculations reflect their view of the nature of perception. Thus Gregory, representing the traditional view of perception states:

> When an artist employs geometric perspective he does not draw what he sees - he represents his retinal image.
> (Gregory 1973:175)

What is suggested here is that the artist 'perceives' a three-dimensional world which has, in a sense, to be deconstructed in order to represent it on a flat piece of canvas. The representational artist seems to be able to train himself to ignore the sensory signals which indicate three dimensionality and concentrate on the flat image, the image on the retina. According to the traditional theory of perception this could be done by simply closing one eye in order to negate the parallax of binocular vision, and artists sometimes do this. But generally they work with both eyes open.

Gibson (1979:278-9) describes, first, an explanation of representational drawing according to the traditional theory of perception:

> Drawing is always copying. The copying of a perceptual image is drawing from life. The copying of a stored image in the mind is drawing from memory. The copying of an image constructed from other memory images is drawing from imagination.
> (Gibson 1979:278)

This, it will be noted, is similar to Gregory's explanation - it is to do with the copying of an image either on the retina or retrieved from memory. Gibson goes on to reject the traditional theory, and puts forward his alternative:

> I insist that what the draftsman, beginner or expert, actually does is not to replicate, to print, or to copy in any sense of the term but to mark the surface in such a way as to display invariants and record an awareness.

> Drawing is never copying. It is impossible to copy a
> piece of the environment. Only another drawing can be
> copied. We have been misled for too long by the fallacy
> that a picture is <u>similar</u> to what it depicts, a <u>likeness</u> or
> an <u>imitation</u> of it. A picture supplies some of the
> information for what it depicts, but that does not imply
> that it is in projective correspondence with what it
> depicts.
>
> (Gibson 1979:279)

Some of the language is a bit difficult here and Gibson
uses some otherwise common terms in specific ways.
However, the essence of the argument seems to be that the
artist does not copy the world - as Gibson points out, this
would be impossible - but rather makes marks on the canvas
which allows an observer to perceive a similarity with a
scene which could occur in the real world. Whether or not
the scene does occur in the real world seems to be
irrelevant, the central point is that the artist has
constructed an image which we accept as a possible
representation of the world. Hence the image may have
arisen from observation of the view before the artist's easel,
or from the imagination of the artist. What is central is that
the image is constructed on the canvas as opposed to the
traditional theory which seems to involve a deconstruction
of a percept in order to copy it onto a canvas.

Many artists will feel drawn to Gibson's account. This
relates closely to what <u>it feels like</u> to do a representational
painting. The experience of artists suggests that what they
are doing is creating an image on a canvas which will
persuade an observer that it represents a real or imaginary
scene which exists or could exist in the real three
dimensional world.

However, a trap which many psychologists fall into is to
assume that artists are always engaged in the same activity
when they appear to be drawing or painting. Many artists
draw, not in order to make a drawing or notes for a painting,
but as an exercise to improve their levels of perceptual
acuity. Sketching is often seen as a sort of five finger
exercise for visual artists. When they are engaged in this
sort of activity they are doing something different from the
activity described by Gibson. Here the attention is focussed
on the scene out there, not on the marks of the canvas.

In drawing or painting a representational landscape
artists will direct their attention in the most part to what is

taking place on the canvas. The intention is to create an illusion of three dimensional reality. Various devices are used to help to create this illusion. Linear and aerial perspective, texture, the characteristics of some colours to appear to advance or recede in relation to the picture plane and the relative scale of objects are all phenomena which the artist can deploy to create (construct) an illusion. The artist attends to the canvas primarily and to the scene being represented secondarily.

When, on the other hand, the artist is working to develop perception the attention is directed first and foremost to the scene being depicted. It is worth mentioning that some artists refer to this activity as 'extending their visual vocabulary'. It is as though they need to seek experience of an increasing range of visual stimuli in order to maintain their effectiveness as visual artists. In any event, the emphasis is on observation. It is seen as a sort of training session which keeps one's creative abilities in trim. This is the rationale behind the emphasis on the keeping of notebooks by art students. It is felt that by asking them to deconstruct the percept they will learn and understand more about the visual world and at the same time develop their perceptual acuity.

Such procedures are not peculiar to the visual arts. Many writers keep notebooks in which they jot down the occasional overheard comment or line of verse which comes to mind. Similarly musical phrases are often recorded, either electronically or in notation, in an effort to build up a stock of material for possible later use.

Hence we see creative artists as being involved in two distinct sorts of activity. The first is preparatory in nature, to do with building a stock of percepts, extending the visual (or auditory) vocabulary and developing levels of perception. It involves attending first and foremost to external stimuli and deconstructing the percept in order to discover how the parts relate to the whole.

The second form of activity is creative in nature, demands paying attention to the canvas or the work in hand, and involves the construction of a visual image or a composition of musical sounds which may or may not represent a perception of the external world. A piece of music may recall the sound of running water but a painting may be entirely 'abstract' or pure fantasy. The nature of the relationship of the artefact to the perceived world seems to be arbitrary, with many different forms of relationship being represented in the history of the arts.

As will be obvious from the above, the act of creation involves the use of those same perceptual skills which we discussed in the section on 'appreciation'. In creative work, however, the way in which one attends to what one is doing seems to be different, there is a different kind of awareness.

Stumbo (1970:465-73) gives an excellent analysis of what it feels like to be involved in the creative process. He begins by discussing the concept of attention and points out that the way in which he intends to use it is synonymous with the word 'consciousness' as used by phenomenologists such as Merleau-Ponty, Husserl, Heidegger and Sartre. He goes on:

> If we take the basic tenet of phenomenology, i.e. 'Consciousness is always consciousness of something', and substitute 'attention' for 'consciousness', we have the basic assumption of this essay, 'Attention is always attention to something'.
>
> (Stumbo 1970:466)

He illustrates this by pointing out that if a sculptor is attending to the negative space in a work, the positive space cannot be attended to at the same time. He further explains that attention has two poles, the subjective and the objective, and refers his reader to the history of philosophy for evidence that the two features of experience do exist and that one can attend to either or neither of them. He then suggests that there is a third kind of thing to which one can attend. This he exemplifies as a goal which one is striving to achieve.

> A painter, for example, who desires to achieve in his painting an effect of sunlight upon haystacks at a particular time of the day (as the impressionist painter Monet attempted) attends primarily to the goal, with the physical means and the accompanying psychological states being attended to secondarily.
>
> As long as the goal is uppermost in his mind he cannot at the same time directly attend to either the objective or subjective features of that creative undertaking. If the artist could reflect upon the objective and subjective features of the goal-oriented endeavour, he could learn a great deal about the nature

85

of his instinctive or spontaneous reason. Such knowledge would afford insights concerning his style of life as well as his style of painting, drawing or sculpting, and would allow him to make calculated changes in his future artistic endeavors.

(Stumbo 1970:468)

This third kind of attention he calls 'projective' and goes on to discuss the three ways of attending as bases for research procedures. 'Subjective' is concerned with subject matter not opened to public verification as in the arts and some psychology and social science. 'Objective' is concerned to establish general laws as in the natural sciences. 'Projective' allows one to consider an experience where there is neither attention to a physical object nor to the feelings of the body, but rather to a project which entails both. This is to be understood in the sense that a painter,

becomes so absorbed in the painting that he attends only to the painting not as a physical object or a subjective event but as a blend of the two. He does not attend to the canvas, the paint, the turpentine, rules of composition, or his body. He attends to the painting that is moving towards a close.

(Stumbo 1970:469)

Stumbo reserves the word 'project' to describe an undertaking in which a person is attending to objects and feelings only insofar as they are a part of a flow of activities that are moving to a close. There may be links between Stumbo's three types of attention and what Bartley (1980:19) referred to as the 'three modes of personal existence' outlined in the section on appreciation.

This view of the nature of attention during creative activity may seem at odds with the description given above of the two sorts of activity engaged in by artists where attention is focussed either on the scene being depicted or on the work on the canvas. In both these cases, attention, in Stumbo's terms, is objective, not projective.

I think that the difficulty arises from Stumbo's assertion that attention and consciousness are synonymous. It is my feeling that this cannot be the case. It is possible for a painter to attend to the paint on the canvas whilst being conscious only of a process moving towards a conclusion. Attention here can perhaps best be understood if the statement 'attends to the paint on the canvas' is turned round. If one were to say that 'the paint on the canvas commands the attention of the artist', in the sense that the artist's perceptual systems are focussed on the paint on the canvas, then it is not inconceivable that the artist may be conscious of something other than that to which he or she is attending. Thus the artist may be conscious of the process moving towards a conclusion, in a projective sense, whilst attending to the canvas or scene being painted.

The role of the perceptual systems is central here. In the creation of a work of art these systems are clearly directed towards the work in hand. In this sense one is attending to the work. But because this work is directed by the unconscious primary processes, one is not aware of what one is doing. One is conscious, as Stumbo so clearly explains, not of the paint or the turpentine, nor of the feelings of the body, but of involvement in a process moving towards a conclusion. It is because of this that artists can surprise themselves by what they have done; it is in this way that the characters can take over the novel.

There are examples which one could draw from everyday life. When one is driving one is attending to the task in hand, in the sense that one's sensory systems are focussed on the task of driving the vehicle safely. But one is conscious of being on a journey. Or maybe of holding a conversation with a passenger. In any event, one is not usually conscious of the actions and perceptions necessary for driving a car. We say that these are automatic. In fact a different sort of mental activity is involved; our actions are controlled by unconscious rather than conscious processes.

This kind of consciousness Stumbo likens to that of a player in a game of sport who appears to be operating on an entirely intuitive level, aware of neither self, in terms of cuts and bruises sustained in the match, nor aware on a conscious level of the constantly changing field of play. The player is aware only of the game moving to its conclusion. It will be remembered that Bartley (1980:19) referred to this as the 'motoric mode of personal existence'. It is only after the match is over, when a player can analyse a video-recording of the game, that a conscious awareness and analysis of what happened can take place. It certainly cannot take place during the match.

It is difficult to see how Stumbo's 'subjective' mode of attention relates to creation in the arts. One could argue that one projects subjective feelings into the work in hand, but this would be misleading since the activity would be on an unconscious level and consequently there would be no awareness of it. It could be that the area of creative and artistic experience where subjective attention is important is in those art forms where the human body is involved as part of the creative or expressive medium. One thinks of the dance as an immediate example where subjective awareness of, say, one's position in space is essential. It could be that subjective consciousness is central to participation in the performing arts and we will return to this theme in the next section.

This section on engaging with the arts in a creative way has attempted to demonstrate that, of the three ways in which the idea of creativity is conceived and researched, the idea of creativity as a process seems the most useful. Since the concern of this book is with creativity in the arts, the focus has also settled on 'integrated creativity' as defined by Maslow. It is acknowledged that there may be other ways of describing the creative process and different psychological perspectives produce different terminologies and analytical vocabularies. The concern here is to demonstrate that creative activity involves both unconscious and conscious, primary and secondary, intuitive and intellectual processes working together in a dynamic way. This dualism seems essential to the creative process; this is something on which most writers agree. The two modes of mental functioning work together in what I have called elsewhere (Jones 1985:17) a creative dialectic.

Further, this section has described the nature of attention and the state of consciousness of the artist during the creative process. In order to do this it has been necessary to reject Stumbo's assertion that consciousness and attention are synonymous. Indeed, it seems clear that one can attend to one or more things whilst being conscious of something else. The artist, when creating, is conscious of a process moving to a close. This applies particularly to those moments in the creative process when the artist is operating on an unconscious level. There are, of course, moments when an artist will sit back and, in a very conscious way, appraise what has been done. Here the consciousness is not projective but objective. It is only when the artist is involved in what Maslow calls integrated creativity that he is conscious in a projective sense.

The final point I wish to make in this section concerns the nature of creative ability. Most writers seem to agree that everyone is capable of creative activity. As a process it has a universal potential. If one does not now participate in any sort of creative activity, one can learn to do so. Some people experience psychological blocks to creative involvement. It is part of the teacher's role to help people to overcome these. There has, for a long time, been a great deal of mystery surrounding the activity of the artist. There were vested interests in maintaining this position. Increasingly, however, it is being demonstrated that the reasons why most of us do not become involved as creators in the arts are socially determined rather than the result of some sort of genetic or hereditary inadequacy. In discussing the generation of metaphor as the central process of creative thinking Gordon, as long ago as 1961, made the following seminal point:

> Generative metaphors seem to take their inception in essentially subliminal process - a process of which we are not thoroughly conscious at the moment of its occurrence. Thus we tend to slide past the moment of inception, to regard it as mysterious and sacrosanct, to call it inspiration, and to overlook the possible effects of training and discipline upon the metaphor making potential.
>
> (Gordon 1961:116)

PARTICIPATION

As I outlined earlier, I have reserved the term 'participation' to describe a way of engaging with the arts which, on the face of it, is neither appreciation, as I have described it above, nor creation, as defined by Maslow in terms of integrated creativity. There is another way of engaging in the arts; it is that conventionally entered into by the actor, dancer and musician. These I shall refer to as performers. On a different level but similar in nature are the activities entered into by the director of a theatrical production, the conductor of an orchestra and the choreographer of a dance. These I shall refer to as producers.

My concern in this section is with the nature of the activity usually engaged in by participants when an orchestra performs Beethoven's Ninth Symphony, a theatrical company performs Shakespeare's Hamlet or a dance company performs Swan Lake, to quote well-known examples. However, in discussing the nature of participation engaged in by performers, I am concerned to demonstrate that it can be creative on a primary, secondary or integrated level. I am concerned to distinguish between that participation which is creative in an integrated way from other forms of participation.

It is important to remember this distinction. The art forms which are under discussion embrace a very wide range of activities and it is helpful to remember that the concern here is not with a particular art form but with particular ways of engaging with that art form. To clarify this point I will take an example from the area of dance. Peter Brinson, writing in 1981, postulates a very broad concept of the dance:

> 'dance' should comprise the whole range of dance movement in Britain today: theatrical dance, such as classical ballet, jazz, tap, and contemporary dance; ethnic dances of the English, Irish, Scots, Welsh, Poles, Ukrainians, Asians, Africans, West Indians and so on; recreative and social dance from ballroom to keep fit.
> (Brinson 1981:47)

One might include in the above list disco dancing, break dancing, body popping and other forms of expressive movement that from time to time emerge from youth culture. It is acknowledged that involvement in some of these activities can be highly creative in the sense that they demand integrated creativity in Maslow's terms. The concern of this section, however, is to distinguish between integrated creativity and those activities where this sort of creativity does not take place, where, in dance, the steps are pre-ordained or dictated by someone other than the dancer.

Whenever, in conversation, I venture to suggest to performers that what they are engaged in is not creative in the same sense that the composer or playwright is creative, I usually elicit angry and defensive reactions. Performers know that their task requires training, discipline and interpretive inventiveness and believe the fulfilment of these demands to be consonant with creative activity. Producers see their task in a similar way. They feel that they, as it were, create a production. But the fact remains that the original creative act took place some time earlier and was engaged in by someone who is often not even present during the conception and design of a particular production. Is it reasonable, therefore, to suggest, that performers and producers are involved in creative activity in the same way as the playwright, composer or original choreographer?

I want to argue that the nature of their engagement with the arts can sometimes be qualitatively different. I do not, however, wish to attribute any particular or relative value to these different activities. I hope to be able to demonstrate that what producers are engaged in is what Maslow called secondary creativity and that performers can engage in a number of different ways. There is a danger that the term 'secondary' is misunderstood and taken to imply some sort of value judgement. This should not be the case. In terms of their value either personally, societally, artistically or culturally I wish to make no distinction between these different activities, these different ways of engaging with the arts. 'Secondary', as we have defined it, is a Freudian term which refers to the more conscious intellectual mental processes. I mean it in no other sense than this.

One of the problems with this area of enquiry is the paucity of research. There are writings on the history of the various art forms (Bentley 1972, Styan 1981, Braun 1982) which analyse them in much the same way that art historians analyse fine art, and these shed some light on the topic; there is some writing on the performing arts (mainly theatre) in education (Redington 1983, Bolton 1984, Heathcote 1984) which, though mainly concerned with the education of children provides some useful theoretical models; and there is some writing from the aesthetic philosophers (Bolton 1977, Reid 1985, Sparshott 1985) which is interesting but somewhat limited in its usefulness for the purposes of this book. There is very little from psychology to explain the nature of the activity engaged in by performers and producers.

I want to begin by looking at the work of the producers. Their role has not always been the high-status managerial one it seems to be today. Braun points out that at various times the task of taking charge of a production has been assigned to different individuals.

> Ever since Aeschylus supervised the presentation of his tragedies at the Athenian festivals of the fifth century BC it is safe to assume that someone has had overall

responsibilty for the rehearsal of any play that has reached the stage. Sometimes, as in the case of Shakespeare or Racine, it would have been the dramatist; sometimes an actor-playwright such as Molière; later it would have been the leading actor or some other humble functionary like the stage manager or the prompter.

(Braun 1982:7)

The director's role eventually became separated from these other duties and with this separation the director became an important and powerful figure in the design of a production. Indeed, it is recorded (Braun 1982:59-76) that Stanislavsky, when directing Chekov's plays for the first time, often got in the way of what the author was trying to say. He would make alterations to the setting, stage direction and text to the extent that the playwright became exasperated with the director for misrepresenting his intentions. This might lead one to think that it was normal for the director to ignore the wishes of the playwright, that the playwright was somehow incidental to the realisation of the production. Such a view would, I think, be mistaken.

Certainly the nature of the relationship between the director and the playwright cannot be considered as constant or universal. There are a wide variety of ways in which directors relate to living authors. Perversely it is when writers are dead that their work seems most secure. When there is no way in which negotiation can take place directors seem more inclined to honour the intention of the author, insofar as that intention can be ascertained.

The role of a director seems to relate most closely to that of a manager. It is the director's responsibility to bring together actors, set designers, costume designers, dress-makers, carpenters, and lighting and sound engineers in order to realise the director's conception of what the playwright intended. In this sense there is little room for primary process activity, for the entirely individual generation of images and visual or verbal metaphors. The satisfaction which the director derives from the activity must be of a different order to that of the author. Authors can develop psychologically through their involvement in integrated creativity; they can re-order and re-integrate the fragmented split-off parts of their personalities. This would not appear to be possible for those working as directors.

The director can influence the style of a dramatic

production by setting the pace and controlling the appearance of it, in the same way that a designer influences the style of a bridge or an automobile. In a similar way the conductor can influence the style of a performance of a piece of music. Despite having to work to a score there are still many choices which producers can make, starting with the choice of performers and designers. There is considerable room for novelty and innovation in the staging of a production; there is clearly scope for some sort of creative activity to take place. That creativity is generally secondary in nature, that is, it is rooted mainly in the secondary thought processes. I can conceive of no way in which producers can become involved in either primary or integrated creativity if they are directing the performance of a work which was originally created by someone else. The script or score to which they are working and to which they have a commitment is too constraining to allow their own primary or integrated creativity to predominate.

There is remarkably little evidence on which one can draw for a more thorough analysis of the producer's role. There is some writing on the work of theatrical directors but this concentrates on identifying a director's style or approach and relating this to a developing philosophy of theatre. Such evidence provides clues to the way in which directors relate to the people with whom they work but gives no clue as to the mental or psychical processes involved.

The role of the performer is better documented and, interestingly, it is the educationalists who seem to have been most successful in analysing the behaviours of those who involve themselves in performing. I want first to explore the ways in which the activities entered into by performers in the various art forms might relate together. It is evident that in acting, musicianship and dance the body is part of the medium of creation. Participants are involved in an activity where the soma is as important as the psyche.

Bolton describes acting in the following way:

> Acting is normally a complex psycho-somatic activity ... a symbolic representation of meaning achieved by using the body in relation to the physical environment as a medium of expression.
>
> (Bolton 1977:63)

Describing acting in this way makes it possible to see how it relates to some forms of dance, particularly those forms like classical ballet where the dancer is portraying a character, where the dancer is also involved in a psycho-somatic activity. Hamby distinguishes those forms of dance which relate more to drama from those which relate more to music:

> Some works make demands on dancers which, despite obvious differences, are comparable to the demands of plays on actors ... Other dances, being abstract or specifically architectural, make demands on performers which are comparable to the demands of musical composition on musicians.
>
> (Hamby 1984:41)

This analysis allows a systematic way of characterising the different kinds of performing along a continuum from the more recognisably realistic to the abstract; from representational drama at one end to abstract music at the other. Dance, it is suggested, fits somewhere in the middle. At one level dance can be seen as a language of communication, at another it is an almost religious form of abstract expression. Indeed, historically, the relationship between religious expression and the dance has been quite close in both primitive and more developed societies. The Rites of Spring in many pagan societies include a ritual dance round a maypole or some other fertility symbol, a practice which Christianity has singularly failed to eradicate. Sparshott sees dance as follows:

> First one treats dance as a proto-language of gesture and assigns it the functions of expressing grief, joy and such other feelings as a public expression may seem appropriate to. Second, one fastens on the specialness of dance behaviour and ascribes to dance the function of marking 'the sacred' or some such concept. In general dance is made out to be an emphatic celebration of enhanced vitality.
>
> (Sparshott 1985:111)

What the different types of performing have in common is that, in the case of each art form, the performer is involved in a psycho-somatic activity which can involve different forms of attention and different forms of consciousness. The extent and nature of both the somatic and psychic involvement varies for each art form and varies according to the nature of the performance in each art form.

The role of the body can be functional, visual or both. In dance and drama the appearance of the body is centrally important; there is a visual expectation and a visual aesthetic inherent in the art form. The position of the body in space, the expressions and movement of the body and any sounds, musical or verbal, generated by the body can contribute to the effective use of the actor's or dancer's body as a medium of artistic creation.

This is not generally true of music. Here, except for choral work, the body provides the manipulative skills and the energy which causes a musical instrument to issue the correct sounds in the correct sequence - the correctness being pre-determined by a composer and/or a conductor. In choral work the body produces the sounds without an intervening musical instrument. The body has a functional rather than aesthetic purpose. Visual appearance is not important in a medium of expression which is essentially auditory, though there is the convention of a symphony orchestra wearing formal dress and, recently, many pop and rock groups have made much of the visual aspects of their performances. Generally, however, for the musician, manual and pedal dexterity together with sound lungs and control of breathing for singers and the players of wind instruments seem to be the essential somatic attributes.

The nature of the psychic involvement of the musician depends on the activity being undertaken. When, for instance, pianists are learning a new piece one would expect them to attend to the sheet music, the score, and to the sounds being emitted by the musical instrument. There is, however, an intermediate level of activity which needs examination; it is the nature of attention given to the musical instrument being played. Here, one is led to believe, and it has to be said that whilst the evidence seems to be consistent it remains at the level of the anecdotal, the musician is not aware of the instrument being played. It is as though the musical instrument is an extension of the performer's body. The performer knows the motor activities required to produce the correct pitch from an instrument in the same way that a singer knows what muscular activity is needed to produce the correct note. It is a question of producing the correct Gestalt, the correct pattern of muscular activity needed to produce a given musical outcome.

For the musician then, at least when practising, attention is directed to the score and the sounds being produced. At this stage the musician is conscious of being involved in a learning process in a projective way.

When a piece of music has been learned one can speculate that the nature of attention changes. For the solo instrumentalist attention will focus on the musical sounds being produced. For the orchestral musician attention will focus on the sounds being produced in relation to the sounds made by the rest of the orchestra under the direction of a conductor. For both these performers consciousness will be projective; they will be aware of being involved in a process moving towards a conclusion.

It is difficult to see how the orchestral musician can be involved in creative work in an integrated way. In the performance of a work written by a composer there is no possibility of that primary process activity which is a pre-requisite of integrated creativity. What choices are available to the musician - choices concerning phrasing, some freedom with regard to tempo and volume for instance - are not sufficient to allow primary process functioning. One can, however, legitimately suggest that the musician is involved in secondary creativity, in the design of a production of a particular piece of music. The involvement is not as great as that of the conductor of the orchestra but there does exist a window of opportunity which allows each instrumentalist to add something of their own to a particular performance.

There are, of course, some musical forms which allow the musician a great deal more freedom. Jazz provides an example of a musical form which permits creative involvement at an integrated level. It is also possible for the musician to operate as composer and to become fully creative in the integrated sense of the word, to have access to both primary and secondary processes in the production of a work.

This range of different forms of involvement also occurs in drama. I use the term drama here to denote that artistic activity which has action and acting as its central means of expression. This clumsy definition will serve as a starting point.

Bolton (1984:110) distinguishes between what he calls 'dramatic playing' and what he designates as 'performing'. Dramatic playing relates to the sort of fantasy play engaged in by children and some adults. It is the child playing at being mother or a doctor or superman or some invented hero or heroine. It is imaginative play. Contrary to this is the idea of performance where the actor depicts a character created by a playwright. The actor's job in this instance is to convey to an audience by means of verbal and non-verbal signs, everything they need to know about the character in order to comprehend the drama. The actor here is, in a sense, divorced from the role being played; the actor is, according to Bolton, depicting the 'character's distress, not his own'. In such situations the actor's behaviour is not expressive. The audience is watching King Lear's expressive behaviour, not the actor's. Bolton goes on to analyse these two modes of behaviour, dramatic play and performing, as follows:

> So far I have been at pains to make a clear distinction between these two modes. In Chapter Two I asserted that two contrary intentions were involved: the intention to be, to submit to the experience of an event, and the intention to describe, to communicate an event to someone else.
>
> (Bolton 1984:114)

Without much difficulty it is possible to relate Bolton's two categories of drama to Maslow's concepts of primary and secondary creativity. Bolton does not himself make this point but on reading his argument it seems clear that Maslow's conceptual framework provides an explanation for the two dramatic behaviours identified by Bolton.

In discussing dramatic play he makes points which will be familiar to the painter and sculptor as well as to others involved in the arts. It should be remembered that his main concern is with education and with drama as an educational activity. When, however, he describes how some students 'hold back' from fully committing themselves to participate he could be talking about the same inhibition which is often evidenced in a painting or a music class:

> Many kinds of reason prevail in the drama lesson for participants 'holding back'. They may not, for instance, be prepared to risk having any kind of emotional engagement ... or they may not trust each other or the teacher; or the 'hidden curriculum' of the groups own dynamics may cut across the drama's requirements; or

97

the group may concentrate too hard on preparing material for 'showing' so that they miss out almost entirely on 'playing the drama game'; or they may dislike drama or really want to perform a play or are simply not in the mood to submit to the experience.

(Bolton 1984:111)

This reticence, this unwillingness to take what almost amounts to an existential leap of faith, this reluctance to give oneself up to unconscious processes will be familiar to all those who have been involved in or have helped others to become involved in primary process thinking as part of creative activity.

Having distinguished these two approaches to drama which relate closely to Maslow's ideas about primary and secondary creativity Bolton goes on to postulate another mode of dramatic activity. He was faced with the problem of accommodating in his ideas about performing that approach to acting developed by Konstantin Stanislavsky. This approach is summarised by Magarshack as follows:

Stanislavsky realized that creative work on the stage was first of all the fullest possible concentration of the whole of the actor's spiritual and physical nature. Such a concentration, he discovered, extended not only to hearing and sight but to all the other senses of the actor, and in addition, took possession of his body, mind, memory and imagination. The conclusion Stanislavsky arrived at was that the whole spiritual and physical nature of the actor must be centred on what was taking place in the soul of the person he was representing on stage.

(Magarshack 1972:224)

The thesis is that the creative actor 'feels himself into his part' without thinking about it, the process involving unconscious rather than conscious mental activity. Braun (1982:65) describes the approach as a rejection of 'theatrical stereotypes and naturalistic approximations in favour of a corporate search for the inner psychological truth of the character's behaviour, directed towards the revelation of that truth through all the available means of the production'. It is also pointed out that the danger in this approach is that 'for all the perception of behavioural detail the playwright's overall design, what he was saying through the medium of his character's actions, could easily be overlooked'.

Here is a thesis which outlines an approach to acting which goes beyond the secondary activity of performing. The suggestion is that unconscious processes are involved in 'feeling oneself into the character'. Furthermore, the actor becomes emotionally involved in performing a role. Hence, we can see emerging two distinct approaches to performing. There is the technical approach which suggests that actors are detached from their own feelings during performance and, in a secondary way, use technical devices to portray a character; and there is this approach of Stanislavsky where there is emotional involvement and where more primary processes are involved.

This approach exemplifies a situation where both primary and secondary activity come together. Bolton sees the activity where the actor is both 'experiencing and describing' a character involved in action as a dialectic, similar to the creative dialectic I postulated in the section on creativity. He explains it like this:

> The actor, in attempting to subject himself spontaneously to an occurrence and at the same time communicate that occurrence to an audience, is experiencing an unresolvable tension. It seems, however, that the tension for the actor is but derivative of that tension endlessly defined and redefined by psychiatrists, psychologists and social psychologists in terms of inner/outer reality; I/Me, Ego/Self, or Subjective/Objective.
>
> (Bolton 1984:122)

This surely, relates closely to Maslow's notion of integrated creativity. It also relates to that dualism of inner-outer, unconscious-conscious, intuitive-intellectual which was referred to in the section on creativity. But Bolton goes a stage further. He proposes that this form of integrated creativity demands what he calls a heightened state of consciousness:

> Dramatic activity does not supersede direct experience nor is it a second best to direct experience. The potency lies in 'metaxis', a heightened state of consciousness that holds two worlds in the mind at the same time. The fictitious world is not 'given', to be

merely suffered. It is actively construed, so that submitting to its experience is tempered by the treatment of it as an object. Thus the psychology of dramatic behaviour is of a different order from direct experience and independent of any criteria to do with 'nearly real'; it is a form of experiencing that 'brackets off' an occurrence, permitting both submission and an enhanced degree of detachment.

(Bolton 1984:142)

This notion of 'metaxis' relates quite closely to Stumbo's concept of projective consciousness. It is not difficult to see how different forms of consciousness relate to the different modes of participation in acting. One must assume that in each case the performer is conscious in a projective way. There is no subjective consciousness or self-consciousness, indeed, self-consciousness usually prevents involvement. And there is no real objective consciousness; no consciousness of the audience or the lights or the set. Consciousness in this instance is that of being involved in a process moving towards a conclusion as described by Stumbo; it is the 'bracketing off' of experience which Bolton describes.

Attention is directed in a way appropriate to the activity. It is suggested that in dramatic play attention is focused not, as might be expected, subjectively, on self, but rather on the other participants or objects involved in the drama; on the make-believe aeroplane or the twig which becomes a sword, or on the friend who plays another part in the shared fantasy. In 'dressing up' games there may be a subjective form of attention where the mirror permits a concentration on the appearance of self but in the dramatic play which is the concern of this chapter the nature of attention is different. It is directed outwards rather than inwards. It is objective rather than subjective.

In performing in either a secondary or an integrated way it becomes necessary to attend both subjectively and objectively. The actor must attend to self, to position, appearance, movement and expression as well as to the other things that are happening on stage. In this sense it becomes necessary to attend to two things at once; the actor must attend to both self and to the physical and spatial relationship between self and others.

Where, then, does this leave us in this attempt to understand the role of the performer? In the last few paragraphs the emphasis has been mainly on acting and in examining the work of Bolton we have seen how the actor can operate creatively on a primary, secondary or integrated level as suggested by Maslow. I want to suggest that dramatic play is seen as primary creativity; performance which relies on technique and emotional detachment is seen as secondary creativity; and that dialectic which Bolton proposes as a tension between inner and outer states of consciousness and which demands 'metaxis' is seen as integrated creativity.

As far as acting is concerned the participant may be involved on any of the three levels proposed by Maslow. When acting is of a sort which relates to Maslow's integrated creativity it should more properly be considered as 'creation' and would sit comfortably in the previous section. When this activity is 'performing' it becomes a mode of participation which is becoming increasingly concerned with secondary creativity. When it is 'dramatic play' it is primary creativity.

It is difficult to equate the primary activity of dramatic play to other art forms. In the visual arts one could equate it with that activity known as doodling where images are generated without thought or conscious intention. In dance it might relate to that entirely free movement of the disco dancer who dances for the pure exhilaration of uninhibited expression. Musically it may be possible to relate to improvised forms such as jazz or other means of 'doodling with sounds'. All these activities relate closely to the idea of play.

This is not to diminish them. The idea of play is central to primary process functioning. It is an activity easily engaged in by children but difficult for adults. It may be that strategies which help adults to develop their ability to engage in imaginative play will be instrumental in developing their creative potential.

It is not unreasonable to suggest that the sort of attention and consciousness demanded by acting is also demanded by some aspects of dance. The role of the choreographer. does not seem to be considered as central to the production of a performance. Indeed, Hamby almost dismisses the choreographer as coincidental:

> as performance art, a dance achieves its purpose in presentation to its public, and this is made possible only through the mediation of performers. No matter what

101

> vision a choreographer may have or what imaginative
> insight a ballet-master may show in reconstructing a
> work and encouraging, coercing, urging a dancer into a
> part, in the final analysis the outcome rests on whether
> the dancer: (a) sees what is necessary for a given part;
> (b) makes the part his or her own; (c) brings the part 'to
> life' in the movements of dancing.
>
> (Hamby 1984:41)

What is not clear from the above extract is precisely
what is meant by terms like 'makes the part his or her own'
or 'brings to life'. However, one can conjecture that there
will be similarities with acting. In the first place the writer
refers to 'a part'. Where dancers are portraying characters
one can assume, for the most part, that they will be either
performing, in a secondary way, or involved at an integrated
level where consciousness is projective and a degree of
metaxis is required. This is probably true whether the
dancer is playing the leading role in a popular ballet or the
figure of a god in a tribal dance.

Dance at a primary level seems to equate most closely
to other forms of abstract expression. One example already
cited is the free expression of the disco dancer. Ballroom
dancing seems to be more secondary in nature; the steps are
prescribed and must be learned. The dancing for joy of both
children and adults exemplifies primary creative activity
through dance.

It occurs to me, however, that in dance there exists, to
a greater extent than in acting, the possibility that the
somatic involvement could interfere with the projective
nature of consciousness. The demands that the dance makes
upon the body are often so great that there is the real
possibility of the dancer experiencing pain. Such an
occurrence would immediately focus attention on self and
preclude that projective consciousness which is a feature of
integrated creativity. Whether or not it is possible to pass
through the pain threshold and achieve that heightened level
of consciousness referred to by Bolton is a matter of
speculation. Athletes sometimes talk in these terms but
whether or not it is an ability needed by the dancer must
remain open to question.

In this section on participation in the arts an
examination has been undertaken of the different ways in
which producers and performers engage with the arts. It was
concluded that producers, generally, are working on a

secondary level; they are managers who bring together the various component parts which are necessary for a production.

In acting, playing a musical instrument and dancing the performers can be involved in either primary, secondary or integrated creativity. When they are involved in an integrated way they should more properly be considered as engaging with the arts as creators rather than participants. When they are involved at either primary or secondary level they are engaged in an activity which is qualitatively different from that in which a creative artist is involved.

The different sorts of involvement in each art form require different sorts of attention and different forms of consciousness. Generally speaking, the more the participation moves towards integrated creativity, the more the consciousness is likely to be projective. The demands of the art form itself dictate the nature of the attention required. The degree to which a participant needs to attend to self as well as the objective world outside self depends on such factors as the need to relate the body to those of other performers and to objects in the performing area, the need to be aware of the limits of the performing area, the need to control the gesture, movement and position of the body and the need to speak, sing or give forth other expressive sounds. All these demands require a subjective attention. Movement through the performing space demands an objective attention.

The skills required by the performer include that acute perceptual ability demanded by the appreciator as well as the ability to work on a primary, secondary or integrated level.

Whilst some forms of participation can be seen as distinct and different ways of engaging with the arts it must be remembered that some performers can engage in a creative way. When this occurs they are operating in a way similar to any other creative artist, they become creators rather than participants.

What must be underlined here is that it is not the category of activity which determines its character but the nature of the engagement in that activity. Acting, dancing and playing a musical instrument are categories of activity. Within any one of these categories a performer may become involved in any or all the ways outlined above.

CONCLUSION

This chapter has examined the different ways in which people engage with the arts. It has focussed on the demands made upon those who become involved in the arts as well as the value of that involvement to the individual. The skills required for such involvement vary according to the nature of the activity being undertaken.

It has been demonstrated that for all the arts, no matter what the nature of the engagement is, a high degree of perceptual acuity is required. The nature of perception, as it is currently understood, suggests that an individual can improve levels of perception through exercise and practice. Perceptual systems can be developed to the extent that the restricting cultural determinants of perceptual ability can be overcome.

Different sorts of artistic engagement require different forms of consciousness and it has been suggested that projective consciousness, a consciousness that is neither objective nor subjective but involves an awareness of involvement in a process moving towards a conclusion, provides an illuminating explanation of the experience of those involved in the arts at a creative level.

A distinction has been made between attention and consciousness and it has been suggested that the various forms of engaging with the arts demand different forms of attention. Attention is either subjective and directed to physical or mental aspects of self, or objective and directed to the world outside self, to a work of art, another performer, or to musical sounds. The perceptual systems are the means by which we attend to the world.

The nature of the engagement with the arts is characterised by psychological and somatic processes as well as by the nature of attention and consciousness. Creative involvement demands either primary or secondary mental processes or processes where the two sorts of mental functioning combine in an integrated way. Appreciation demands cognitive as well as affective skills. Whilst all activities have a somatic as well as a psychic component, participation in the arts as a performer is seen as a psycho-somatic activity where the role of the body is as important as that of the psyche.

Understanding the nature of engagement in the arts is a complex business. This chapter sits between a discussion on the nature of the arts and the next chapter which will deal with access to the arts. It was necessary to analyse the nature of engagement in artistic activity before attempting to relate these to educational activity in the arts. The next chapter forms a bridge between this analysis and the education section; it is not central to the argument of this book but is important in demonstrating the extent and nature of artistic activity. It is concerned with Britain but the way in which artistic provision is categorised will provide a useful framework for readers from other countries to carry out a similar analysis.

REFERENCES

Barron, F., 1955, 'The Disposition Towards Originality', Journal of Abnormal and Social Psychology, vol. 51, 1955

Barron, F., 1958. 'The Psychology of Imagination', in Coopersmith, S. (ed.), Frontier of Psychological Research - Readings from Scientific American, San Francisco, Freeman

Bartley, S.H., 1980, Introduction to Visual Perception, New York, Harper and Row

Bentley, E. (ed.), 1972, The Theory of the Modern Stage: An Introduction to Modern Theatre and Drama, Harmondsworth, Penguin

Beveridge, W.M., 1935, 'Racial Differences in Phenomenal Regression', British Journal of Psychology, 26, pp. 59-62

Beveridge, W.M., 1939, 'Some Racial Differences in Perception', British Journal of Psychology, 30, pp. 57-64

Bolton, G.M., 1977, 'Psychical Distancing in Acting', The British Journal of Aesthetics, vol. 17, no. 1

Bolton, G.M., 1984, Drama as Education: An Argument for Placing Drama at the Centre of the Curriculum, Harlow, Longman

Braun, E., 1982, The Director and the Stage: From Naturalism to Grotowski, London, Methuen

Brinson, P., 1981, 'Adult Education Through Dance', in Jones, D.J. and Chadwick, A.F., Adult Education and the Arts, Nottingham, University of Nottingham, Department of Adult Education

Bruce, V. and Green, P., 1985, Visual Perception, Physiology, Psychology and Ecology, New Jersey, Lawrence Erlbaum

Child, I.L., 1970, 'The Problem of Objectivity in Aesthetic

Value', in Pappas, G. (ed.), Concepts in Art and
   Education, London, Macmillan
Cohen, D., 1977, Creativity, What is it? New York, M. Evans
Dennis, W., 1960, 'The Human Figure Drawings of Bedouins',
   Journal of Social Psychology, 52, pp. 209-19
Ehrenzweig, A., 1968, The Hidden Order of Art, London,
   Weidenfield and Nicolson
Freeman, J., Butcher, H.J. and Christie, T. (eds), 1968,
   Creativity - A Selective Review of Research, London,
   Society for Research into Higher Education
Gibson, J.J., 1966, The Senses Considered as Perceptual
   Systems, Boston, Houghton Mifflin
Gibson, J.J., 1979, The Ecological Approach to Visual
   Perception, Boston, Houghton Mifflin
Gordon, W.J.J., 1961, Synectics - the Development of
   Creative Capacity, New York, Harper and Row
Gregory, R.L. and Wallace, J.G., 1963, Recovery from Early
   Blindness, Exp. Psychol. Monogra., Cambridge
   (England), Whole No. 2
Gregory, R.L., 1970, The Intelligent Eye, London,
   Weidenfield and Nicholson
Gregory, R.L., 1973, Eye and Brain: The Psychology of
   Seeing, London, Weidenfield and Nicolson
Hamby, C., 1984, 'Dance and the Dancer', British Journal of
   Aesthetics, vol. 24, no. 1
Hebb, D.O., 1949, The Organization of Behavior, New York,
   Wiley
Heathcote, D., 1984, in Johnson, L. and O'Neill, C. (eds),
   Dorothy Heathcote, Collected Writings on Education
   and Drama, London, Melbourne, etc., Hutchinson
Herskovits, M.J., 1948, Man and His Works, New York,
   Knopf
Herskovits, M.J., 1959, 'Art and Value', in Redfield, R.,
   Herskovits, M.J. and Ekholm, G.F., Aspect of Primitive
   Art, New York, The Museum of Primitive Art, pp. 42-97
Hochberg, J.E., 1978, Perception, New Jersey, Prentice Hall
Hoggart, R., 1985, 'False Populisms, False Elitisms', Arts
   Express, no. 12, February 1985, London
Holmes, A.C., 1964, Health Education in Developing
   Countries, London, Nelson
Hudson, L., 1966, Contrary Imaginations - A Psychological
   Study of the English Schoolboy, London, Methuen
Hudson, W., 1960, 'Pictorial Depth Perception in Sub-
   cultural Groups in Africa', Journal of Social Psychology,
   52, pp. 183-208

Jones, D.J., 1978, 'Teaching Art to Adults' in Adult Education, vol. 51. no. 1, Leicester, National Institute of Adult Education

Jones, D.J. and Chadwick, A.F. (eds), 1981, Adult Education and the Arts, Nottingham, University of Nottingham, Department of Adult Education

Jones, D.J., 1985, Creativity, in the series 'Adults: Psychological and Educational Perspectives', Nottingham, University of Nottingham, Department of Adult Education

Kant, I., 1933, Critique of Pure Reason, 1781, translated by N. Kemp Smith, London, Macmillan

Latta, R., 1904, 'Notes on a case of successful operation for congenital cataract in an adult', British Journal of Psychology, 1, pp. 135-50

London, I.D., 1960, 'A Russian Report on the Post-Operative Newly Seeing', American Journal of Psychology, 73, pp. 478-82

MacKinnon, D.W., 1962a, 'The Personality Correlates of Creativity: A Study of American Architects', in Proceedings of the Fourteenth Congress on Applied Psychology, vol. 2, Munkguard

MacKinnon, D.W., 1962b, 'The Nature and Nurture of Creative Talent', American Psychologist, 17, pp. 484-95

Mackinnon, D.W., 1965, 'Personality and the Realisation of Creative Potential', American Psychologist, 20(4), pp. 273-81

Magarshack, D., 1972, 'Stanislavsky', in Bentley, E. (ed.), The Theory of the Modern Stage, An Introduction to Modern Theatre and Drama, Harmondsworth, Penguin

Martindale, C., 1976, 'Creativity: Its all in the head', Psychology Today, March 1976, vol. 2, no. 3, pp. 16-19

Maslow, A.H., 1968, Towards a Psychology of Being, New York, Van Nostrand Reinhold Company

May, R., 1975, The Courage to Create, London, Collins

Redfern, H.B., 1986, Questions in Aesthetic Education, London, Allen and Unwin

Redington, C., 1983, Can Theatre Teach, Oxford, Pergamon

Reid, L.A., 1985, 'Art and Knowledge', British Journal of Aesthetics, vol. 25, no. 2

Rogers, C.R., 1961, On becoming a person, London, Constable

Ross, M., 1978, The Creative Arts, London, Heinemann, Educational

Rumelhart, D.E., McClelland, J.L. and the PDP Research

Group, 1986, Parallel Distributed Processing. Explorations in the Microstructure of Cognition, Vol. 1, Foundations, London, MIT Press

Segall, M.H., Campbell, D.T. and Herskovits, M.J., 1966, The Influence of Culture on Visual Perception, Indianopolis, New York, Kansas City, Bobbs-Merrill

Senden, M. von, 1932, Raum und Gestaltauffassung bei operietan Blindgebornen vor und nach der Operation, Leipzig, Barth

Sparshott, F., 1985, 'Some Dimensions of Dance Meaning', British Journal of Aesthetics, vol. 25, no. 2

Stumbo, H.W., 1970, 'Three Bases for Research and Teaching in the Arts: Subjective, Objective and Projective' in Pappas, G. (ed.), Concepts in Art and Education, London, Macmillan

Styan, J.L., 1981, Modern Drama in Theory and Practice, Volume 3, Expressionism and Epic Theatre, London, New York, etc., Cambridge University Press

Symes, C., 1983, 'Creativity: A Divergent Point of View', The Journal of Aesthetic Education, vol. 17, no. 2, Summer 1983, pp. 83-96

Thouless, R.H., 1933, 'A Racial Difference in Perception', Journal of Social Psychology, 4, pp. 330-9

Underwood, G., 1976, Attention and Memory, Oxford, Pergamon

Wilding, J.M., 1982, Perception, From Sense to Object, London, Hutchinson

Williams, R., 1983, Keywords, London, Fontana

Wollheim, R., 1968, Art and its Objects - An Introduction to Aesthetics, New York, Evanston, London, Harper and Row

Chapter Five

ACCESS TO THE ARTS

Whilst the previous chapter was concerned with different ways of engaging with the arts this chapter is concerned with access to the arts. The original draft title for this chapter was 'Arts Provision', but the term 'provision' implies a definition of the arts as a commodity, which I want to avoid. In choosing to use the word 'access' I am deliberately allowing myself the opportunity to go beyond simply describing the different individuals and agencies who organise, promote or otherwise bring into being arts activities and events; I am providing a framework for also discussing those factors, be they social, psychological or educational, which encourage or inhibit participation in artistic activities.

In discussing access to the arts I will attempt to infer a definition of the arts which is inclusive rather than exclusive. I will certainly not restrict myself to the narrow definitions which inform much state provision. As John Pick points out,

> We often speak as if the arts are the same thing as the subsidised Arts, and as if excellence can be found nowhere within commercial or media productions.
>
> (Pick 1986:1)

In order to broaden the base of this chapter I will consider access by looking at state provision, commercial or private provision, the media, education and voluntary activity. In this way I hope to cover the same ground as Muriel Nissel in her book, 'Facts about the Arts'. In her summary of available statistics (Nissel 1983:1) she includes the performing and visual arts (including crafts), literature, film and broadcasting but excludes what are known as heritage arts.

I am aware that there may be some overlap between the various categories I have decided to use. I could include the BBC in the section on state provision but prefer to consider the media together. Much work by Regional Arts Associations takes place in educational settings but I prefer to look at education as a separate entity. The framework I have chosen is ad hoc and should be seen as nothing more than this.

The arts industry is a large undertaking. Eschewing problems of definition for the moment and including those activities which, by popular consent, are acknowledged as part of the arts, we have a massive output from:

i)   the state-subsidised sector involved in music, video, theatre, cinema, publishing and the promotion of the visual arts and crafts;
ii) the same range of activities in the commercial sector;
iii) the media, notably radio, television and film but not forgetting short stories and other literary work in the press;
iv) the contribution of the education sector to promoting and facilitating access to all of the arts and most crafts.
v)   much voluntary activity from brass bands and male voice choirs to community arts activities;

If one wanted to be all-embracing one could include the contribution of military bands to the availability of music and the contribution of the churches to music, painting, sculpture and the crafts. To quote John Pick discussing the art industry,

> There is not just one arts economy in Britain - even the different realms of the subsidised arts work quite differently - and the subsidised arts economy is a small part of the whole economy of the arts; and it is not, as it likes to claim, invariably at the generative core of the wider economy.
>
> (Pick 1986:96)

A word needs to be included here about the type of analysis which follows. I do not intend to offer a quantitative analysis. Figures showing the extent of a given activity in a given year soon become out of date and, whilst they may have some value in showing the relative size of the different areas of artistic activity, they are not important for the purpose of this book. Anyone interested in acquiring quantitative data for a particular form of arts activity should consult Muriel Nissel's (1983) book for clues to the sources of up-to-date information. My intention here is to attempt a qualitative analysis of arts activity focusing particularly upon those factors which inhibit or encourage participation. Figures are only included where they illustrate a point.

It may be useful at this juncture to distinguish two philosophies which underlie much of the educational work undertaken in the promotion of the arts. One philosophy, as mentioned in the previous paragraph and written about by Jor (1976), seeks to demystify the arts. This involves taking steps to ensure that members of the public have the necessary knowledge and background understanding to appreciate, say, the language and structure of a Shakespeare play or a T.S. Eliot poem, the iconography of a Renaissance painting, or the structure and harmonics of a Mozart concerto. This is the traditional approach to arts education and is usually very Eurocentric. It assumes that the vast majority of the population are simply uneducated when it comes to understanding and appreciating the arts. What prevents them from gaining greater access to the arts is their own educational inadequacy. This, therefore, is the problem which must be addressed by the arts funding bodies. It is a deficit model in that it assumes that the public are inadequately educated in the arts.

The other philosophy, written about by Simpson (1976) is concerned with the democratisation of the arts, or of culture, and seeks to broaden our definition of artistic activity. Unlike the 'demystification' philosophy, the 'democratisation' philosophy does not simply accept a concept of the arts as a given which people need only be helped to understand. It instead asks us to accept as legitimate art a whole range of different activities and artefacts, from folk music and dance to pop music and ballroom dancing, from corn dollies to the totems of punk rockers, from the Punch and Judy show to street theatre. Moreover, the democratisers of the arts acknowledge the contribution of the ethnic minorities to the cultural life of the nation. The folk and classical traditions of the different immigrant groups are seen as having equal status with grand opera or classical ballet. This is a much more populist view of arts development which accepts the creative potential of all of the populace rather than the few who have been accorded the status of artist.

These two approaches to arts development are often seen as mutually exclusive, but this need not be the case. Within the education sector it has always proved possible to promote both the artistic heritage and the creative development of the individual, the classical and the popular, the experimental and the personal. There is no reason why arts providing agencies should not adopt a similar approach to their educational activities. It is not simply a matter of creating bigger audiences for traditional art forms but rather a matter of awakening the artistic consciousness of the nation to both its own potential as a producer of art and to the vast range of artistic activity which we can enjoy as appreciators.

This leads to the final point I wish to make in this chapter. I hope to demonstrate that the opportunties which exist to engage with the arts are mainly opportunities to appreciate them. Opportunities to create and to participate are limited. Generally speaking, the arts establishment provides arts activities for audiences; creation and participation are the prerogative of those professionals who are employed by the arts providers. Educational activity is seen by many arts promoters as concerned with demystification rather than democratisation.

THE STATE

For the purposes of this chapter I am using the term 'the state' to refer to all those institutions which receive public monies and use them for the benefit of the community at large. It is not a tidy concept but something of a catch-all which can include both central and local government and a whole range of national, regional and local quangos (quasi-autonomous non-governmental organisations). The Arts Council of Great Britain and the Regional Arts Associations are obvious examples of such quangos. Nicholas Pearson identifies the state as follows:

> The State ... is a complex set of relations which shape and are part of a wide range of economic, social and

cultural activities. The State is not a discrete organisation or machine. It is a set of practices, relations and forms of authority bound up with many aspects of daily life. It is not a discrete "thing" that can be specifically identified and described on an abstract or theoretical level. It has to be understood in its particular forms.

(Pearson 1982:3)

The principal organisations through which the state intervenes in the promotion of the arts at a national level are The Arts Council of Great Britain, The Crafts Council, The British Film Institute and, to a lesser degree, the Design Council. Of these, the Arts Council is by far the largest and most influential organ of state intervention in the arts. Of course, the local authorities, through their leisure or recreation departments, are instrumental in providing arts activities at a local level and their contribution should not be underestimated. In terms of national policy, however, the Arts Council would appear to be the most influential body.

The Arts Council was granted a Royal Charter of Incorporation on 9th August 1946. It was to continue the work of the wartime Council for the Encouragement of Music and the Arts (CEMA). The Council was granted a new charter in February 1967 in which its objects were laid down as:

a) to develop and improve the knowledge, understanding and practice of the arts;
b) to increase the accessibility of the arts to the public throughout Great Britain;
c) and to advise and co-operate with Departments of Government, local authorities and other bodies on any matters concerned whether directly or indirectly with the foregoing objects.

(ACGB 1967)

The Arts Council receives monies from central government which it uses to further these objects. Nowadays, in the regions, it works mainly through the Regional Arts Associations which also raise money from the local authorities. It has responsibility for the National Companies (National Theatre, English National Opera, etc.) and in 1985 was granted a supplemental charter to enable it to administer the South Bank complex after the abolition of

113

the Greater London Council.

The Council has the freedom to define the arts as it feels fit and to disburse monies subject to whatever conditions it or its panels decide. The Arts Council is concerned with standards. It is in large part responsible for setting the value systems for the arts in contemporary Britain. In formulating these value systems it occasionally adopts some of the spurious ways of defining what is and what is not art which were outlined in an earlier chapter. Thus, it promotes serious art rather than popular art, a distinction made by one of its former Secretaries General, Sir Roy Shaw.

> The popular arts are not now considered appropriate for public subsidy, but they were during the second World War, when there were two organisations for distributing the arts. For the high arts there was the Council for the Encouragement of Music and the Arts (CEMA); for the popular arts there was the Entertainments National Service Association (ENSA). The CEMA tradition was continued and developed by the Arts Council, but the ENSA tradition was largely allowed to lapse.
> (Shaw 1987:138)

The Council also makes a point of supporting only professional arts activities. This is another of those nonsensical distinctions which bedevil the arts subsidy business. By adopting this policy the state, via the Arts Council, excludes from its patronage many folk arts, many amateur choirs, brass and silver bands - despite their achieving excellent standards of performance - and many art forms from both the black and white ethnic minorities where there is no 'professional' tradition. This policy has had a far-reaching effect and is in no small part responsible for alienating many people from involvement in the arts. Nicholas Pearson makes the point as follows:

> the State has been involved in supporting and promoting not only 'professional' definitions of art but the 'professionalisation' of art.
> While on the one hand the increasing level of State involvement in art has promoted art as part of public culture (public exhibitions, public museums, public education) it has also been part of the removal of the public from active involvement in the creation of

that culture.

The involvement of State power in the support of the professionalisation of art and of the authority of the art professional has marginalised the role of the public in aesthetic matters, and in the active development of a public art culture.

(Pearson 1982:44)

What seems to have happened is that the Arts Council has assumed the role of the custodian of the national artistic culture and in so doing has excluded the majority of the population from participating in what it, the Arts Council, defines as art. Kelly puts it another way:

Through a long and complex process, the state has assumed a role of patron of the arts and custodian of a specific national culture, and the establishment of the Arts Council of Great Britain in 1945 is but one example of the ways in which the state enacts that role. The establishment of the BBC and later the IBA, and the regulatory frameworks within which they are required to operate, provide other examples, as does the establishment of the Sports Council. The state has also assumed the role of 'director' of this national culture through its ability to emphasise or constrain activities by means of funding allocation and licensing restrictions. This ability enables it to construct a specific dominant culture, while apparently dealing evenhandedly with all cultures and favouring none.

(Kelly 1984:43)

Thus the state has taken upon itself the prerogative to set the agenda, to decide what is or is not art, and, as suggested above, to play an influential role in establishing the value system within which the arts, at least the state-subsidised arts, will operate. In doing so it has defined the arts in a very narrow way, a way which does not accord with the cultural interests and perceptions of large numbers of the population. Writing in 1970 John S. Harris saw this paternalistic approach to cultural development as one of the important functions of the Arts Council.

The scope of a patronage programme - the determination of which arts are to be supported - is of much importance. The Arts Council has confined its support activities to a relatively few areas - professional opera, ballet, drama, art, music and poetry and, more recently, literature. It decided early that amateur participation in the arts could be fostered most appropriately by the schools and universities and by volunteer bodies functioning in local communities.

(Harris 1970:321)

There is no doubt that the Arts Council is aware of this important aspect of its work. Occasionally it sees fit to expand its horizons and put money into ventures which are normally deemed to be outside its remit. This was exemplified quite recently when the Council backed a production of a well-known musical comedy. Some of those involved in the Council's work would like to extend the sphere of their activity even further. Roy Shaw shows an unexpected populist leaning when he suggests:

I would particularly like to see public funds used for the training of popular entertainers - the comedians, singers, jugglers, acrobats, conjurers and clowns - as is so successfully done in the Soviet Union, where circus is an immensely popular art.

(Shaw 1987:139)

Of course, the Council does not operate in a vacuum. It operates within the context of a developing culture within a capitalist society. It influences and is, in turn, influenced by those other activists in the culture industry. Commercial arts providers, the media, education and the many voluntary organisations - from a local art appreciation club to a radical Arts Laboratory, a male voice choir to a youth club pop group - all play a part in determining the nature and extent of national artistic activity. But it is the Arts Council which is, perhaps, most influential in determining and maintaining what we think of as the high arts.

The driving force behind much of the Council's work is its chartered obligation to increase the accessibility of the arts to the general public. This means, if one thinks of the three ways of engaging with the arts outlined in the previous chapter, that it is concerned mainly with developing opportunities for appreciation of the arts. It does this by putting the arts, in a physical sense, within the reach of more people and by developing its educational work to help more people to enjoy and understand the arts. One has to remember that here I am using the term 'the arts' to denote only those art forms legitimised by Arts Council patronage. They tend to be the arts of the past. The Arts Council would, I feel sure, argue that this was because, in simple numerical terms, at any given time works of art from the past outnumber contemporary works. Consequently more money must be spent on maintaining the availability of the heritage than in promoting the new.

Arts funding bodies generally have to live with the dilemma of deciding how to allocate their resources between the arts of the past and contemporary work. They feel it important to retain the possibility of listening to a performance of a Grieg concerto or enjoying a production of a Restoration Comedy, and increasingly they are concerned to provide opportunities to promote classical work from the ethnic minorities. At the same time they acknowledge that it is part of their role to promote new work by new artists. There is a problem in maintaining the availability of an ever growing national archive in all the art forms. Choices have to be made about where to invest the national contribution to the arts economy. By and large, the Arts Council puts most of its resources into the maintenance of those companies and artists which promote the European tradition. It allocates a small proportion of its expenditure for the promotion of the non-European artistic tradition. Increasingly it devotes a proportion of its resources to educational work which seeks to demystify the dominant European culture for the benefit of those members of the population who have not had the necessary educational induction into the European artistic heritage.

The Arts Council's involvement in education goes back to its roots in CEMA. Some would agree with John Pick (1986:189-96) that the Arts Council has always, almost by definition, been involved in educational work. Others would see this interest in forging links with educationalists as stemming from the formal adoption of an education policy by the Council in February 1983 (ACGB 1983). This movement towards the adoption of an educational policy stemmed, in part, from the following exhortation in the Redcliffe-Maud report, Support for the Arts in England and Wales:

> Meanwhile, we must reject the long established fallacy that 'arts support' and 'education' are two separate things. More positively, we must insist that those

117

responsible for them are natural allies, and see to it that they collaborate at national, regional and local levels.

(Redcliffe-Maud 1976:23)

The year of 1976 saw not only the publication of this report, but also four publications from the Council of Europe by Finn Jor (1976), Stephen Mennel (1976), Raymonde Moulin (1976) and J.A. Simpson (1976) together with Naseem Khan's (1976) book on the arts of ethnic minorities. These all contributed to a climate of opinion which helped Roy Shaw, the secretary general of the Council and a former professor of adult education, to ease into place the education policy which he had been wanting to develop. This was done after much consultation within the field and was further helped by the publication of the Gulbenkian report, The Arts in Schools - Principles, Practice and Provision (Calouste Gulbenkian Foundation 1982).

One of the effects of adopting an education policy was to increase the interest in education of the regional arts associations. It would be wrong to suggest that prior to this they had shown no interest in education at all, though this was certainly the feeling of some educationalists. What had changed was that there was now an education department at the Arts Council and it had a budget to disburse. Principally it funded collaborative ventures between arts providing agencies and educational providers so that they could, in the spirit of the Redcliffe-Maud Report, become natural allies and work out a joint approach to promoting the arts. What they both felt they had been doing separately they were now able to do jointly. And this inevitably led to a re-appraisal of much of their earlier work in this area. Residences and 'artist in schools' schemes were examined with a more critical eye and their strengths and weaknesses evaluated. New forms of collaboration were tried and there was a great deal of activity in the regions to raise levels of awareness amongst teachers about what their colleagues in the arts associations had to offer. In a similar way artists and those working in the arts associations were more fully appraised of the aims and objectives, the working practices and constraints and, not least, the organisation and structure of education in both the compulsory and post-compulsory sectors.

Such joint ventures were described, from an adult

education point of view, as follows:

> Joint ventures are schemes which bring people into contact with the professional arts or artists in organised learning situations arranged by arts providers and adult education providers. The working links between the providers, together with all the meetings, working parties, cross-memberships and so on, are examples of co-operation.
>
> (Adkins 1981:4)

Adkins (1981:5) goes on to categorise these areas of co-operation as involving appreciation courses addressed to the arts, practical arts courses and arts in the community. One assumes that his category of practical arts courses includes both the creative and the participatory. Usually, such activities were funded jointly. When they took place in the compulsory sector of education they were, as a matter of principle, extra-curricular. It was rightly felt that the arts providing agencies should not be putting monies into the normal school curriculum which was the responsibility of the local education authority.

By offering resources, both financial and advisory, the Arts Council was once again in a position to set an agenda for educational development in the arts in the country as a whole. By offering matching grants the Council was often able to unlock additional resources from the regions in order to promote both artistic and art educational policy. In this way it was certainly fulfilling its obligation to make the arts more accessible. But by putting conditions on the award of grants, by deciding that in a particular year, say, photography would be the educational priority, the Council ensured that it retained the initiative in deciding which arts were to be promoted.

It is important to note that in referring to the Arts Council we are not simply referring to the eighteen members, chairman and vice-chairman appointed by the government. The Council's work, on a day-to-day basis is carried out by its officers and guided by its advisory panels. The members of these various groups bring their influence to bear on the work of the Council though, it has to be said, the ultimate power and authority rests with the Council of government appointees.

The Arts Council, then, as an organ of the state, promotes those activities which it deems to be arts

119

activities either directly, as with the national companies, or through the regional arts associations. It exercises its influence through these bodies to not only promote the arts but also to promote an idea of what the arts are. It becomes involved in educational work in order to make these arts more accessible to the public at large. Recently it has adopted a policy for ethnic minority arts and is becoming increasingly involved in promoting non-European art forms. The majority of its work, however, is still concerned with the maintenance of a European tradition of high art and it is seeking to extend its influence in this work.

In 1984 the Arts Council published a policy statement entitled 'The Glory of the Garden'. This statement acknowledged an imbalance in the distribution of funds throughout the country and proposed steps to correct this.

> Nevertheless, after forty years it is time to come to grips with Keynes' first priority, to decentralise and disperse the dramatic and musical and artistic life of the country. The measures required to do so include the institutional, the administrative and the financial.
>
> (ACGB 1984:v)

The policy to date has had some effect and gone some way to redressing the balance, but there is still a long way to go to correct a situation where 'no theatre company in the regions enjoys an Arts Council subsidy equal to one-tenth of that given to either of the two national theatre companies' (ACGB 1984:iv).

Those other agencies mentioned at the beginning of this section, The Crafts Council, The British Film Institute and the Design Council, operate in a way similar to that of the Arts Council. They will not be given separate consideration in this section but it must not be forgotten that they are equally influential in facilitating the State's intervention in the arts. However, the history of film is much shorter than that of other art forms and it cannot be viewed in quite the same Eurocentric way as other art forms, much of the work of the early years coming from the United States. It should be acknowledged that film, in its relatively short history, has grown to be an international medium of expression and as such is nothing like so rooted in a single ethnic tradition as many other art forms. It is, nonetheless, the beneficiary of state patronage and control, just like the other art forms we have been discussing above.

In film we have an art form which, almost from the start, was promoted as a commercial proposition. The Hollywood legend bears testimony to the wealth and reputation generated by the film industry. In the next section we will focus on the role of the commercial sector in providing access to the arts.

COMMERCE

One would be forgiven for thinking that the only arts activities worth talking about were those promoted by the arts subsidising agencies like the Arts Council. We are led to believe that those activities which fall outside this sphere are mere entertainment, something of a lesser order. Such a view is clearly untenable. Much of what is provided in the commercial sector, and for that matter by the media, is of equal value and importance to that coming from the subsidised sector, no matter what criteria are used to make the judgement. Further, the historical record bears testimony to the role of private enterprise in preserving and promoting the fine and performing arts.

The scale of private sector arts activity is vast. John Pick (1986:102) points out that in 1983, when central government spending on the arts was £299,000,000, and local authority spending (including libraries) was £573,371,000, consumers spent £1,830,000,000 on audio records and tapes, £450,000,000 on arts and crafts, £650,000,000 on books, £124,000,000 on cinema, £560,000,000 on photography, £223,000,000 on musical instruments, £2,206,000,000 on television and £1,445,000,000 on video. This represents a large amount of our national wealth circulating in the arts economy. Appleyard underlines this point as follows:

> But the fact remains that the scale of the arts industry is large, and when electronic dissemination is taken into account, there has never been such a huge potential audience. It is in this context that the constant grumbles of the arts world should be seen. Their complaint is the malaise of affluence, not poverty.
>
> (Appleyard 1984:53)

If we accept a broad and inclusive rather than a narrow and exclusive definition of the arts then it is clear that arts patronage has become much more broadly based. This expansion began before the Arts Council was founded. To a certain extent it was a product of industrialisation and the breakdown of the pre-industrial class system. As Janet Minihan points out:

> The transition from a select, largely aristocratic patronage to a middle-class, and finally a mass, audience was the prerequisite for official interest in the arts.
>
> (Minihan 1977:xi)

It was this growth of interest in the arts in the private sector which paved the way for the wartime experiments with CEMA and ENSA and which led, eventually, to the foundation of the Arts Council. Since then the commercial arts world has continued to operate alongside the state subsidised sector. Many of the traditional offerings in the theatre have continued, albeit on a reduced scale. Live theatre was hit badly by the advent of television and the music hall has declined almost to a point of extinction. Recently, however, there has been something of a revival in pub cabaret whilst the social club circuit has continued to provide a livelihood for variety acts.

The real expansion in the private sector has been in the electronic media. It is not unreasonable to suggest that more people nowadays experience music via radio, television and audio discs or tapes, than go to live concerts. Television and video have provided an alternative to what was an ailing film industry and graphics and 'paint-box' software for computers is providing a new medium in which the creative visual artist can work. I will deal with the media more fully in the next section. It is enough to record here the influence they have had on the commercial art world.

The commercial theatre has always been an important part of the nation's artistic activity and, indeed, before the advent of government subsidy was responsible for maintaining the dramatic heritage. It was the entrepreneurial theatre actor-manager who brought Shakespeare to the people before the Royal Shakespeare Company was even thought of. And theatre provided for a truly popular art form. Janet Minihan reminds us:

> The theatre brought together a range of social classes under its roof, if not always in the pursuit of culture. In

its crudest form, as travelling acts, sideshows and circuses, the theatre in fact offered a genuinely popular lower-class entertainment.

(Minihan 1977:4)

When the visual arts moved away from their historic dependence on the patronage of the church and the aristocracy it was the private gallery owner who brought the works of artists to the notice of the public. Whilst the commercial art promoters can be held responsible for some of the worst excesses of the international art market it would be foolish to deny them any place in the development of the arts in the United Kingdom, or elsewhere for that matter. They have made, and still make, an important contribution to our cultural and artistic development.

The commercial art world, much like the subsidised art world, is concerned mainly with the appreciation of the arts. Ignoring for the moment the idea of art as a commodity - the trade in works of art as investments - the private sector arts promoter is concerned to persuade us that art is something we can enjoy and is worth paying for. By and large the commercial arts world is not concerned to foster creative involvement in the arts. A publisher or producer will, of course, nurture what is considered to be new talent with a view to a pay-off at some time in the future. But, generally, they want to engage the public in the role of audience not the role of creator. They want to fill theatres, cinemas and concert halls, sell books or paintings, records or videos and generally persuade the general public to part with money in return for what is hoped will be an enjoyable and aesthetic experience.

The private sector arts industry, therefore, does not enjoy the same freedom, some would say self-indulgence, as the subsidised arts world. They have to attract and to please their audiences and, perhaps more importantly, cultivate the attention of those influential critics who become the arbiters of taste in the free market sector of the arts economy. They are criticised for pandering to the lowest common denominator, for providing sentimentality and spectacle rather than the staging of serious dramatic productions or the mounting of challenging exhibitions. This is certainly true for some theatrical producers and for some gallery owners and publishers for some of the time. But, as I suggested earlier, it would be wrong to write off everything that comes from the commercial arts world as inferior. The

123

commercial theatre still plays an important role in bringing serious theatre to the general public.

In the same vein, there are still gallery owners who are prepared to bring the work of new and unknown artists to a wider audience, to forego a quick profit for a more risky investment in the future. And new writers can still find publishers who are willing to give them an opening. In recent years there has been a great expansion in privately owned galleries promoting the crafts.

It should also be remembered that the commercial sector promotes the folk as well as the classical tradition. The contribution made by this sector is broader than that of the state. But in the end, the commercial operator in the arts has to make a profit. Unless financial solvency can be maintained, no commercial art promoter can operate. And the money to keep these operators in business comes from the general public, or rather that section of the general public which is sufficiently interested in the arts to be willing and able to pay for their pleasures. It is stating the obvious, but nonetheless worth saying, that in periods of high unemployment there are many who do not have the necessary disposable income to pursue their interests in the arts in the commercial sector.

THE MEDIA

The media have already been referred to in the previous section, in particular, the electronic media. The great difference which the development of the electronic media has made to the arts is that now it is possible for most people in Britain to enjoy their art at home. Music, literature, drama and the visual arts have all been seen as a proper concern of television and radio. It is likely that more people enjoy drama on television than ever go to a theatre. Again the media invite the public to participate in an appreciative rather than a creative role, though there are some educational programmes which encourage participation in creative work. And the media are not solely concerned with the classical European tradition. They promote the folk tradition as well as the work of artists from ethnic minority groups.

One of the great successes of television must be the contribution it has made to drama. From the popular soap opera to the screening of classical drama from this country and abroad, television has made its distinctive contribution. Purists worry about standards. Roy Shaw demonstrates an ambivalence to television when he writes on the one hand,

> Some of the popular arts (such as most television sit-coms) aim at giving little more than amusement, which has been cruelly defined as the happiness of those who cannot think.
>
> (Shaw 1987:18)

And on the other hand,

> In 1976, when I was drafting my first Arts Council annual report, I wrote that television drama was the real national theatre.
>
> (Shaw 1987:139)

Whilst it may be true that some of the dramatic offerings on television are little more than amusement, there is also a long tradition which seeks to uphold the highest artistic standards of the day. In discussing the attitudes of Lord Reith when he was in charge of the BBC, Janet Minihan says:

> He refused to pander to popular tastes which he despised and refused to allow the BBC to become a mere purveyor of popular entertainment, like the cinema or music hall. He was willing to court criticism by pursuing a course openly intended to educate and elevate public taste.
>
> (Minihan 1977:207)

One could paraphrase this so that it was clear that what Reith wanted was for the public to share the tastes and artistic pleasures which he himself enjoyed and valued. These were, in his opinion, higher than the tastes of the public at large. It was his mission, he felt, to 'elevate' their taste. Television, at least in its early days and, arguably, even now, provides a vehicle for imposing one set of cultural values on the nation. Much like the Arts Council, the controllers of the television companies are able to set the agenda, to decide what is and is not to be accorded the status of art, to promote this view of art and to educate the general public so that they in turn accept this view of the nature of art.

125

Both the BBC and the IBA are legally obliged to provide educational programmes. Their educational programmes are broadcast on both television and radio for both schoolchildren and adults. These programmes contribute to the educational and cultural development of the nation, even though they may be providing only a partial view of the wide range of artistic activity which makes up the contemporary cultural scene. Additionally the broadcasting companies provide talks and discussions about the arts, promote dialogue about contemporary cultural issues, and bring to the notice of the public at large some of the developments which are taking place in the various forms of artistic expression. Janet Minihan (1977:207) notes that from as early as 1923 the BBC included 'literary, music, film and drama critics among its broadcasters'. Discussions of the arts featured prominently, and still do, in the BBC talk programmes.

The BBC and the commercial radio and television networks now operate at a regional and local level and this enables them to promote the art of the region. The locally relevant and the locally created work of art can be promoted through the electronic media to the local and the regional audience. Music and drama with a regional flavour can be included in the broadcasting schedules.

A special word needs to be said about radio drama. The 'radio play' has developed as an artistic genre in its own right. It is something more than literature read from the printed page but it lacks the visual aspect of television or theatre drama. As a low cost medium it has afforded writers an opportunity to find an outlet for their dramatic talents without the need for the expensive sets and costumes of a full scale theatrical production.

In a similar way the video is becoming recognised as a form of art. By the term video I do not mean those plays or films made specifically for television. I mean rather those short visual experiments which exploit the technology of video-recording to provide an aesthetic experience. From starting out as a way of providing visual content when pop music was being played on television the pop-video has developed to an extent where the visual content is now as important as the music and the two components combine to form a distinctive televisual art form. The new micro-computer technology has provided video artists with a whole range of special effects which are unavailable to the film-maker and were unavailable to early television drama.

126

The contribution of the print media to promoting the arts has largely diminished. Newspapers and magazines are not seen as important outlets for works of poetry or literature, though what are known as women's magazines carry a great deal of fiction. Occasionally we see a story or a novel serialised in a newspaper or journal, and some of the quality newspapers sometimes print poetry, but the advent of cheap printing processes and the paperback book mean that writers no longer look to the press, as Dickens did, to find an outlet for their work.

It should be noted, however, that some photographers have made their names through their work for the press. The colour supplements of Sunday and other newspapers, and more recently colour printing in ordinary newspapers has extended the range of possibilities for photographers to practise their art.

One can debate whether or not one includes the hi-fi system, the compact disc player and the tape machine as part of the media. They are included here for convenience. High quality methods of reproduction have meant that music can be recorded and played back of such a high quality that it would be difficult to conceive of the experience being better if one attended a live concert. Again purists will maintain that a recording is not the same as the experience of a live concert, that the production somehow loses something in the process of being recorded. This may be true. Maybe some of the atmosphere of a concert is lost. On the other hand maybe all that is lost is the background noises, the coughs and splutters of a live audience and the occasional mistake by the musicians.

There is a tendency, on the part of commentators on the arts, particularly those connected with state provision, to ignore the contribution of the media. This may be partly due to the way in which they choose to define the arts and partly due to the difficulty of quantifying the extent of the contribution. In any event, one is left with the feeling that often the media are somehow left out of the equation when the arts are discussed. Such a distortion of the total national picture of arts activity is indefensible. It is important that here we acknowledge the large and important range of arts activity promoted by the media.

EDUCATION

If one were to write a comprehensive history of the relationship between the arts and education one would have to go back as far as Plato and Aristotle, if not further. And this would only account for the development of the relationship within a European tradition. The Arts have almost always been thought of as a proper concern for the educationalist. Within the European as well as within other traditions the idea of the 'educated man' usually includes an interest if not a proficiency in one or more art forms. Hence, in most schools nowadays arts subjects are still prominent in the curriculum. Provision is made to teach children to create, appreciate and participate in a range of art forms and craft areas. From time to time particular art forms may be under threat - currently in some areas the provision of music lessons for those wishing to learn to play an instrument is being seen as an optional extra for which a fee has to be paid - but the desirability of including the arts in the curriculum has never been seriously challenged.

Similarly, within the liberal tradition of adult education the arts have always maintained their position as an essential component of the adult education programme. Writing in 1978 Mee and Wiltshire (1978:33) estimated that some 48% of all non-vocational adult education courses could be categorised as being concerned with craft and aesthetic skills. The usual pattern nowadays is for classes aimed at developing skills in the areas of creation and participation to be provided by the local education authorities and appreciation classes to be provided by the Responsible Bodies. There are, of course, exceptions and the picture occasionally changes. Higher education too plays its part. Apart from degree courses in arts subjects there are usually a whole host of clubs and societies devoted to the arts in universities and polytechnics. What is more, these institutions offer arts activities from cultures other than our own and promote both the folk and the classical tradition. Thus one can study Russian literature or Chinese art, African music or Indonesian dance, American film or Aztec architecture. It is within adult and higher education that all art forms from all cultures are accepted as proper areas of research, study and enjoyment.

In the primary schools creative work is seen as an important means of helping the child develop an identity through self expression. It is argued that involvement in creative work is developmental in psychological terms and leads to the more rounded development of the individual than would a solely intellectual or academic education.

The place of the creative arts in the primary and the secondary school curriculum has been championed by writers such as Robertson (1963), Read (1964), Ehrenzweig (1968), Field and Newick (1973), Ross (1978), and Barrett (1979). All these writers stressed the value to the individual of involvement in the creative process. Often, however, the arts courses in secondary schools were dominated by an examination syllabus which precluded creative expression. The subject matter of examination pieces was set by the examiners. In the visual arts the size of the work, the time available for completion and often the medium were prescribed by the examination board to the extent that the examination candidate became involved in a process that would have been anathema to a professional artist, so little resemblance did it bear to the creative act. The problems of assessment in art examinations were never really resolved and remain to a large extent a measure of a candidates ability to conform to a preconceived notion of 'good' art within a European tradition. Examination boards are slowly acknowledging that we live in a multi-cultural society and there is hope that examinations in the arts will reflect this growing awareness. New forms of examination are being developed in response to the increasingly held belief that a few pieces of work produced under examination conditions are no basis on which to judge a person's creative ability.

Art education in primary schools has managed to retain some sort of artistic and educational integrity, though occasionally considerations of formal artistic structure were disregarded in the name of free expression. Generally, however, freedom from the constraints imposed by examiners allowed a much more experimental approach.

Creative work in schools is usually confined to the visual arts and crafts with perhaps some creative writing and occasional improvised drama sessions. The compulsory sector of education usually sees its engagement with the arts as being more appreciative in nature. Appreciation is a more academic exercise, more at home within a scholastic educational tradition, and, involving as it does a great deal of written work, more easily examinable. Hence, examinations in literature, music and some of the visual arts are concerned with history, analysis and appreciation rather than creation.

Many schools provide opportunities for participation in the arts and at best this can be a truly creative experience. The school play and the school orchestra are means by which the pupil can gain experience of the performing arts. Because of the nature of the exercise, however, these activities can only involve a small proportion of the total number of students. For many people, their experience of the arts in school has been mainly academic in nature.

Art education in secondary schools is in a state of flux at the moment. In recent times it has never really enjoyed high status and in schools dominated by examinations it is often thought of as an easy and non-vocational option. There is no doubt that the fact that the majority of children and young people come into contact with the arts at school has an effect on the cultural life of the community. It is the nature of that effect that one may wish to question. Harris takes an optimistic view:

> The contribution of British education to greater public understanding and appreciation of the arts is of the utmost importance. Youth in the elementary and secondary schools can acquire a lifelong interest in music, theatre, and the visual arts, a concern which later will induce them to support artistic enterprises in their own communities.
>
> (Harris 1970:5)

Whilst it is incontrovertible that many people gain a lifelong interest in the arts from their school experience it can also be argued that the majority of adults are alienated from the arts by this same experience. Figures are hard to come by but Muriel Nissel (1983:144) refers to the General Household Survey of 1980 which demonstrates that in the year in question only 5% of the population visit theatre, opera and ballet, less than 1% visit classical concerts, and 3% visit museums and galleries. This is hardly a testimony to the effectiveness of universal arts education in schools. Educationalists would argue that arts education in schools is more to do with developing the full potential of the individual rather than providing future audiences for arts activities. Arts funding agencies might do well to examine closely the efficacy of their investment in school-based activities.

It would seem that on leaving school young people put aside those activities which they associate with school and interest themselves in what they consider to be more adult pastimes. If their parents do not themselves participate in the arts then it would not be surprising if the young person did not see such participation as an adult activity. If the adult role model to which they relate does not include arts activities then it is reasonable for young people to associate the arts with school rather than with adult behaviour. If we wish to increase participation in the arts there is a strong case for expanding adult education provision. In this way it will be possible to influence the adult role models to which young people aspire.

When Redcliffe-Maud put his faith in the education service as follows, he may have been mistaken:

> The excellence of our artists, professional and amateur, and our increasing enjoyment of old and contemporary art depend in each case more on education than on anything deliberate arts patronage can do. A revolution, therefore, in educational policy over the next ten years which brought the arts nearer the heart of the curriculum in British schools (and teacher training institutions) is what I would dearly like to see.
>
> (Redcliffe-Maud 1976:23)

In any event, ten years after this was written the government were considering omitting the arts altogether from the proposed national core curriculum and relegating them to subsidiary status. Whilst there is a strong case to suggest that the inclusion of the arts in the school curriculum is essential for the full development of the individual it may be more sensible for the arts funding bodies to concentrate their educational activity in the adult sector. The 'artist in residence' schemes which have formed the main plank of the regional arts associations' educational work in schools have to some extent suffered from a confusion of aims.

One view sees the aim of these residences as being of benefit to the artist; a sort of fellowship which allows artists to continue with their own work in the context of a school or college. The second view extends this idea. Placements are short term and the host institution is able to make reasonable demands of the artist in residence. Coonan explains the situation thus:

> the artist may be expected to perform a number of

public duties. 'Open studio' visits by the public (already a discretionary feature of 'fellowship' residencies) may be supplemented by a measure of teaching, lecturing or the execution of specific commissions for the host ... It is fair to say that such short placements stress the idea of public benefit alongside individual benefit to the resident artist, although there is evidence from past placements that too short an attachment may result in frustration both for the artist and host.

(Coonan 1985:2)

It would be wrong to suggest that there exists a universal dissatisfaction with the educational policies of the arts funding agencies, indeed, most educationalists welcome the opportunity to collaborate with them. The situation is more one of honest joint endeavour to work out the best way for the arts funding agencies to relate to the education service in order to promote the arts. There is agreement that something must be done to halt a perceived drift towards the solely intellectual and technological in both the education service and society at large. Hutchison puts his faith in creative involvement in the arts:

But if there is to be a further move away from the instrumental technological view of education, the view which allows examinations to determine the curriculum and insists on the priority of the cognitive over the affective; if there is to be a further move towards the humanist conception of education as lifelong personal development, and the full realisation of human potential, there will have to be much more opportunity to practise the arts as well as study them.

(Hutchison 1982:142)

There is clearly a role for adult education in expanding the opportunities for the creative involvement of adults as well as maintaining those opportunities for appreciative and participative involvement. The quality of much adult education work in the arts is questionable. It is not too alarming to suggest that much adult education work in this area could be seen as remedial; it is intended to provide an opportunity to develop that creative potential and energy which an academic secondary education allowed to dissipate. But even the adult education service is not always committed to developing creative ability. Too many classes assume that participants are incapable of genuine creative activity, focus on the making of a product rather than the learning of a process, and resort to the copying of postcards or other reproductions as a way of ensuring that participants have something to hang on the wall. The problems associated with teaching adults to work creatively will be dealt with later. For the moment I want only to suggest that adult education's record in this area is not all good. When it comes to appreciation courses, however, the picture is much better. Here there exists a long and creditable record of involvement in promoting the arts which predates the establishment of the Arts Council itself. Janet Minihan makes the point:

> Influential work (to enlighten the average wage-earner and his family) of this nature also proceeded outside museums, in classes of the Workers' Educational Association and the University Extra Mural Departments and in the tours of 'Art for the People'. The British Institute of Adult Education, a voluntary organisation founded in 1921, inaugurated Art for the People in 1935. The scheme, operating on the simple principle that art should go to the people who cannot go to art, was largely a private enterprise. The truckloads of pictures, displayed in small towns and rural areas lacking public collections, were on loan almost exclusively from private owners.
>
> (Minihan 1977:183)

In 1949 the Arts Council took over the administration of the 'Art for the People' scheme with a certain amount of disquiet. The annual report for 1948-9 records the following:

> In absorbing the 'Art for the People' scheme the Council was conscious of a certain caution. While the union was an obvious and à happy one, there remained the danger, evident to many on both sides, that by losing its identity in a large official organisation, the scheme might also end up by losing its traditional advantage of simple working and an unofficial approach.
>
> (ACGB 1949:12)

This note of warning turned out to be prophetic. Robert Hutchison (1982:99) notes that whatever the original intentions, Arts Council exhibitions are not, on the whole, found nowadays in schools, shops, canteens and factories. Having taken over part of the role of adult education, the Council found that it was unable to deliver the goods. The adult education service itself has not really filled this gap. The Regional Arts Associations are beginning to arrange touring exhibitions for rural areas but are not, as yet, exploiting venues where people who have no demonstrable interest in the arts foregather.

Much of the above commentary on education and the arts assumes a 'high culture' definition of the arts, a definition with which the arts funding agencies would feel comfortable. If, however, we broaden the definition then the picture begins to look much healthier. If we allow our concept of the arts to include the interest of young people in rock, pop, reggae and folk music, in cinema, radio, television and video, in break dancing, body popping and disco dancing, and in posters and spray-paint graffiti, then one can see a much wider interest in the creative and expressive arts than would appear from our earlier analysis. But it is an interest and a commitment that has largely developed in spite of rather than because of school experience. Moreover, it is often an expression of adolescent protest which is violently anti-school. It is rarely, if ever, accepted or legitimised as art by either the education or the arts establishment. Such a reaction contributes to the liminality of much adolescent creative expression.

The last area which must be mentioned in this discussion of the contribution of education to access to the arts concerns facilities. In our schools and colleges we have an enormous capital investment in buildings and equipment which can be pressed into service for the arts. I say 'pressed into service' deliberately because the experience of many arts promoters suggests that it is not easy to gain the willing cooperation of educational bureaucracies. Despite this occasional reluctance to open their doors to arts organisations there are a growing number of examples of arts bodies making effective use of the theatres and halls, the playing fields and exhibition spaces which are found within the education service.

Some education authorities, of course, positively court the arts funding bodies and in so doing enhance the quality of arts provision within their own service and bring their local communities into closer contact with the arts generally. It is worth mentioning the experience of

Cambridgeshire and Leicestershire, both counties with large rural populations and both counties which developed a philosophy of community education. In these two local education authorities the educational buildings were seen as a resource for the whole community and as a place where the arts should be seen and enjoyed. Theatres were built instead of assembly halls, prominent architects engaged to design school buildings and works of art collected for display in schools and community colleges. It is not unusual to come across a Sickert or a Hockney whilst walking through a Leicestershire community college. And making the arts a normal feature of school life in this way has had the effect of minimising the incidence of vandalism and malicious damage of works of art.

The education service, then, is seen as instrumental in promoting the arts and in the promotion of a culture. With varying degrees of success, schools and colleges pass on a set of cultural values which reflect the dominant culture of society. Opportunities to experience the art forms of minority cultures within the education service are few and far between. The arts funding agencies together with educationalists are jointly working out ways of promoting the arts within the education service. Hitherto, this effort has been concentrated on activities in schools, but it is suggested that it might be more effective to divert these energies and resources into the artistic education of adults. The artistic education of children is and will continue to be catered for in schools. The artistic education of adults, it is suggested, will help to provide the culturally active role models to which young people might aspire. Adult education has a central role to play in the maintenance or development of culture.

THE VOLUNTARY SECTOR

This section is about all those activities which are the product of voluntary activity and initiative and which aim to involve people in the arts. Much of the work in this area is not documented or otherwise recorded. Much of it is concerned with the folk tradition rather than high art, though one should not forget that Brass Bands and Male Voice Choirs somehow manage to continue a classical tradition within a local community context. The nature of the involvement can be either creative, appreciative or

135

participatory.

In many countries there is a strong tradition of local or community involvement in activities which can easily be accommodated in a broad concept of the arts. Song and dance are prominent in many cultures; not the singing of opera or the dance of ballet but the folk songs of working people and the dance of celebration, either round a maypole or in groups of eight for a reel. These are songs and dances which grew out of the community, songs to help people through a day's work, hauling in the fishing nets or working at the loom, and dances to celebrate when work is over, to celebrate the seasons of the year, the high days and holidays, to make the rains come or to cure a sick child.

Similarly there is a tradition of drama, from Greek theatre to the mediaeval mystery plays, a tradition of popular drama which is found in many countries of the world. Story telling also forms part of this folk tradition; the myths and legends associated with many aboriginal tribal groupings are passed on as part of an oral tradition, a tradition which, as noted earlier, Jung sees as reflecting the collective unconscious of the tribal group.

The visual arts are also to be found within this folk tradition. Customs like well dressing, the making of corn dollies, the carving and painting of totem poles, sand painting, the modelling of fertility symbols, cave painting and various forms of face and bodily decoration all bear witness to a strong and developing tradition which uses visual media as a means of expression.

Part of this tradition concerns the way in which we present ourselves to the world. Hands, feet, face, hair and clothing have always been subject to decoration and other forms of adornment, indeed the whole body has been seen as a suitable object for decoration. The presentation of self has been one of the more significant ways in which people have been able to become involved in creative activity, creating their own image to face the world. In developed countries this opportunity for creative expression has largely been taken over by the fashion industry.

In some cultures the preparation and presentation of food is still regarded as a creative act, but the activity is developing into one which is the preserve of experts rather than the everyday experience of the household. The responsibility for depriving large sections of the community of opportunities to become involved in creative activity, either in the home or in the street as part of a community

136

celebration, lies at the door of industrialisation. The presentation of food, of self, and of the home have all been industrialised. What were creative pursuits of the individual are now the bases of big businesses. The garden remains, perhaps, the one area where the individual living in an industrialised society can find an opportunity for creative expression, for realising a dream or a fantasy.

Whilst, in one sense, industrialisation has been responsible for taking the creative arts out of the household, other opportunities are arising for involvement in creative work. Amateur music, dramatic, theatrical, art and choral societies are still a part of the activities of many communities. Writers clubs flourish and there have been many attempts to by-pass the dominance of commercial publishers. Instead of having to demonstrate a potential for commercial success in the open market the small presses are providing opportunities for work from a community base to be disseminated. The significance of this is important. It is, to a certain extent changing the value structure of the arts. This point has been underlined by Mog Ball:

> Small presses have been and are multiplying. Once upon a time publications from all but the most established publishers were objects of dubious value. Could the writing be worth reading if it had been passed over by people who knew what was good? (The writer was sure to have tried the establishment first, of course.) Could it be worth publishing if the writer had actually contributed to the cost of production? (Despite the fact that many a famous literary figure had started out by doing just that.) The confusion was between what was good and what would sell.
>
> (Ball 1984:9)

The emergence of the small presses has been one aspect of cultural development in both Europe and the United States which owes a great deal to the development of the community arts movement. It is impossible to arrive at a date when what we now know as community arts first came into existence. It was born of the many attempts in the 1960s to bring arts to a wider audience. The arts labs, arts centres and arts workshops of that period had as their aim a wish to claim back the arts for ordinary people, to redress the balance of what was increasingly being seen as an arts world which only appealed to an educated elite. This movement gained strength and political force during the sixties and seventies and, in the United Kingdom, made claims on state money to finance a range of activities which were community based. It was argued that an Arts Council of Great Britain could not serve only that section of the population which were interested in the art forms favoured by the arts establishment. Weight was given to the movement by the Council of Europe, and Simpson, in his 1976 publication, quotes the Council for Cultural Co-operation as follows:

> The aim should be to establish in communities within national states a means not only of responding to aspirations for cultural enrichment, not only of assessing public demand by analysis and research, not only of evaluating cultural development programmes as they proceed, but of awakening the community as a whole to the possibilities of achieving a fuller and more rewarding life.
>
> (Simpson 1976:48)

These are fine words but Simpson clearly felt that this statement, sounding as it does like an idealised pronouncement from a supra-national body, needed to be put into some sort of realistic context. He felt it necessary to remind his readers that,

> we confront a hard reality. Obstructing all the planning and efforts which we have outlined in this chapter there lies one great barrier. The reintegration of creativity into everyday life, the recovery by each individual of a voice in his own socio-cultural situation, and the promotion of communications sytems which are consistent with these aims, all these objectives are blocked by a stubborn fact. This is the reluctance of a large majority of the people to be moved to take part as active members of a cultural democracy, motivated to the point at which they will interrupt their routine of adaptation to the mechanics of a consumer society.
>
> (Simpson 1976:63)

This all sounds a little pessimistic and there is no denying the fact that there are problems. However, the community arts movement did succeed in mobilising a band of socio-cultural animateurs who began to make an impact on the cultural activity of many small communities. On the whole they were either voluntary or funded by arts funding organisations rather than by the education service. This freed them from the restrictions of class size, regular attendance and fee structures which are a normal part of the adult education service. To a large extent they succeeded where adult education failed, they managed to empower local communities to take charge of their own cultural development.

The range of activities which are encompassed by a community arts label is wide. In the Community Arts Information Pack compiled by Ros Rigby (1982) there is mention of everything from the traditional arts and crafts to mural and print workshops, fire shows, circuses, festivals and carnivals. Roy Shaw may have over-simplified a very complex operation, but nonetheless encapsulated the essence of the movement:

> Community arts is the activity of artists in various art forms working in a particular community and involving the participation of members of that community.
>
> (Shaw 1977)

This statement reflects the means but not the ends. It describes only the method by which cultural development and cultural democracy were to come about. The problems were enormous, especially those arising from different conceptions of the arts within different ethnic groups. The Notting Hill Carnival illustrates the point. Kwesi Owusu (1986:4) describes how the carnival in Trinidad emerged as a cultural symbol of the emancipation of black people from slavery. State attempts to control the Notting Hill carnival are seen as a form of cultural repression. Such attempts are described as echoing both the 'cultural repression of the Caribbean colonial history, and the history of repression of popular culture and events of mass jollification in England.' He goes on:

> For the present, the Notting Hill Carnival and other offshoots across the country stand as significant symbols, crucial antitheses to this history of state repression. Their survival and development are therefore not the concern of the Black community alone, but of all who appreciate and cherish the vitality of popular creativity. (Owusu 1986:15)

Now, if one were to suggest to the kindly officers of the Arts Council and the Regional Arts Associations that they were involved in the repression of genuine cultural and artistic expression I feel sure that they would be horrified; they feel as though they are dedicated to promoting the arts. So what is going on?

In the first place, they have a concept of the arts which is the product of a Eurocentric education and which denies them any expertise in art forms or other types of cultural expression from non-European cultures; they may not possess an adequate means of perceiving such works. Secondly, they have committed their revenue funding to the maintenance of a largely European idea of high culture to the extent that any attempt to shift resources to other cultural activities is met with dismay if not hostility from their traditional supporters; the political dimensions of such a move would be difficult to handle in a situation where resources for the arts are, in any case, diminishing.

Lest I be accused of being unfair to the arts funding agencies I should point out that in recent years they have developed policies to promote the arts of ethnic minorities and are acquiring staff and consultants with the expertise necessary to make informed judgements about these art forms. The point however remains; artists from ethnic minority groups feel as though they are neither understood nor appreciated by those who hold the purse strings of state aid.

Of course, the same can be said of many amateur artists and art groups in the European tradition, especially if they work in the folk rather than the high art tradition. The amateur brass bands and choirs are generally ignored by the arts funders. And this is what this section has been about. It has been concerned with that wealth of cultural activity which goes unrecorded in the reports of the Regional Arts Associations or the Arts Council; activity which is concerned with creation and participation in the arts rather than solely with appreciation and the development of audiences. It is a voluntary activity which embraces both the high art and folk tradition and which allows the arts of ethnic minority groups to find expression. The community arts movement addresses itself to the same sort of constituency and whilst some community artists are paid, the work is concerned with mobilising voluntary creative effort. Many of these activities are on the fringe of adult education and can be categorised as non-formal adult education. The next chapter explores the nature of adult education in greater detail.

REFERENCES

ACGB, 1949, The Annual Report for 1948-9, London, Arts Council of Great Britain

ACGB, 1967, The Charter of Incorporation granted by Her Majesty the Queen to The Arts Council of Great Britain, London, Arts Council of Great Britain

ACGB, 1983, The Arts Council and Education: A Policy Statement, London, Arts Council of Great Britain

ACGB, 1984, The Glory of the Garden - The Development of the Arts in England, London, Arts Council of Great Britain

Adkins, G., 1981, The Arts and Adult Education, Leicester, Advisory Council for Adult Continuing Education

Appleyard, B., 1984, The Culture Club - Crisis in the Arts, London, Faber and Faber

Ball, M., 1984, 'Small is Confident', Arts Express, no. 10, December 1984, London

Barrett, M., 1979, Art Education - A Strategy for Course Design, London, Heinemann Educational

Coonan, R., 1985, 'Artists in Residence', Education Bulletin, no. 17, London, ACGB

Calouste Gulbenkian Foundation, 1982, The Arts in Schools - Principles, Practice and Provision, London, Calouste Gulbenkian Foundation

Ehrenzweig, A., 1968, The Hidden Order of Art - A Study in the Psychology of Artistic Imagination, London, Weidenfeld and Nicolson

Field, D. and Newick, J., 1973, The Study of Education and Art, London, Routledge and Kegan Paul

Harris, J.S., 1970, Government Patronage of the Arts in Great Britain, Chicago and London, The University of Chicago Press

Hutchison, R., 1982, The Politics of the Arts Council, London, Sinclaire Browne

Jor, F., 1976, The Demystification of Culture: Animation and Creativity, Strasbourg, Council of Europe

Khan, N., 1976, The Arts Britain Ignores: The Arts of Ethnic Minorities in Britain, London, Community Relations Commission

Kelly, O., 1984, Community, Art and the State: Storming

the Citadels, London, Comedia

Mee and Wiltshire, 1978, Structure and Performance in Adult Education, London and New York, Longman

Mennel, S., 1976, Cultural Policy in Towns, Strasbourg, Council of Europe

Minihan, J., 1977, The Nationalisation of Culture - The Development of State Subsidies to the Arts in Great Britain, London, Hamish Hamilton

Moulin, R., 1976, Public Aid for Creation in the Plastic Arts, Strasbourg, Council of Europe

Nissel, M., 1983, Facts About the Arts - A Summary of Available Statistics, London, Policy Studies Institute

Owusu, K., 1986, The Struggle for Black Arts in Britain. What Can We Consider Better than Freedom, London, Comedia

Pearson, N., 1982, The State and the Visual Arts, Milton Keynes, Open University

Pick, J., 1986, Managing the Arts? The British Experience, London, Rhinegold

Read, H., 1964, Education Through Art, London, Faber and Faber

Redcliffe-Maud, Lord, 1976, Support for the Arts in England and Wales, London, Calouste Gulbenkian Foundation

Rigby, R., 1982, Community Arts Information Pack, Manchester and London, The Shelton Trust (Manchester) and the Council of Regional Arts Organisations (London)

Robertson, S.M., 1963, Rosegarden and Labyrinth - A Study in Art Education, London, Routledge and Kegan Paul

Ross, M., 1978, The Creative Arts, London, Heinemann Educational

Shaw, Sir R., 1977, ACGB Annual Report, London, Arts Council of Great Britain

Shaw, Sir R., 1987, The Arts and the People, London, Jonathan Cape

Simpson, J.A., 1976, Towards Cultural Democracy, Strasbourg, Council of Europe

Chapter Six

ADULT EDUCATION AND CULTURAL DEVELOPMENT

In the same way that our concept of the arts can be seen as a social construct so also can our concept of adult education. When speaking of adult education it is tempting to include only those adult education activities which go on in recognised educational settings. But this would be to ignore all that educational activity which goes on outside the educational world in the workplace, in community centres, in theatres, museums and art galleries, on radio and television and in the home. This chapter explores the nature of the relationship between adult education and culture and, more precisely, between adult education and the arts as an aspect of culture. The chapter starts by looking at some aspects of adult education which are relevant to the theme of this book. Different ways of defining adult education are considered and attention is paid to the purposes of adult education. Aspects of adult learning and adult teaching are discussed with reference to the arts. The chapter then goes on to provide a practical means of identifying whether a given educational activity develops or preserves a particular form of cultural expression. A range of common adult education practices will be examined in order to demonstrate how they can be seen as a means of either cultural conservation or cultural development. Finally, the chapter invites practitioners to accept a theory of cultural development as a basis for the design and analysis of adult education programmes in the arts.

It is not intended to do justice to all the writers and theorists who have contributed to the thinking on adult education. The ideas which are discussed in the following paragraphs have been selected because of their relevance to the purpose of this book - a consideration of adult education in relation to its cultural and artistic context.

ADULT EDUCATION

Definition

Whenever people discuss the idea of adult education there is not always agreement about what they mean by the term. It is agreed that we usually mean something more than the 'education of adults'. Jarvis points out that:

> The education of adults was seen to be any educational process in which those who regard themselves and are regarded as socially mature participate while adult education was seen to contain connotations of liberal education.
>
> (Jarvis 1983:53)

Jarvis regards liberal education as a humanist ideal to which adult education should aspire. But as a term, 'adult education' carries other connotations. As mentioned above, adults learn in a whole variety of settings, some of which are part of an organised educational system. The term 'adult education' is usually reserved for adult learning which is organised by some agency or other.

It is, no doubt, an area where discussion is likely to continue. Many writers have offered definitions of the term and there have been a number of attempts to develop a typology of adult education, a means of categorising adult education activity. These have been summarised by, amongst others, Houle (1974:1-225), Legge (1982:1-10), Groombridge (1983:3-19), Rogers (1986:xii-xv and 1-20), Elsey (1986:6-20) and Long (1987:17-49). It is not within the scope of this publication to analyse the competing merits of the various definitions and typologies which have been offered in the past. It is felt necessary, however, to spend a little time in discussing some of the more common ways in which adult education activity is sometimes classified.

When attempting to categorise adult education activity writers seem to focus on different aspects of provision as the basis for their categorisation. Some focus on student motivation and we have distinctions between vocational and non-vocational adult education. This particular distinction is often used by administrators who tend to see the descriptors 'vocational' and 'non-vocational' as applying to the activity in the class rather than student motivation. Thus examination classes are seen as vocational and non-examination classes are seen as non-vocational, irrespective of the reasons why students may be attending them. Whether or not a course has an examination at the end of it can never be an indicator of whether or not a given student is attending for vocational or non-vocational reasons. Whilst many teachers will be familiar with this distinction it is only relevant to the theme of this book insofar as a prescribed examination syllabus may promote one view of culture rather than another. Thus the administrator's vocational course, with an examination at the end of it, may not be as creatively liberating as a non-vocational course.

In his book Teaching Adults, Alan Rogers focuses on the providing agency to distinguish between three different sorts of adult education activity. He categorises adult education into three sectors as follows:

> formal - courses and classes run by schools, colleges, universities and other statutory and non-statutory agencies making up the educational system;
> extra-formal - courses and classes run by formal agencies outside the educational system, e.g. government departments, industrial training agencies, trade unions and commercial concerns;
> non-formal - educational activities provided by voluntary agencies and informal groups.
> (Rogers 1986:xii-xiii)

Most if not all the adult education activities which concern the arts can be accommodated in one or other of Rogers' categories. Excluded are those unorganised activities which take place in the home or between friends. Whilst these are not the concern of this book the extent to which they go on should not be underestimated. Many people learn craft or artistic skills from friends, relatives or neighbours; they acquire their learning outside organised adult education structures and in doing so take charge of their own learning activity. Tough (1968, 1978 and 1979) has shown the extent of these self-directed learning projects though we have, as yet, no real idea about what they may contribute to the cultural life of a community. It is known that many traditional crafts and many folk songs and tales are passed on in this way from generation to generation. The oral traditions has been instrumental in the development of folk culture. The concern here, however, is with adult education activities which are arranged by an organising agency, whether or not that agency is part of a formal educational system and whether or not those activities are classified as vocational or non-vocational.

Purpose

The purpose of a given adult education activity provides another dimension on which to base a system of categorising adult education activity. Purpose, in this instance, is defined in terms of the relationship between adult education and society. Adult education is seen as either contributing to social change or as conserving the status quo. The term 'conservative' is used here in the sense of opposed to change. Those who do not see adult education as a means of social change tend to focus their attention on the 'development of the individual' as the purpose of adult education. This latter view is associated with the liberal tradition of much adult education work in the early part of this century. Long sees these two philosophical views of the purposes of adult education in terms of a continuum.

> It is significant that philosophical thought regarding the aims and objectives of adult education in the United States is distributed along a continuum from a scholastic approach to the 'liberation of the mind' (existential and liberal) to various applied forms of political/economic and social liberation (radical).
>
> (Long 1987:27)

The two views are seen by some writers as being mutually exclusive. Keddie (1980:45-64) argues that an emphasis on the development of the individual must be at the expense of any societal or community development. The view that the liberal tradition, with its emphasis on individual development and the idea of the 'educated person', corresponds with a conservative approach to adult education is echoed by others who see such approaches as diametrically opposed to the radical approach. Thomas presents the two views as polarities:

> At one extreme is the view that any system of adult education, which is to be effective, must challenge established economic and social assumptions. At the other is the view that adult education contributes to the preservation of the existing system.
>
> (Thomas 1982:6)

This polarisation is later refined into a continuum similar to Long's:

> it can be suggested that interpretation of the relationship between adult education and society can be grouped under the four headings of revolution, reform, maintenance and conservation. The characteristics of each group shade into those of its neighbour on the continuum, but each group displays certain distinct and peculiar features.
>
> (Thomas 1982:7)

In a similar vein Rogers (1986:45) distinguishes between the 'conformist view and the liberation view of education'. Those who advocate a radical approach to adult education relate much of their thinking to the Brazilian adult educator Paulo Freire. Freire (1972a, 1972b and 1973) saw adult education as a means of liberating the oppressed peoples of Brazil. For him education could not be neutral. If it was not concerned with liberation it was concerned to maintain a status quo which, in the case of Brazil, was oppressive. The dominant elite of the country espoused the values of a non-Brazilian culture. They were seen by Freire as colonisers. The Brazilian people were seen as the colonised who had been socialised to accept the values of a dominant and alien culture. Freire makes what, in terms of the theme of this book, is a seminal point:

> It is not a coincidence that the colonizers refer to their own cultural practices as an art, but refer to the cultural production of the colonized as folklore. Similarly, the colonizers speak of their language, but speak of the language of the colonized as dialect.
>
> (Freire 1973:50-1)

Freire's philosophy has evolved from a mixture of Christian and Marxist thinking. It espouses certain humanist

147

values which see individual development as an important purpose of adult education. But he goes further than this. He sees the purpose of education as an attempt to liberate adult students so that they can take charge of their own lives and, in so doing, bring about social change. At the heart of his philosophy lies the idea of 'consciensization' which involves helping adults to become aware of their own biography in relation to society as a whole. It is concerned to help them to see how their situation in life is the result of social processes which they themselves can effect. This philosophy, whilst having as its main aim the liberation of the oppressed, does not regard the development of the individual as in any way antithetical to this aim. Indeed, the consciensization of the adult participant in the educational endeavour is seen as an important part of the process.

It is not the case that a concern to develop the abilities of the individual necessarily precludes a concern to bring about change in society. Or, to put it the other way round, a concern to change society cannot be effective without a concern to bring about change in the individuals who comprise that society. One can see how, in the past, certain practices associated with the liberal tradition were, in themselves, conservative. Value systems associated with an educated elite were passed on to the adult student. In an attempt to induct the uneducated into the ways of the educated it was felt necessary, not to enable people to think for themselves, but to ensure that they thought in a particular way - a way which reflected established value systems. This was certainly true of many appreciation classes in the arts. They reflected the high culture view of established artistic practices. Such approaches to the teaching of adults provide the sort of evidence on which Keddie's (1980) thesis is based. But it would be misleading to assume that all appreciation courses were organised in this way.

It is sometimes argued that classes concerned with appreciation are, almost by definition, conservative. They are usually concerned with already established artists and works of art. The intention seems to be to provide the student with the tools necessary to understand and gain enjoyment from these works of art. This involves introducing students to those value systems which have pronounced these works to be good. Students in this situation often assume that these value systems have a universal currency; that they can be used to assess any work of art from any society or from any historical period. It is assumed that these values are permanent and immutable. It is in this way that appreciation classes can serve to reinforce a particular set of established values in the arts.

It is only when these value systems are set in a historical and social context that the adult student can be freed from a dominant set of cultural norms. Seeing a particular set of cultural values as belonging to a particular historical period and a particular geographical location makes the point that such values are both transient in nature and culturally determined. After all, there is nothing wrong in helping someone to learn how to enjoy a symphony by Brahms or a poem by Eliot. We have a rich cultural heritage which can be enjoyed by those who learn to appreciate it. But it should never be assumed that so-called high culture is the only or the best form of cultural expression. It is simply one among many and it is part of the role of adult education to make them all accessible. It is when only one value system is presented, and presented as the only value system, that appreciation classes can be said to be conservative.

Classes which aim to develop creative ability, on the other hand, are concerned, again almost by definition, to challenge value systems, to encourage the new and experimental and to develop the cultural tradition. It has to be said that not all adult education courses which purport to be creative do in fact develop creative ability. Many are superficial in their practices and do no more than teach students how to conform to a predetermined set of values. They concentrate on technique, on helping students to produce pictorial representations which reflect the Western European Renaissance tradition. Success in such courses is judged solely in terms of the mastery of the medium and any value judgements related to the content of the work of art are never articulated. Such classes are not really creative, at least not in the sense that the term has been explained in an earlier chapter. Many courses which set out to be developmental lose their way when they meet the competing demands of a group of adult students. This is not an unusual phenomenon. Thomas refers to it as follows:

> Numerous instances occur, however, where activities planned to be instrumental are transformed into ends in themselves, or where, from the very beginning the concept of purpose is forgotten and activities are

undertaken for the sole purpose of meeting the
recreational needs of adult students.

(Thomas 1982:4)

Thomas goes on to point out that the vast majority of
adult educators do not see adult education as an instrument
of social change. They regard the structures and value
systems of society as accepted, as a given, as 'a static
framework which provides the boundaries within which the
activities of adult education should be carried out'. This is
also true of many of those involved in higher education.
Degree courses in the fine arts often set out to ensure that
students conform to a prescribed set of values rather than
to liberate their creative energies.

When, however, creative classes eschew a superficial
pre-occupation with technique and concentrate on the
development of an ability to generate images, visual or
verbal metaphors, then students may find themselves
working outside not only their own and their teacher's but
also society's field of artistic experience. They are
developing novel forms of expression for which there may be
no developed value base, indeed their work may spring from
and demand new ways of perceiving the world. They are, in
every sense, learning to become involved in the creative
process and may be contributing to the development of the
artistic tradition.

In an article in which she bemoans the lack of Arts
Council support for writers' workshops Victoria Neumark
makes the case for a creative approach to adult education
courses in the arts and in doing so re-values the work which
comes from such courses.

In attempting to help working class people articulate
their own concerns, writers' workshops stimulate
working people to claim writing as something they do,
rather than something thrust upon them. They can, as
Paulo Freire said, seize the world, organise thought,
shake up consciousness; begin with what the middle
class writer to The Times has at his or her fingertips. ...
The task is not to solidify literary merit, it is to release
a language in which literature may one day be written.
So why no Arts Council grant?

(Neumark 1986:11)

Whether or not the work of participants in such creative

classes gains public acceptance is, in a sense, immaterial. The success of such courses is judged in terms of the extent to which participants are able to work outside their previous experience, maybe outside the experience of the teacher, and outside the dominant cultural norms.

An important point should be made at this juncture. It is as follows. It is not possible to predict the direction which a creative activity will take. Unlike those who take a radical approach in other areas of adult education where there is often a fairly clearly defined idea of the ends to be achieved, in creative art courses the end is to enable participants to be creative, rather than to create a particular form of art. It is change for the sake of change rather than change to achieve a particular end. If an adult tutor succeeds in helping students to operate creatively then it is not possible to predict what they will create or how the works they create will affect the dominant culture. Here is an area of education where the purpose is seen in terms of individual development and where the effect on society and on artistic value systems will be real but unpredictable. Such an approach clearly poses problems of evaluation. The temptation is to evaluate the works of art rather than the quality of the learning that has taken place. This aspect of the creative education of adults will be dealt with later. For the moment let us go on to consider some explanations of how adults learn and assess their usefulness in terms of arts courses.

Adult learning

It is not so long ago that it was felt that the adult's ability to learn declined with age and that learning was something that mainly happened in childhood. It was believed that 'you can't teach an old dog new tricks'. Our education system, together with those of most developed nations, is founded on the premise that childhood is the best time to learn. This is often known as the 'front end model' or the 'apprenticeship' model of education. The assumption is that an initial burst of education can equip a person for life; that compulsory education between the ages of 5 and 16 is all that is required to maintain a literate and otherwise educated population. Increasingly, however, this view of learning potential is being challenged. It is becoming accepted that learning goes on throughout life and that education can be a lifelong process. Greater knowledge about the learning potential of the adult and the accelerating pace of change in society are but two of the factors which have highlighted the desirability of accepting education as a cradle-to-grave undertaking. Terms such as 'recurrent education', 'continuing education', 'lifelong education' and 'permanent education' have entered into the vocabulary not just of educators but also of politicians and social commentators.

With this growth of interest in adult learning there have been parallel developments in adult learning theory. Rogers categorises these theories in the following way:

> There are the behaviourist theories, mostly of the stimulus response variety of varying degrees of complexity. There are the cognitive theories, seen by some more as a variant from the behaviourist theories but based on different views of the nature of knowledge. And there are those theories that have been called humanist; these rely on the analysis of the nature of personality and society.
>
> (Rogers 1986:45)

Rogers goes on to describe behaviourist theories as 'teacher centred', cognitive theories as 'subject centred' and humanist theories as 'learner centred'. The idea of 'centring' the educational effort is helpful and illuminating. It allows us to describe the orientation of the educational process in terms of either the teacher, the subject or the student and in so doing provides us with a means of assessing the appropriateness of a particular educational activity. If, for instance, the concern was to develop creative ability in the student there would be little point in trying to achieve this by using a teacher centred approach.

There have been many other attempts at categorising adult learning. Bloom (1965), Belbin and Belbin (1972) and Gagné (1975) have all developed learning hierarchies which have been adequately summarised by Rogers (1986). The problem with them is that they cannot come to terms with the sort of learning that takes place on an arts based course. Most of these writers come from an intellectual tradition which sees learning in terms of either the acquisition of psycho-motor skills or the acquiring and manipulating of cognitive knowledge. They may acknowledge that learning to reason is also a valuable adult education activity but they remain mute on the subject of creativity and the arts.

The best known and most widely used taxonomy of educational objectives is that developed by Bloom (1965). Here the objectives of educational enterprises are seen as being either cognitive, concerned with the acquisition of knowledge, affective, concerned with emotional responses and attitudes, or psycho-motor, concerned with the acquisition of skills. None of these categories can adequately accommodate much of the educational work that goes on in the arts. The development of creative ability can be seen neither as a cognitive nor an affective objective, nor is it merely the acquisition of a psycho-motor skill; this would put it on the same level as learning to drive a motor car and that clearly is inadequate. Similarly it is impossible to view the development of heightened levels of perception as fitting neatly into any of Blooms categories. Yet, many adult educators are still taught to use this taxonomy as the basis for their curriculum planning. Brookfield makes the point forcibly:

> It is difficult to outline in advance objectives that clearly relate to an adult's development of critical consciousness, to the internal mental re-arrangement that follows from flash of insight, or to a growing appreciation of lyric poetry. To equate the development of artistic sensibility with the number of books read, the number of museums visited, or the number of concerts attended is simplistic and misconceived in the extreme.
>
> (Brookfield 1986:212)

The process of learning is complex and it may be impossible to devise a simple taxonomy of educational objectives which can accommodate all the different forms of learning. The ways in which adults learn are so varied, culturally determined and often constrained by very individualised emotional blockages that it becomes impossible to make any general statements about the nature of adult learning activity. In any event, the usefulness of such statements is limited. It may be that it is necessary to find another starting point for educational planning and it may be that such starting points spring from a knowledge of the individual learner and of the demands of the subject. In this case the term 'subject' will refer to a particular art form and the nature of the desired engagement with that art form.

153

If, for instance, one wanted to learn how to be a painter, then it would be legitimate to ask what it takes to be a painter. There is a body of research about the nature of the creative process which could provide a starting point and there is equally research about the nature of perception. A freedom to experiment with paint would also seem important and it may be considered worthwhile for the student to know at a cognitive level what is involved in working as a painter; to know about the nature of the creative process before learning how to become involved in it. Finally it would seem important for participants to be aware of the cultural and artistic context in which they are working and to be familiar with the value systems inherent in that culture. It is important that the value system is seen not as immutable, but as culturally specific. It may be that this, together with knowledge about the strengths and weaknesses of the adult student, is the starting point for the planning of a learning strategy and not a taxonomic structure which does not seem to fit the task in hand.

The sort of changes which take place in a person who embarks on a programme of adult learning cannot all be predicted. If they are involved in the creative arts it may be that their whole sense of identity and their view of the world changes. This is what Mezirow (1977 and 1981) calls a perspective transformation. When a student's view of the world is contradicted by experience of the world, then that particular perspective can be transformed. The mismatch between experience of and knowledge of an activity can lead to a period of reflection during which the adult student questions earlier knowledge in the light of the new experience. Such a period of reflection leads to a re-orientation to the world and the development of new strategies for coping with life. Hence many assumptions and misconceptions about the nature of creative activity have to be re-assessed in the light of the experience of becoming involved in the creative process. Conventional value systems are challenged and the adult participant comes to terms with this new orientation to the world. This can prove very difficult for some adults. The learning process can be very painful as, indeed, the creative process can be for the artist. When the adult student is involved in a learning activity it is difficult enough. When that activity is directed to becoming involved in the creative process, a process which in itself can evoke feelings of anxiety, then the process is doubly difficult.

There is a danger in the arts, as well as in other areas of adult learning, that the student will become a mirror image of the teacher; that the learner will end up doing no more than reflecting the beliefs, attitudes and actions of the teacher. In the arts this is evident when the works produced by the student are indistinguishable from those produced by the teacher. It is important that the student is encouraged to move beyond the teacher's field of experience. However, this leap into the unknown is often the cause of great anxiety to both students and tutors; to the students because the work appears to be out of control and to the tutors because they have no basis on which to make the expected value judgements about the work. This can lead to a certain amount of role conflict if the students' expectations are that the tutor will make aesthetic judgements about the work produced. Such judgement would be no more than a reflection of the tutor's own subjective value system which may not be appropriate for the work under consideration. The student who created it is the person who is best able to judge the completed work.

With so much talk of stress and anxiety it is a wonder that anyone decides to embark on an adult education course in the arts. There are, of course, rewards. Again this is an area where different people will gain different rewards for their effort. Some will gain satisfaction from the acquisition of a new skill or new knowledge, others will have their lives transformed by re-assessing themselves in relation to society, and yet others will become involved in activities which may promote social change or cultural development. In any event, if the adult education experience has been successful they will be different people at the end of it from what they were at the beginning.

Facilitating adult learning

This section could have been called 'Adult Teaching' but the term teaching has fallen out of favour in the context of adult education. It is felt to be too teacher-centred and to have connotations of the school-room which are out of place in the adult sector of education. I have, therefore, borrowed the above phrase from Stephen Brookfield (1986) to describe a section of this chapter which examines the role of the tutor in adult education.

The way in which a teacher operates will depend on

that teacher's philosophical approach to adult education. The particular view of adult education will inform the way in which any learning transaction is organised. Much has been written recently about the distinctive nature of adult education. Brookfield identifies six principles of effective practice in facilitating adult learning:

> Voluntary Participation - Participation in adult learning is voluntary; adults engage in learning as a result of their own volition ...
> Mutual Respect - Effective practice is characterised by a respect among participants for each other's self-worth ...
> Collaborative Spirit - Facilitation is collaborative. Facilitators and learners are engaged in a co-operative enterprise in which, at different times and for different purposes, leadership and facilitation roles will be assumed by different group members ...
> Action and Reflection - Praxis is placed at the heart of effective facilitation. Learners and facilitators are involved in a continual process of activity, reflection upon activity, collaborative analysis of activity, new activity, further reflection and collaborative analysis, and so on ...
> Critical Reflection - Facilitation aims to foster in adults a spirit of critical reflection. Through educational encounters, learners come to appreciate that values, beliefs, behaviours, and ideologies are culturally transmitted and that they are provisional and relative ...
> Self Direction - The aim of facilitation is the nurturing of self-directed empowered adults ...
> (Brookfield 1986:9- 11)

This list of Brookfield's is not without a history. It is based in part on the principles of andragogy developed to a large extent by Knowles (1980) and refined and developed by the Nottingham Andragogy Group (1983). Knowles based his theory of andragogy on four assumptions about adult learners which he sees as distinctly different from child learners. These are as follows:

> - It is a normal aspect of the process of maturation for a person to move from dependency toward increasing self-directedness, but at different rates for different

people and in different dimensions of life.
- As people grow and develop they accumulate an increasing reservoir of experience that becomes an increasingly rich resource for learning - for themselves and for others.
- People become ready to learn something when they experience a need to learn it in order to cope more satisfyingly with real life tasks or problems.
- Learners see education as a process of developing increased competence to achieve their full potential in life.

(Knowles 1980:43-4)

Self-directedness is assumed to be an indicator of adulthood. Knowles appears to define adulthood, not so much in terms of chronological age, but in terms of individuals accepting responsibility for the direction of their own lives. He sees the role of the adult educator as dependent upon an acceptance that adults are self-directed.

However, as Brookfield (1986:93) points out, the evidence does not really support this view. He points to the many political regime's in the world where people are not free to exercise control over their own lives. In such situations, as Freire (1972b) has pointed out, self-directedness becomes a goal of education rather than a condition of adulthood.

Among the many critiques of Knowles' view of andragogy, the Nottingham Andragogy Group is cited by Brookfield (1986:100) as providing a development of the concept of andragogy which relates most closely to the mode of facilitating learning outlined in his book. The Nottingham group extend Knowles' four assumptions about adults to a list of nine assumptions which underpin andragogy as a theoretical approach to the education of adults.

1. Human beings are social beings, which means that their nature derives from their interactions or transactions within their social and historical contexts; therefore, whilst contributing towards the creation of self, society and history, they are, in turn, influenced by what they and others have created, i.e. the entire context.
2. An adult person who is thinking, learning and critically reflecting is a more adequate social being.

157

3. The potential for continuing development of thought, feeling and self during adulthood entails qualitative change in thinking and thought structures which distinguishes the adult's development of various forms of competent thinking from that of the child or adolescent.
4. Creative and critical thinking rather than the uncritical reception of others' thinking is preferable because these modes of thinking foster the full development of the adult.
5. Creative and critical thinking are most appropriately fostered by a combination of group and individual self-directed learning.
6. A continuing re-integration of the cognitive and the affective domains is an essential ingredient for effective adult learning.
7. Knowledge can be seen as both an open system and a closed system. When it is seen as an open system it is something to which the learner can add or which can be altered by critical thought.
8. Learning involves thinking, discovery, enquiry, critical reflection and creative response.
9. Education is not about transmission, but rather it is about selection, synthesis, discovery and dialogue.

(Nottingham Andragogy Group 1983:36-7)

One of the problems with this list is that it would leave the painter and the potter out in the cold. It stems from a careful and considered critique of that sort of educational activity which traditionally goes on in universities and other centres of academic excellence. It is based on a view of education which assumes that all learning is cognitive and condemns that sort of cognitive learning which asks participants to accept uncritically the views of others as empirical fact. The list can accommodate much of that activity in the arts which is concerned with analysis criticism and appreciation, the sort of activity on which university arts departments are built. But it cannot accommodate creative activity.

It is, perhaps, important to put this list of assumptions in its context and to acknowledge that it was assembled by a group of adult educators who were involved in an academic study of adult education in a university education faculty. As a consequence it seems to assume that learning is an intellectual activity concerned with the development of academic skills. It is, perhaps, because of this, that the list cannot really accommodate all the creative activity that goes on in adult education. There are aspects of the list with which one would have no quarrel, indeed, one would agree with almost everything that is there. Criticism of the list arises from sins of omission rather than commission.

Assumption No. 1 is totally acceptable. Assumption No. 2, however, totally ignores the creative potential of adults. It has to be acknowledged that our education system emphasises intellectual development at the expense of creative development. As long ago as 1966 Hudson's seminal book, 'Contrary Imaginations', demonstrated admirably that our compulsory schooling system could not really cope with the encouragement of creative development, and little has really changed in the emphasis of educational activity since that date.

Research by Martindale (1976) has demonstrated that the creative process is a known form of mental functioning which can be identified in terms of cortical arousal. Research by Ornstein (1975) has shown that creative mental activity is probably located in the right hemisphere of the brain, a hemisphere which our education system to a large extent ignores.

To state, as assumption No. 2 does, that an 'adult person who is thinking, learning and critically reflecting is a more adequate human being' is, in a sense, incontrovertible. To omit all reference to creative activity is to continue to support the assumption that education is only about intellectual development. This is to ignore the fact that the values of a civilised society are enshrined in the art forms of that society just as much as in the social and economic structures. It is to ignore the fact that creative ability is a universal potential which remains under-valued and undeveloped in most adults. And it is to ignore the fact that already, according to Mee and Wiltshire (1978:33) some 48% of all adult education courses in the United Kingdom could be categorised as being involved with 'Craft and Aesthetic Skills'.

If an objective of adult education is to bring about social change then it would be a mistake to ignore change in the perceptions and the creative output of the members of that society. Cultures are remembered by, amongst other things, their art forms; the arts are felt to reflect the distinctive nature and style of a culture. Whether these art forms are those of an aristocracy or those of the ordinary

159

people they tell us something about the nature of that society and the way it viewed itself. In an age of mass communication it is even more important to acknowledge that society's view of itself is to a large extent fashioned by those who create the artefacts. Such a societal view may be accurate or it may be a fiction. Empowering adults to create their own view of their world is as fundamental a purpose of adult education as is raising their levels of consciousness about their history in relation to that of their culture.

If we return to the Nottingham group's list it will be clear that the rest of the assumptions are based on a view of human development and human potential which ignores one half of the brain. Even when the term 'creative' is mentioned it is in connection with academic enquiry rather than with the arts. Thus, assumption No. 3 ignores creative and participatory activity altogether and Nos. 4 and 5 refer to intellectual pursuits. Assumption 6 speaks of the re-integration of the cognitive and the affective and this is helpful to creative activity in the arts, though this is not mentioned. Assumption No. 7 is concerned with knowledge of a cognitive kind. Assumption No. 8 gets nearest to any sort of creative activity but even here we only have mention of 'discovery' and 'creative response'. Finally assumption No. 9 makes the point that education is not just about transmission of knowledge but about 'selection, synthesis discovery and dialogue'; again edging towards the creative but unwilling to make the leap.

My criticism of the Nottingham group's list, therefore, is not that it is in any way wrong but that it does not go far enough. It may be thought possible to argue that creative activity is not qualitatively different from other forms of mental activity and it is therefore included in the list. This would, however, be to ignore the wealth of evidence concerning the distinctive nature of the creative process and the different ways in which we make sense of the world. Malcolm Ross argues for creative work with schoolchildren as follows:

> We make sense of our lives in two ways. We use our minds to collect and sort information and ideas. We call this kind of understanding "conception"; its process is logical reasoning and we use discursive and conventional language when we want to represent it or communicate it. We also arrive at meaning emotionally

- life makes sense (or nonsense) to us intuitively. Instinctively. We say it feels right. We represent or communicate our feelings in images. We do not have to choose between logical meanings and emotional meanings - all human beings use their reason AND their feelings, their minds and their bodies. So it should be in education: we should train children to make sense of their experience both rationally and emotionally so as to fully understand the world they live in and themselves as individual personalities with a place in that world.

(Ross 1978:62)

It may also be argued that it is impossible to develop a theory of andragogy which includes all forms of adult learning, and that the Nottingham groups formulation is concerned only with intellectual activity of an academic kind. This point, however, would not be supported by an examination of the text. The claim is that all human learning operates in the ways suggested.

The list therefore is perhaps best considered as incomplete. Reference to perceptual development and the development of creative ability need to go alongside the other forms of mental activity which are encouraged. It has to be acknowledged at some point that adults are creative human beings and it is part of adult education's task to nurture and develop creative potential.

Brookfield's list, on the other hand, is not written in a way which makes it specific to a particular form of learning. It is presented in a way which does not preclude creative activity and in this respect it is more helpful to those involved in adult education in the arts.

The Nottingham Andragogy Group goes on to identify 'twelve salient features which are essential to the andragogic process':

1. Non-prescriptive
2. Issue centred
3. Problem posing and knowledge creation
4. Praxis
5. Continuous negotiation
6. Shared individual and group responsibility for learning
7. Valuing process as part of learning
8. Dialogue

161

9.   Equality
10. Openness, trust, care and commitment
11. Mutual respect
12. Integrated thinking and learning
       (Nottingham Andragogy Group 1983:40-2)

It is difficult to find anything in this list which is inappropriate to adult education work in the arts, though, again, it is clear that the list implies a view of learning and of knowledge which is cognitive rather than creative. I am not sure in what way a creative painting class can be 'issue centred' unless the issue is different for each member of the class. It cannot be the job of the teacher to tell adult participants what to paint about. This must arise from their experience and their current concerns.

It is important, in the creative arts, to get away from this notion that adult education which focuses on the individual is somehow wrong. Every artist has an individual statement to make, a subjective comment to communicate. But this occurs within the context of first, the class group and second, society in general. The essential message of a work of art arises from the artists' unique experience and knowledge of society within particular geographical contexts. It both reflects and communicates to society. Its creation, however, can be an intensely private, personal and subjective activity. What artists, psychologists and philosophers have come to call the creative process is not a group activity. There is no reason why this should make it, somehow, undesirable in educational settings.

The fifth salient feature mentioned by the group concerns 'negotiation' and it is worth spending some time looking at this idea. Most people who write about or discuss adult education make a point of signifying the importance of negotiation. The idea is that the learning transaction, what goes on in the studio or classroom, is negotiated between the tutor and group members. Readers may sometimes be forgiven for assuming that such negotiation means that the students are encouraged to take sole charge of what takes place, that it is they who decide what will or will not go on in an adult class.

The danger here is that participants will negotiate away all the difficult and threatening aspects of the learning exercise and participate in only those activities which are comforting and undemanding. This happens already in many adult education courses where a sort of collusion takes place. Though it is never articulated in this way, the unspoken agreement seems to be that the students will continue to attend the course so long as the teacher does not make any threatening or inhibiting demands on them. If, of course, the students cease to attend, then the class may fail and, in many cases, the part-time teacher will lose income. It is not surprising that some part-time teachers allow themselves to be manoeuvred into a situation where they preside over a course where little or no learning takes place, where participants become dependent on the teacher and the aim of the course becomes, not learning, but the production of artistic goods. It is almost assumed that the professional teacher or artist has nothing to bring to the negotiation; that the participants themselves are the final arbiters and the role of the teacher is to do some of the work for the students when it gets difficult.

There is, of course, a sense in which the participants are the final arbiters of what takes place. One cannot force anyone to learn and, in the final analysis, participants must be willing to enter into an agreement with a tutor and other members of the group before a learning activity can take place. But this does not mean that the tutor has no role.

It is the job of the tutor, initially at any rate, to make the group aware of the nature of the undertaking on which they wish to embark. It is true that once the members of a group have decided that they want to learn, say, how to make pots, then the room for negotiation is immediately narrowed. There are certain processes which must be learned and certain abilities which must be developed. It is the role of the tutor to point these out to the group, to make them aware of potential difficulties and to negotiate a learning programme with and for the group.

This process is sometimes made more difficult if the group has misconceptions about the nature of both the learning process and the creative process. This is also true of those academic areas of enquiry where groups expect tutors to tell them what to think about a particular subject. There is often a need for a great deal of discussion before a programme of action can be devised. The resulting programme could be characterised as a compromise but it is better to see it as a synthesis of the expressed needs of the group tempered by the knowledge and experience of the tutor. Brookfield puts it like this:

In most educational programs there will be some

163

curricular areas and programmatic activities that represent a direct response to the expressed needs of learners, others that reflect the educator's view of what ought to be minimally present in any education or training programme.

(Brookfield 1986:98)

It may be that prior to this planning process there will need to be a diagnostic period. To a certain extent it depends on the nature of the engagement with the arts, but if creative development is to take place then blocks to creativity need to be identified. The tutor and the group will need to know whether or not levels of perception are under-developed and whether time will need to be spent on exercises aimed at heightening perceptual awareness. It is unlikely that all participants will present the same level of expertise or the same level of perceptual acuity. The programme of activity which is developed will need to take into account the particular strengths and weaknesses of each participant. An andragogic approach would see this negotiation and collaboration as central to the learning transaction.

This discussion of the facilitation of learning in adult education has been fairly general in nature. There is no doubt that different subjects demand different kinds of learning transactions from both the tutor and the student. As has been pointed out, much of the writing in this area assumes that learning is all cognitive. The learning of processes or the development of physiological abilities, such as perception, are often not considered by educational thinkers. The next section is about the facilitation of learning in the arts. One cannot end this section, however, without some sort of definitive statement about the facilitation of adult learning. For this I turn to Brookfield again:

This critical philosophy regards the facilitation of adult learning as a value-laden activity in which curricular and programmatic choices reflect normative preferences. It sees adult education as a socialisation agent of some force, capable of confirming values and behaviors uncritically assimilated in earlier periods or of prompting adults to challenge the validity of their received ideas and codes.

Developing in adults a sense of their personal

power and self-worth is seen as a fundamental purpose of all education and training efforts. Only if such a sense of individual empowerment is realised will adults possess the emotional strength to challenge behaviors, values and beliefs accepted uncritically by a majority.
(Brookfield 1986:283)

This formulation will serve well the purpose of this book. The inclusion of the term 'behaviours' allows us to include a whole range of educational and developmental activities which other formulations exclude. Empowerment, here, is concerned with enabling the adult learner to function as an artist in any or all of the recognised or unrecognised artistic media. The next section concerns this activity.

ADULT EDUCATION AND THE ARTS

Chapter 4 demonstrated that people engage with the arts in one of three ways, as either appreciators, creators or participants. The nature of the learning activity in which they wish to become involved, to a large extent, depends on the nature of the engagement with the arts. For all these modes of engagement there are four areas of development or learning to which attention must be paid. These are not seen as learning objectives, since it would be impossible to say if or when they had been fully achieved. They are seen, rather, as areas of personal development in much the same way as physical exercises are seen as a means of bodily development. And, to continue the analogy, in much the same way that the body can never be developed to such an extent that its performance can be maintained without further exercises, so also these abilities to which I will refer need continued attention. It is not like learning to ride a bicycle, once learned never forgotten. It is more like keeping one's psychic and somatic abilities at a high level of performance. In this sense it is an iterative process.

It will clarify the issue if I identify the four areas of development. I have referred to them before (Jones 1985:20-4) in terms of the visual arts. Here I want to try to discuss them more generally so that they refer to more if not all currently accepted art forms. They are as follows:

1. The development of perceptual acuity.
2. The development of an ability to exploit the

165

potential of a medium of expression.
3. The development of an ability to become involved in the creative process.
4. The development of an awareness of the nature of artistic activity and the relative nature of the value systems within which the arts operate.

Let us look at each of these four areas in greater detail.

The development of perceptual acuity

In the section on 'Appreciation' in Chapter 4 I dealt at length with the nature of perception and introduced the idea of six perceptual systems. Prior to discussing these systems I introduced the idea of 'attention'. I mention attention here because it can be important for engaging with the arts. As was pointed out earlier, it is possible to perceive without paying attention and it is possible to perceive subliminally. However, if a tutor in adult education is working with a group of participants in order to help them engage with the arts, it may be important to raise the idea of attention with them. Decisions may need to be made about the sort of attention that is appropriate for the task being undertaken.

Given that the sort of attention, or 'mode of personal existence' to use Bartley's (1980:19) terms, adopted by the learner is appropriate for the task in hand, then one can begin to address the idea of raising levels of perception.

Different art forms require different sorts of perceptual acuity as do the different ways of engaging with the arts. The adult group and the tutor have to decide what forms of perception are appropriate for the activity in which they are to become engaged. The sort of attention appropriate for the development of perceptual acuity is objective, focusing primarily on the world out there. In this instance the 'world out there' can include the sounds made by a musical instrument, the pigment and the canvas. The intention is to improve the ability to discriminate between perceivable phenomena.

The development of perception is not usually considered to be an objective in education, indeed, the whole world of perception and the arts is more often than not disregarded in both pedagogic and andragogic thinking. If perception was thought to be equal to thinking in its educational importance then the task of adult education might be considered to be

166

remedial in nature, as important as basic education adult programmes. But this is rarely the case. Arnheim makes the point:

> Today the prejudicial discrimination between perception and thinking is still with us. We shall find it in examples from philosophy and psychology. Our entire educational system continues to be based on the study of words and numbers ... The arts are neglected because they are based on perception, and perception is disdained because it is not assumed to involve thought.
>
> (Arnheim 1969:2-3)

Consequently, in adult education in the arts, it is important to spend time in developing those basic perceptual skills which are essential to artistic activity.

The visual system is important in many art forms for the appreciator, creator and the participant. The visual arts of painting and sculpture, together with many of the crafts, theatre and dance, all depend on heightened levels of visual awareness. Indeed, it could be argued that the literary arts also require a minimal level of visual perception in the sense that one normally reads by using the eyes. But this is of a different order. In poetry and literature the concern is not so much with the visual presentation of the work, though in some instances this may be considered to be important, but in using words as a medium of expression. Since the first hieroglyphs and pictograms, words have been written down and have been communicated visually as well as orally. But such communication does not require the same heightened level of visual perception as the visual arts. The sensitivity, here, is a sensitivity to the components of language. The sort of sensitivity required for the literary arts will be dealt with later.

It was noted above that developing visual perception is important for engaging with many art forms, yet rarely is this acknowledged in the structure of courses. It is possible to devise exercises aimed at developing the visual perceptual system but this is rarely done in what to me seems the most obvious case of art appreciation courses. It never seems to occur to the teachers of such courses that participants may not be able to perceive the features of a painting which are being discussed. This problem may arise, in part, from a teacher centred approach where the content and processes of the course are decided by the teacher

167

without consultation. Where discussion of the curriculum takes place it may happen that participants will reveal that they are simply unaware of some of the subtleties of form to which the teacher is referring. But even this would require a certain amount of confidence on the part of group members. It is much better, clearly, if the teacher or facilitator can raise the subject for discussion.

It can be argued that tonal and colour exercises, drawing exercises and explorations of form and texture are as important to the student of theatre or dance as they are to the student of painting. But again, rarely is this acknowledged by teachers in this area. Any visual training or perceptual development usually takes place by default. It simply happens (or not) as a result of watching these art forms. Would it not be better if the agreed structure of such courses whether in appreciation, creation or participation, recognised the importance of developing levels of visual awareness? Especially when art forms from different cultures are being dealt with. It is more than likely that the level of perceptual ability which a student brings to a class, being as it is, culturally determined, is simply inadequate to cope with works of art from another cultural context. And might not this be part of the reason why some art forms are misunderstood and undervalued by arbiters of taste who themselves are capable of only a unicultural form of visual perception?

The auditory system of perception suffers from neglect in much the same way as the visual. As a child in school I used to enjoy singing but often got the tunes wrong. I was told, at an early age, that I was tone deaf and this knowledge put paid to any interest in music that I might have developed. It was not until much later in life that, still enjoying singing, I realised that I knew when I went wrong. How could I be tone deaf if I could recognise such errors in my performance? I realised that my childhood problem was not to do with perceptual ability but with memory. I simply could not remember the tunes accurately. Unable to sight read I relied on my memory of a tune to reproduce it. I often got it wrong but I was not aware that it was wrong. The listener heard a wrong note and assumed that I could not perceive that it was wrong, that I was indeed tone deaf. To me the note was right, but it was right in the context of an incorrectly memorised melody. According to my own memory of the tune the note was correct and it is true that I could not hear what was wrong with it. Over the years, with more exposure to music and with an improving auditory memory I became aware that I was not tone deaf and that it was possible to work at improving both my levels of auditory perception and my auditory memory.

I tell this story to make a point that is true for perceptual systems other than the auditory one. For some reason many people believe that they should be able to memorise the appearance of an object or the sound of a piece of music. For some people this is indeed possible but for most of us we need to make regular reference to the object or melody in order to remind ourselves what it looks or sounds like. Thus many people feel inadequate or feel some sense of failure when they cannot draw, say, a tree from memory. They know what trees are. They think that they know what they look like. They simply cannot understand why they cannot draw one. They explain this in terms of a failure of perception or skill rather than a failure of memory.

The role of memory in creative work has not been fully explored. It may be that we make judgements about ability by unwisely focusing on an imperfect memory of what may in the first place have been an incompletely perceived phenomenon. In any event both students and teachers should be aware that memory is a factor to be considered in education in the arts. If it is felt to be important then it is possible to develop exercises to improve both visual and auditory memory. If it is not felt to be important then care should be taken to ensure that learning procedures do not rely too much on a highly developed ability to remember. Remembering what a tree looks like is a very difficult task, as is remembering what a piece of orchestral music sounds like. Such feats of memory are important for producers, performers, participants in the arts but may not be necessary for creators and appreciators.

This consideration of the role of memory has been somewhat of a digression from the discussion of auditory perception. It was felt, however, that the topic did not warrant a section to itself and including it here enabled one to make the point that many apparent failures of perception may, in fact, be failures of memory.

The auditory system of perception is important in many of the performing arts and some of the literary ones. Again, it does not matter about the nature of the engagement. Whether or not one is appreciating, creating or participating in music, theatre or dance it is important to have one's

169

auditory system finely attuned. That literature which is heard aloud also demands a keen auditory sense.

It is perhaps in this area that cultural differences in perception are most clearly marked. Much oriental music, to the western ear, seems strange to the point of being simply unmusical. Unaware of the subtleties of form and the nuances of expression the untutored ear might dismiss such music as grating, wailing noises. What is and is not included in our concept of music is often determined by perceptual factors; if we are unable to perceive a given work we tend to dismiss it as not music rather than attempt to increase our levels of perception so that we can better cope with it.

Even within a single social grouping there may be perceptual differences between a youth culture and an adult culture with adults dismissing much of what teenagers enjoy as unmusical and young people dismissing much of what adults enjoy as boring. This can be interpreted in terms of generational differences with the youth culture anxious to do and enjoy something different from adults but the effects of different types and levels of perceptual ability should not be underestimated.

In adult education the task can, as was suggested above, be considered to be almost remedial in nature. It is to do with raising levels of perception so that participants can better discriminate between different sorts of sounds. Most of us can distinguish between one type of musical instrument and the next, between a violin and a trumpet, but some people can distinguish the sound of one violin from that of another. And these are instruments with which those of us aware of the classical tradition in Western music are familiar. How much more difficult is the task when faced with musical instruments from cultures other than those in which we live and work? Just as the painter needs to be able to distinguish between colours that are very similar, so the musician needs to be able to distinguish between sounds that are very similar. Clearly, in those art forms where sound is important, the development of auditory perception becomes an important consideration for adults engaging in the arts as either appreciators, creators or participators.

The savor system involves both tasting and smelling. It is difficult to know just how important this perceptual system is in the arts. If one includes food in our concept of the arts then the system is obviously central. However, whilst we sometimes refer to them as 'culinary arts', in Western societies the preparation, serving and consumption of food is not usually considered as an art form, except, perhaps, by a few devotees. In many Eastern societies, however, food plays an important part in many rituals and religious rites and the preparation of food is seen as a form of creative expression.

Whilst food does not rank with other art forms as worthy of government support, as a form of cultural expression food is undoubtedly important. The distinctive nature of an area is often reflected in typical regional dishes. Seasonal and festive foods add to the appreciation of an occasion and many traditional festive dishes have symbolic meanings arising from their origins in our pagan past. The Easter egg and the Christmas cake are more than simple means to keep body and soul together. They carry with them a whole array of symbolic meaning which place them firmly in a Western European cultural tradition. Whilst food may not be considered to be an art form in contemporary society, it can certainly be seen as a form of cultural expression.

Whether or not the sense of savor is important in other art forms is debatable. There have been experiments with the sense of smell in the theatre but they did not seem to come to anything. The smell of joss sticks or burning incense may be important to certain sorts of Indian or Oriental musical or dramatic performances. I know someone who loves the smell of old books and swears that the aesthetic pleasure of reading them is enhanced by the aroma. But, by and large, the sense of savor is neglected in the accepted art forms of contemporary European society; neither the appreciator, creator nor participant in the arts as they are practised today requires a highly developed savor system for the practice of their art.

Educationally it might be thought important to increase levels of perception in the area of savor. As was pointed out in an earlier chapter, food has managed to cross cultural boundaries far more readily than other forms of cultural expression. Food from all over the world is now available in our towns and cities and our sense of savor seems more easily to be able to break free from its culturally determined roots. If one uses the term culture in its anthropological sense, then the development of the sense of savor would be an important educational task in the development of the whole person; it would help us to break free from our culturally determined preferences for particular tastes and smells. If one uses the term culture in its artistic sense, however, the savor system has, as yet, little to offer the world of the arts.

The haptic system is important in many art forms as well as in most of the crafts. Where artistic expression involves making something with the hands then the haptic system is central. The appreciation of hand-made works also demands a high level of perceptual awareness in the haptic system. Tactile sensitivity is important to both the appreciator and the creator. The potter, the sculptor, and the modeller as well as the weaver and the silversmith, the calligrapher and the woodworker all need a highly developed sense of touch. A similar level of awareness and sensitivity is required to appreciate the work of these creators.

But the haptic system also involves pulling and pushing, lifting and kicking. Most manual tasks require an operator to do such things. One has to take care not to go too far in asserting the need to develop the haptic system. Where delicate or complex manual tasks are required it is important. One cannot, however, go as far as saying that the high level of awareness which is required to draw the bow across the strings of a violin or to carve an intricate piece of jewellery is also required to lift a paint brush. Adult groups will need to decide for themselves the extent to which they need to attend to the development of haptic awareness.

In some of the performed arts a highly developed haptic system is also required. It is through the haptic system that we gain information about the way in which we make contact with the ground or floor. Hence those involved in the dance, mime and acting may need to pay attention to developing the haptic system.

The level of perceptual acuity required will, as in other cases, depend on the nature of the art form and the nature of the engagement with that art form. Where the engagement with the art form demands it, then exercises can be undertaken to develop the haptic perceptual system.

The basic orientation system enables us to gain information about our position in space in relation to gravity. It also allows us to detect speed and acceleration. This is important to those performing in the theatre and to dancers but not to those sitting on seats watching the dancers, the appreciators. It is a perceptual system important to those performers who engage in a great deal of posture and movement. It is not essential, other than in avoiding falling over in our everyday lives, for appreciators or creators; the director and choreographer do not themselves require a highly developed basic orientation system.

With the <u>homoeostatic</u> system we are getting into an area where there may be no particular relevance to the arts which is distinct from relevance to everyday life. Information about our feeling of well-being is of no greater or lesser importance to those involved in the arts than it is to anyone else. If this perceptual system is important it may be important for reasons contrary to those discussed in relation to the other systems. We have already noted that dancers and other performers sometimes experience pain. It is possible that one might want not to develop the homoeostatic system but to suppress it so that feelings of pain and stress might be overcome.

Before concluding this section I want to include a word on language. In the visual arts and in music it is easy to see that the principal perceptual sensitivities required are visual and auditory respectively. This begs the question, what sort of highly developed perceptual system is required for the literary arts? Clearly the concern is not simply to do with seeing the print on the page or, in the case of the blind, feeling the braille characters. Nor is it a question of being able to hear a poem read aloud or the short story on the radio. What we are concerned with here is not one of the perceptual systems described above, though they are necessary at a basic level in order to perceive the work, but rather a sensitivity to language itself.

As a medium of creative expression language presents something of a special case. It is set apart, first, by the fact that it is transmitted in the two distinct ways, speech and writing. Second, language changes over time; it has an historical dimension. The language of Shakespeare is not the language of today. And third, it is more culturally specific than perhaps any other creative medium. And this is not just a question of national linguistic differences. Within a national or international language there will be different linguistic forms. English can be spoken in many dialects and with many different sorts of grammatical construction. Some cultural groups use elaborated linguistic codes whilst others use more restricted ones. Much vocabulary can be specific to a sub-culture; many new words, or new usages of established words, arise, for instance, from the youth culture. Terms like 'ghetto-blaster' for a portable cassette tape machine, 'body-popping' for a form of dancing and 'fanzine' for a cult magazine are examples current in the UK.

This presents special problems for the teacher in the arts. In order to appreciate the literary arts one has to know the language in which they are presented. Whether this is the language of Shakespeare, or the language of the West Indian youth of Birmingham, the obligation to know or learn the language remains. Appreciation can only occur if communication can take place. This is just as true of the folk art tradition as it is of the high art tradition. Appreciation requires, at the very least, a passive knowledge of a language. The appreciator is not required to speak or to write the language but must be able to understand it and be sensitive to variations of construction and meaning.

The participant in the arts, the actor, reader or singer must be able to speak the language in which the work of art is composed and ideally should be able to understand and be sensitive to the nuances of sound and meaning. This, though, is not always the case. The opera singer may be performing in an only half understood language and the actor only half comprehending the Shakespearean dialogue being performed. This is perhaps more true in educational settings than in the professional theatre but even the professional cannot be expected to be thoroughly familiar with all the languages and linguistic forms that are used in drama and opera.

The creator must be comfortable in the language. This is not to say that it is necessary to have a huge vocabulary or feel at home with very complex sentence structures. It is to say, rather, that for the creator the language of creation must feel as though it is the natural means of creative expression. It must feel right. It must be aesthetically satisfying. The creator must feel able to exploit the components of language. This does not require linguistic analysis or a knowledge of grammatical structures. The short story writer does not need to know about adjectival and conditional clauses, about assonance and alliteration, about metaphor and simile. The oral tradition of many cultures would be dead if this were a necessary prerequisite. The creator need only feel satisfied that the language, the creative medium, is, like any other creative medium, appropriate for the task of creation within a given cultural context.

This formulation in respect of language is the nearest we can get to a comparison with perceptual development in other art forms. It is a more cognitive sort of sensitivity than is sensitivity in the six perceptual systems, though, we do, on occasion, say that a person has 'a feel for language'. This implies a more affective approach. I do not, in this publication, intend to explore linguistic philosophy in any depth. My purpose in the above few paragraphs has been to do no more than map out the special nature of language as an artistic medium. We all feel that we are familiar with language because we use it every day, but, as with the six perceptual systems, there is a sense in which we can increase our sensitivity to language as a medium of artistic expression. Part of the role of the tutor in adult education is to work with adult participants to devise ways of doing this.

The starting point for this section was that the arts depend for their creation, performance and appreciation on, amongst other things, heightened levels of perceptual awareness. It has been argued that for each art form and for the different ways of engaging with that art form there will be some sensory systems which are more appropriate than others. It is, therefore, important for the adult educator with the group of participants to design exercises which will develop the appropriate perceptual systems. Such exercises will be discriminatory in nature, inviting participants to discriminate between phenomena which are increasingly similar. Colours or tones which are close together, tastes or smells which are very similar, textures and surfaces which are very alike, musical sounds which are almost indistinguishable one from the other all provide the raw material for such developmental exercises. The aim of the exercise is to develop perceptual systems to the extent that an individual is able to appreciate the subtleties of visual, tactile and auditory phenomena which comprise a work of art. Such a heightened awareness should be able to transcend the cultural determinants of perception and permit the adult student to gain enjoyment from artefacts emanating from many different cultural environments.

The development of an ability to exploit the potential of a medium of expression

One of the great disservices done to education in the arts by publishers and broadcasters was to persuade the interested public that creative activity was all a question of learning a technique. Books and television programmes with titles like

175

'How to Paint Trees', 'How to Paint in Water-colours' and 'Portrait Painting in Oils' are still to be found. They are however, founded on a false premise. They assume that creative activity in the visual arts is about learning how to use a particular medium of expression. Further, they assume that there is only one way to use a given medium.

This section is mainly about creativity in the arts. Appreciators do not themselves manipulate a medium, though experience of doing so may enhance appreciation. Participants in the arts play a sort of intermediary role. A musician, dancer or an actor is part of the medium with which the creator works. The composer, choreographer or dramatist realise their creations through the medium of these participants. The participants themselves also exert some control over the performance. They manipulate either their own bodies in the case of a dancer or actor or they manipulate (play) a musical instrument in the case of a musician.

It is perhaps as important for performers to develop an ability to exploit the potential of their own bodies and of their musical instruments as for the painter to develop an ability to exploit the potential of paint. Performers both control and are controlled. They are in control of what they do but what they do is to a large extent prescribed by the director and the originator of the work.

If it is accepted, as was suggested earlier, that the musical instrument operates as an extension to the body of the musician, and if it is further accepted that performers need to learn to exploit the potential of their bodies as a medium of expression, then the sort of attention appropriate for the participant, the performer in dance and in music, is subjective. The self, the soma, the body of the performer is the medium to be exploited in any creative work and it is to this that attention must be paid. The choreographer, the conductor and the director, on the other hand, must direct their attention to the corps de ballet, the orchestra with their instruments or the members of the cast, together with the sets and lighting which, constrained by the demands of the script or musical score comprise the medium in which they work. Attention here is objective.

Similarly, the creative artist, unlike the performers, is required to focus on the chosen medium of expression in an objective way in order to learn how to exploit its potential. I use the term 'exploit the potential' deliberately. I want to avoid any suggestion that there is only one way to use a given medium. Such an assumption, often held by adult students, arises from the technicist approach to teaching art. It is comforting to believe that one only needs to learn how to put paint on canvas in order to become a proficient painter. This is clearly a cruel deception.

The adult educator has the task of persuading an adult group to approach the medium of expression in an exploratory way, to invite the group members to explore its potential without feeling inhibited or discouraged. There may be a minimal level of knowledge required before starting; participants may need to know the solvent for a particular type of paint and the fact that certain grounds need some preparation before they will accept pigment. But even here, one is not talking in absolutes and it would not be surprising to find a painter who exploited the use of the 'wrong' solvent on an unprepared ground. In a similar way, in the creative writing class participants should feel free to ignore whatever rules of grammar or construction may be constraining them. The criteria by which they should judge their activity are not derived from some culturally specific rules of grammar but from concerns about the transmission of meaning in an aesthetically satisyfing way. There are, of course, questions about how one decides if a particular piece is aesthetically satisfying and these will be dealt with later in the section on evaluation.

The purpose of this section is to suggest that it is important to move participants in a creative learning transaction away from the idea that creativity in the arts is about learning only one way to use a given medium, about learning a technique. The interaction between an artist and the medium of expression is unique. It is unique to a given artist with a given medium in a given cultural context. There is no point in adopting the work of a particular established artist as a model to be emulated, though many adult students would like to do so. They would like to do Constable landscapes or Rembrandt portraits. The objective is, rather, to encourage every participant to develop their own way of interacting with their chosen medium of expression. This is true whether that medium is paint or stone, words or music, or, as in the case of dance, the human body itself.

It would be a mistake to think of the medium in which an artist works as no more than a means to an end, a vehicle for transmitting meaning. It is, rather, an integral part of the work of art and itself contributes to the aesthetic response of the appreciator. It is part of the meaning. The medium is part of the message.

The medium can also be part of the stimulus for a given work. Exploring the possibilities of a given medium can provide a starting point for involvement in the creative process. Some teachers use the medium as a means of helping students to become involved in creative work. Brightly coloured pieces of scrap paper, home made musical instruments, a box of theatrical costumes can provide a starting point for creative activity in art, music and drama. One should not assume that works of art always arise from a need to communicate something of which the creator is conscious, an acknowledged need to transmit meaning. In many cases the content of a work arises from unconscious primary processes once work has begun. The medium, as Redfern points out below, can itself be a stimulus.

> And here, in view of the deeply ingrained assumption on the part of most teachers (and others) that an art work invariably springs from its author's actual emotions and thoughts - an idea that would have been unintelligible before the eighteenth century and that even today is foreign to Chinese and Indian art theory - the possibility needs to be stressed that inspiration may be derived from the medium itself.
>
> (Redfern 1986:78)

An understanding that there is no single way to use a medium helps to overcome attitudes that certain forms of cultural expression are 'wrong'. It is not unusual for some forms of musical expression, either from different countries of from, say, the youth culture, to be considered as 'not music'. The West Indian steel band is as valid a form of musical experience as is the symphony orchestra, the rock music guitar as valid as the violin. There is no absolute way in which we can say that one art form is somehow superior to others. They are merely different cultural forms of musical expression. The radical approach to adult education would see it as part of the educator's role to alert participants to this. The point has already been made in respect of school education in the Gulbenkian report, Arts in Schools.

A cultural education, therefore, is one which:

a. helps pupils to understand cultural diversity by bringing them into contact with the attitudes, values and institutions of other cultures as well as exploring their own;

b. emphasises cultural relativity by helping them to recognise and compare their own cultural assumptions and values with these others;

c. alerts them to the evolutionary nature of culture and the potential for change;

d. encourages a cultural perspective by relating contemporary values to the historical forces which moulded them.

(Gulbenkian Foundation 1982:39-40)

This perspective is something new in art education. Earlier statements on art education tend to ignore the cultural context and concentrate solely on personal development. A survey from the Department of Education and Science in 1971 spoke of modifying the 'conception of art as being mainly composed of painting and drawing'.

An ever widening variety of materials is being used in schools and developments in sculpture, ceramics, textiles and printmaking and photography have led to more interest being taken in art, a wider range of pupils attracted, and the encouragement of much hitherto untapped talent.

(DES 1971:95)

The concern here is more with materials and numbers of students participating. There is no mention in the report of the cultural context in which this art education was taking place. A worry is expressed about art education keeping up with the rapid changes taking place in the art world. But this is conceived in terms of solely Western art and the task of art education is to ensure that the new generation knew about it. Thus, implicit in this Government report is a belief that art education is about cultural socialisation, a process by which young people learn about the artistic values of a dominant culture. The widening of the artistic experience to include new materials was seen as doing no more than contributing to this socialisation process.

The Gulbenkian report, on the other hand, sees education in the arts as operating in a cultural context where there are relativities rather than absolutes. The use

179

of different media in artistic expression is seen as stemming from different cultural traditions. Implicit in this assumption is that there is no one way to use a particular medium and the task of education, in our case adult education, is to free participants from the cultural constraints which may inhibit their view of the potential of a given medium. It is to empower them to make their own statements in their own way within their own cultural context and to enable appreciators of these works to accept and enjoy what might otherwise seem alien forms of expression.

Whilst this section has primarily focused on the development of an ability to exploit the potential of a medium of expression it has addressed the topic within a context which acknowledges cultural diversity in the use of media. Teaching in this area is not easy. Participants in adult education often have expectations which are in conflict with those of the tutor. They sometimes want to be shown 'how to do it'. Such expectations have been raised by the publications and television programmes mentioned at the beginning of this section. It may be that at the beginning of a course time will need to be spent in talking through these issues in order to free participants from these self imposed constraints. Or at least to give them a choice, to decide for themselves the constraints within which they choose to work.

Such discussions are doubly difficult when participants have the expectation that they have enrolled for a practical course. Discussion and enquiry of the kind advocated are not what they have enrolled for. It is important to ensure that advance notice of the course makes it clear that, whilst the concern is to develop creative ability, a necessary prelude to this is a discussion of the nature of the processes involved so that the group can come to a decision about the ways in which they wish to tackle the work.

The development of an ability to become involved in the creative process

Many teachers find this educational objective one of the most difficult to achieve in adult education. It is relevant only to those people who wish to engage creatively in the arts, though appreciators may gain some additional understanding of the work of the artist from experience of creative activity. Further, the concern is with that integrated creativity, described by Maslow (1968:135-45), which involves both primary and secondary process thinking, that creative dialectic which moves between conscious and unconscious activity.

Adults do not readily give up conscious control of their work to become involved in primary process thinking. The integrated creativity of the artist is not easy to achieve by adults who often believe that education involves only cognitive secondary processes. They work under a misconception about the nature of artistic activity. They sometimes seem to think that it is just a matter of learning a set of rules for good composition. The aim here is to enable participants to become involved in the same sort of integrated creativity as the creative artist. Opportunities for adults to do this are very rare. The chapter on access to the arts demonstrates that most opportunities to engage with the arts are opportunities for appreciation. They, thus, keep those wishing to engage with the arts in a passive role. This point is underlined by Hutchison:

> Even with the great growth of arts and adult education provision since the Second War, the distribution of opportunities for artistic expression and development is patchy, and the questions posed by this uneven distribution are directly related to the relative importance accorded by government agencies to amateur and professional work, and to the expectations surrounding that work. To push the argument further: distinguished psychologists, Fromm, Jung and others, have argued that people have a need to express their grasp of the world of the senses - be this expressed through song, dance, drama, music, painting or whatever - and whether this expression is conducted individually or collectively, whether it is called art or ritual, it is something that everyone needs to join in, not simply have served up by 'professionals'.
>
> (Hutchison 1982:54-5)

Adult education provides one of the few opportunities outside higher education for adults to become active participants in creative work.

It should be made clear at this point that this section is not about that sort of activity which develops levels of perception or extends the artist's visual, auditory or tactile

181

vocabulary - the sort of activity where the visual artist attends first and foremost to the scene to be painted and deconstructs the percept in order to see how the parts relate to the whole. It is concerned, instead, with that integrated creative activity which involves working with a medium in order to construct a work of art which may or may not represent the appearance or sensation of something perceived in the world, be it perceived aurally, visually, haptically or by the savor system. I make this point because the two processes can appear the same. Someone drawing may be either developing levels of perception or creatively developing an image, a visual metaphor. This section is about the latter activity. Since it is concerned with creative modes of engaging with the arts it includes a consideration of the process by which we learn to become involved in participation in creative drama and dance as well as the more obvious forms of creative activity in the visual and literary arts.

It will be remembered that in Chapter 4 we referred to Stumbo's (1970:469) proposal that there were three sorts of consciousness: subjective, objective and projective. The sort of consciousness required for creative work is projective in Stumbo's sense of the term. We also argued that attention was different from consciousness and that one could attend to one thing but be conscious of another. The sort of attention required for creative involvement is primarily objective and focuses on the work in hand, the canvas or the musical score, rather than on a scene, object or sound to be depicted. This means that it is important to try to ensure that participants are not working on a level where they are overly conscious of, or attending to, either their own feelings or some external object or phenomenon which is the stimulus for their work. The sort of consciousness required is that of a process moving towards a conclusion. The primary focus of attention is the work of art being created.

One of the difficulties encountered by many adult participants in the creative arts arises from their unwillingness to give up conscious control of their work. They display a sort of ego rigidity which prevents them from escaping from secondary process functioning. They feel secure in the world of the conscious and are inhibited from leaving it in order to explore the much less predictable world of the unconscious. If they are to enter into a creative dialectic and become conscious in a projective way then they often need the security, support and encouragement which a mature group of adult learners can provide.

Success in this area depends to a large extent on the development of a trusting and sympathetic group. That part of andragogical theory which stresses mutual support and encouragement is central here. The anxiety states which arise from involvement in the creative process are easier to cope with if they are both shared and anticipated. It helps if adult learners know, at a cognitive level, about the nature of the creative process; if they know that giving up conscious control often involves feelings of anxiety which the creating adult must tolerate. Opportunities for the group to discuss the nature of creative activity can provide a means of sharing anxieties about the work being undertaken.

It is difficult for those who have never operated creatively to know what the experience feels like. Like many other activities, real knowledge of the nature of the creative process only comes with the experience of it. The role of the teacher or facilitator, therefore, is to work with the group in order to design situations where participants are encouraged to work at a primary level.

With the particular emphasis I am giving to primary process functioning the reader would be forgiven for thinking that I was discussing only primary creativity. This emphasis stems from a belief that operating at a primary process level presents the greatest area of difficulty for adult students. Secondary process functioning is more normal for most adults in educational settings. Applying their intellectual powers to a given problem is what they expect to do; it reflects their earlier experience of education. Primary process functioning, on the other hand, is strange and threatening and not at all what they expect to do. To be told not to think often contradicts everything which the adult student understands about the nature of the learning process. I want to make it clear, therefore, that the emphasis here is with integrated creativity and I am only stressing the nature of primary process functioning because it often presents the greatest problems.

How, then, does one help a learning group to become involved in the creative process? One can devise situations where the secondary cognitive processes are of no help. Setting problems for which there is no known or rational solution is one way. Asking people to draw what something feels or sounds like, for instance, is to present a problem to which there is no ready-made answer. Participants cannot rely on past experience to provide a solution to the problem and as a consequence they are thrown back onto their creative resourcefulness. The setting of impossible problems can lead to creative involvement in the pursuit of answers. Dependence on the more intellectual secondary thought processes will be of no help in these situations. The only way to tackle such a problem is to have the confidence to rely on primary process activity.

Analogies may be drawn between primary process functioning and doodling, that meaningless scribbling on the telephone pad or blotter whilst engaged in conversation. In a situation like this the doodler is operating on a primary level. The secondary, more conscious processes are taken up with the conversation to which conscious attention is directed, the primary processes are busy generating scribbled visual images for which there is often no rational explanation. The doodler has been out of conscious control of the work and has still managed to produce a series of visual images without 'really thinking' about them. Finding ways to occupy the conscious mind often allows unconscious processes to be released.

Working quickly sometimes helps. If one deliberately sets a fast pace for an exercise then often the participants have no time to think about what they are doing, no time to operate on a secondary level. They are forced to resort to primary process activity, to that sort of mental functioning which does not require logical deductive reasoning but demands, rather, the intuitive flash of insight. Indeed, this sort of primary process thinking is often associated with intuition and insight rather than logic and reason.

It should be remembered that the creative process is a dialectic process and demands involvement in secondary processes as well as primary ones. As I said earlier, the primary ones tend to be the more troublesome. There can be some advantage, therefore, in using the more familiar secondary thought processes as a means of accessing the more difficult primary process functioning necessary for integrated creative activity. It is possible to start with an idea, with a thought, at a conscious level, of what the work of art might be like or about. This is quite a legitimate starting point so long as one acknowledges that it is important to move from here into a primary process phase of activity, to let unconscious processes take over. Much conceptual art begins in this way. The initial concept is, however, always modified by the unconscious functioning of the primary processes.

Tolerating the feelings of anxiety which are attendant upon this phase of the creative process can prove a difficulty in the adult group. Participants who had enrolled for what they assumed might be a pleasant recreational activity are suddenly faced with stressful emotions which represent the opposite of this. Feelings which are familiar to artists can be dispiriting to the adult student.

Who has not experienced the grey feeling of the 'morning after' when having to face work done on the day before? Suddenly the ignored gaps and fragmentation and the apparent chaos of undifferentiation push into consciousness. Part of creative capacity is the strength to resist an almost anal disgust that would make us sweep the whole mess into the waste-paper basket.

(Ehrenzweig 1968:21-30)

If there is a week to wait between class meetings, a week to worry about what is going to happen to the work which at the moment seems to be in such a mess, a week before being able to become once again involved at a creative level in order to resolve the unfinished fragmented aspects of the work, then the feelings of anxiety can become extenuated to the point of being unbearable. It is small wonder that some adult students feel unwilling to continue with an activity which gives rise to such unpleasant emotions. They vote with their feet and cease attending.

Part of the capacity to overcome these feelings stems from a knowledge of the nature of the creative process. Knowing that anxiety and unease are a normal part of creative activity, that they in no way signal failure or inadequacy, and that even professional and full-time artists feel the same, can go a long way to alleviating the feelings of depression which may arise from prolonged states of creative anxiety.

These problems are often made worse by the fact that creative work is usually a solitary activity. In an adult group, reliance on processes which seem out of one's conscious control can feel threatening. After all, one does not want to make a fool of oneself in front of the whole group. The dynamics of the group must be sympathetic for involvement in primary process thinking to take place. Much has been written about group activity and behaviour in

185

educational settings. Writers like Klein (1956, 1961), Trist and Sofer (1959), Herbert (1961), Bion (1961), and Richardson (1967) were all part of that movement, prominent in the sixties, which acknowledged that much of what happens in education happens to people, not in isolation, but in groups. The unit of research, therefore, becomes the interactive group rather than the individual. Much of the initial work in this area was done by Bion at the Tavistock Institute of Human Relations. It was here that he developed his theories of group behaviour.

Bion (1961) found that the ways in which a group behaves shift and alter. It is not possible to predict the way in which a group will behave but it is possible to categorise different types of group behaviour. He found that there were three basic assumptions on which groups operate. This is not a matter of conscious choice for the group. The particular mode of behaviour at any given time usually evolves and is not the outcome of a conscious decision. These three basic assumptions Bion calls 'dependence, fight-flight, and pairing'.

The dependent group demands the attention of a leader, usually the teacher in educational settings, though not necessarily so, to solve its problems for it. The teacher, it is assumed will do all the work and rescue the group from the threat of the learning task. The 'pairing' group operates in much the same way, though here the group relies on two of its members to solve its problems for it. Classically the group sits back whilst two of its members engage in discussion - it is from this discussion that, so the group assumes, a solution to the group task or problem will arise.

In contrast to these first two modes of operating the 'fight-flight' group is more active in its behaviour. In this case the members attack or run away from reality. The object of their fight or flight may be the leader of the group or another group member. It may be the task in hand. In any event, the members of the group become either very aggressive towards this person or task or they take flight, either literally, by moving away or not attending, or by avoidance, by not facing up to the demands of the task to be undertaken.

These three basic assumption groups, in one way or another, avoid confronting the task. Contrary to these groups is the 'work group'; a group which accepts the task to be undertaken and is willing to work together to become involved, in this case, in the creative process. In adult education it is not difficult to recognise these group stereotypes. The group that discusses last night's television programme on art, no matter how legitimate this may appear, rather than getting down to painting is involved in 'flight' from the task. The group that argues that the task they are about to undertake is useless and the teacher and other group members are incompetent for having suggested it, is involved in 'fight'. Non-participation, avoiding any interaction with other members of the group is also an effective form of 'flight' from the task.

Clearly, in all adult education activities, it is important for the group to see itself as a work group and to get down to the task in hand. In classes in the creative arts the need for such an attitude may be even more important. The mutual support and encouragement which is generated when the members of a group decide for themselves to tackle a particular problem is invaluable when the group is intending to take a step into the unknown realms of unconscious thought processes.

Given that the group dynamics are supportive and that the group wishes to operate as a work group, two assumptions which cannot be taken for granted and which may need to be discussed at length, then the group can begin to experiment with ways of developing creative ability. Implicit in what has been written above is the principle that no other member of the group can interfere with the images generated by one of its members. These images are individual to their creator; they are a unique and personal statement about that individual's view of the world at a particular point in time. The individual artist is in sole charge of the work.

There are those who believe that it is possible to become involved in a sort of group creativity. I am not sure about this and it may be that some art forms permit this whilst others preclude it. I can see that in dance and in drama it is possible for a group to work together to create a work of art. Whilst the experience of each member of the group may be different they at least end up with one created artwork. This may also be true in music, though I feel less sure here. Except for the case of jazz and other improvised art forms a piece of music is usually the product of one composer, not a group.

I cannot, however, see how this could be the case in the visual arts or in literary art forms. If I create a painting or a poem, if the imagery is generated from my own unconscious

187

processes and is about my own perception of and interaction with the world I inhabit, then I would, in the first place, resent anyone else interfering with my personal vision and, in the second place, see no point in trying to develop a sort of hybrid work of art, a mongrel with two or more different progenitors.

This in no way implies an anti-social or anti-community attitude. I would, needless to say, respect other people's work and their right to create their own images. Further, I would be fulsome in my support and encouragement for their creative work and their creative development. What I can see no point in is their daubing at my painting or my adding an occasional adjectival clause to their poem. It seems to me that there are some art forms which are simply inappropriate as group activities, other than in the sense of a group of people involved in their own creative work but from time to time offering each other mutual support and encouragement. I have, in the past, drawn an analogy between a creative arts group and a mathematics group. Each person in the group may be working on a separate problem but this does not mean that they are any less of a group. There will be times in the course of the lesson when the group reasserts its identity, when interaction between the members of the group is at a maximum. There will be other times when group interaction is at a minimum, when each member of the group is totally absorbed in their own work.

Where the emphasis is on process, either the creative process or the processes involved in solving a mathematical problem, then everything should be done to facilitate the development of expertise in that process, even if this means foregoing some group interaction in order to allow individual primary process involvement. If, on the other hand, say, a community arts project wishes to foster a communal spirit, then no doubt joint activities can be devised which will achieve the desired end, but this may be at the expense of creative development.

There are art forms, particularly in the performing arts, which seem more appropriate for these activities. If other art forms are chosen, then it must be acknowledged that outcomes are to do more with community cohesion than with creative activity. It almost goes without saying that participants should be aware of this. To persuade people that they are learning creative skills when they are, instead, learning to work in and with a group would be unethical. At the very least it would lead to a confusion of objectives which might make it impossible to arrive at an agreed learning strategy.

The creative process is a complex and difficult human activity. The section on 'Creativity' in Chapter 4 gave a detailed account of its nature. In facilitating learning in the area of creative development the facilitator needs to work with the adult group to devise ways of directing attention and attaining the appropriate form of consciousness. But the greatest difficulties arise from the anxiety states which are an inherent part of the creative process. It is these which more than anything else challenge the adult learner. Children seem to be able to cope better with these feelings. It seems as though adults have such high personal aspirations, so much of their status and identity invested in the learning transactions, that these feelings of anxiety are often associated with failure and personal humiliation. It is part of the role of the adult teacher to persuade participants that rather than signalling failure such feelings may signal success, that they may indicate an involvement which can honestly be described as creative and that they may be no different from the anxieties and uncertainties felt by creative artists over the centuries.

The development of an awareness of the nature of artistic activity and of the relative nature of the value systems within which the arts operate

This section is about cognitive development. It represents the only aspect of creative and artistic education to which all the principles of andragogy outlined previously clearly apply. It is about learning in the sense of the term familiar to academics and intellectuals. The title of the section gives an indication of the areas where learning is felt to be most important; learning about the nature of the creative process and learning about the relative nature of values. In addition to this, however, one should mention some of the instrumental learning that might take place.

I am referring to the learning of the names of tools and equipment, the names of processes involved in the creation of a work of art and I am referring to the development of a language for talking about work in progress. This latter is vitally important in adult education. I still remember the times when, as a young art student, I did not understand

189

what seemed to be the simplest of statements made by some of my tutors. They would look at my painting and with a knowing nod say 'Yes, it works'. It was a long time before I had any inkling of what was meant by this statement. Adult students may also be made to feel inadequate by such behaviour and leave the class as a consequence.

The language used to describe colour or harmonic relationships also needs some explaining. A discord in either colour or sound needs to be understood as a feature of the composition and not some sort of mistake. At a very simple level it is important to evolve a language to enable participants in an adult learning group to communicate about their work. The names of colours and the names of musical notes, a means of discussing movement in dance and a means of discussing movements in music, and the names and characters of the raw materials of any art form must be learned or, at least, a terminology must be agreed between the members of the group.

This is important for all three different ways of engaging with the arts. Appreciators may, in addition, need to know the language of analysis; they may need a conceptual framework which will help them to relate the various parts of a work to a whole. The extent to which analysis is undertaken may itself be a culturally determined phenomenon. It would not be unexpected to discover that in some cultures appreciation was concerned more with response to a work of art than with analysis and historical periodisation.

There is, then, a level of cognitive learning required which is basic to the art form with which one is engaging. It has to be recognised that a student's orientation to a work of art, as either an appreciator, creator or participant, is unique and may not be the same as the tutor's orientation. Language is the medium through which we communicate our particular orientation to a given work. In educational settings we need to be able to communicate our feelings, our responses to art, in words so that discussion can take place about them. The professional artist may eschew such dialogue, claiming that the work itself communicates all that is necessary. This is a reasonable position to take and one often articulated by artists. But it is of little help to the educator. It has to be acknowledged that, in contemporary developed societies, the dominant mode of communication is linguistic. Language, therefore, is the medium through which members of a learning group communicate about their learning. Such communication is facilitated if terminologies and expressions are explained and agreed amongst members of the group.

Whatever conventions are used to transmit meaning about works of art will be culturally derived, and this ought to be acknowledged. Raymond Williams makes this point:

> It is characteristic of educational systems to claim that they are transmitting 'knowledge' or 'culture' in an absolute, universally derived sense, though it is obvious that different systems, at different times and in different countries, transmit radically different versions of both.
>
> (Williams 1986:186)

Whatever the cultural context in which an adult group is working, the group itself will modify their perceptions of the nature of that culture. If they begin to add to our understanding of that culture or to influence the value systems espoused by that culture, then they are participating in cultural development. Such activity, according to Jarvis, is not at all unusual:

> The human being is not a passive recipient of his cultural heritage, he does not have it imprinted upon a "tabula rasa" type of mind; but he receives, processes and externalises ... During the process, he accepts some aspects of culture, modifies others and even rejects some of the information with which he is presented. But he does more than merely processing what he receives, he is frequently active in pursuit of knowledge ideas values and beliefs enshrined in objectified culture.
>
> (Jarvis 1983:10)

One cannot accept this statement totally since it implies that this questioning goes on at all times and in all situations. We noted earlier that some adults live in a state of oppression where the possibility of questioning cultural norms does not exist. What Jarvis does is point to the possibility of liberating adults so that they can question and perhaps modify the cultural climate in which they live.

In the previous section it was stated that adult students can better cope with the anxieties of creative involvement if they know that they are a normal part of the process. Knowledge about the nature of the creative process can

191

come from a number of sources. Writing by artists themselves, by critics, psychologists and philosophers can be studied as a way of arriving at an understanding of the nature of the creative process. The section on 'Creation' in Chapter 4 covers much of this writing. But the writing itself must be examined as a product of a particular cultural context. Thus, a Freudian explanation of creative activity has to be seen, not as the definitive explanation, but as one explanation offered in Western Europe in the early part of the 20th century. It is a psychological explanation put forward when the discipline of psychology was in its infancy.

Our knowledge of human behaviour is constantly changing and, as with other areas of human knowledge, it is best not to think in terms of absolutes. What the adult tutor should be concerned to do is to offer the best explanations we have to date about the nature of the creative process. As with culture, the relative nature of knowledge should be acknowledged and discussed. Other cultures will have different explanations of the nature of creative involvement. One arrives at understanding, not by looking for the definitive explanation, the fact of the matter, but by pondering on the different explanations for a given human behaviour and understanding how they belong to and are derived from their cultural context. It is quite legitimate to say that this explanation of creative work is right for the Australian aborigine whilst this other explanation is right for the Japanese potter. Participants in adult classes will work out their own understanding which they will relate to their eventual experience.

A knowledge of what has been written about creative activity, it has been suggested, will help adults to tolerate the anxiety states which writers on the subject seem to agree is an integral part of the creative process, a feature of integrated creativity. When an adult group gains experience of creative involvement they will match this experience against their acquired knowledge. This may result in the members of the group modifying their own understanding of creative activity. It may also result in their adding to our understanding of the nature of the creative process.

The difficulty here is in ensuring that what our students are referring to is the same process as that referred to by other writers on creativity. The only way to do this is by matching individual experience against that communicated in the discussions and writings of others. It would not help matters to describe as 'creative' an entirely different form of human behaviour, say, copying. But this is sometimes done. Teachers will sometimes assert that their students are operating creatively when, in fact, they are doing no more than becoming involved in the mechanical process of copying someone else's work, no matter how intricate this process might be.

In order to be able to say whether or not a given activity is or is not creative it is necessary to identify indicators of creative involvement. Such indicators can be derived from the literature on the subject. Involvement at an unconscious level is an important feature of primary process activity and can be taken as an indicator that adult students are developing an ability to become involved in the creative process. How one recognises whether or not a student is working on an unconscious level will be dealt with in the section on evaluation. For the moment it is important to point out only that the group can, from a study of the available literature, come to decisions about how it will monitor its progress, about how it will decide when individuals are or are not involved creatively.

The last area to be discussed in this section is concerned with values. It has already been established that values in the arts are culturally determined and it has been acknowledged that it is important for participants in an adult learning group to be aware of this. In Chapter 3 it was suggested that there are three sorts of value systems concerned with the arts and these were identified as 'commercial', 'artistic' and 'subjective'. It is important for students to be able to distinguish between the different value systems and to understand the basis on which they make judgements about works of art created by both themselves and by other people.

The commercial value of a work of art is of only passing interest in the sort of educational enterprise we are discussing. Such value is established by market forces and says nothing about the merits or demerits of the work as art. The fact that someone is prepared to pay millions of dollars for a painting does not make the painting any better or any worse. It usually means that works by this particular artist are rare, that they seldom come onto the market and that it is necessary to pay a high price to acquire one. Adult students can be forgiven for thinking that high commercial value equates with a high artistic value. This may or may not be the case. It is important for them to be able to distinguish between the different sorts of value.

Artistic value, it was suggested, cannot be identified in an objective way. It is not possible to say that a work of art has artistic merit which will always be evident. Tastes in the arts change and what is considered to be good in one century is not necessarily so considered in the next. Values in the arts are relative. Like other cultural values they change over time and are different from country to country. This can be demonstrated by looking at the historic record. It is important for those involved in the arts as appreciators, creators and participants to understand the relative nature of artistic value.

Adult students can be misled by authoritative assertions that a particular piece of work is of high quality whilst others are of inferior quality. It is important to challenge those who make such statements to reveal the value base on which they are making their decisions, to identify the criteria they are using. The criteria can usually be seen to be specific to a particular period and a particular culture.

What I have called subjective value is probably the most difficult sort of value with which students need to come to terms. Having the confidence to make subjective value judgements about one's own work and about the work of others requires a certain degree of sophistication in one's understanding about the arts. Adults involved in a learning transaction should be helped to a situation where they are able to articulate their feelings about a work. It needs to be understood that saying that they don't like a particular work is to do no more than express a preference. But it is a preference which is just as valid as that made by an eminent and experienced art critic, provided that levels of perceptual acuity in both cases are adequate for the task.

It is difficult for the adult student to accept that there are no absolute rules for evaluating a work of art. Life for all concerned in art education would be so much easier if there were. We could simply apply the criteria and come to a decision about whether or not the work was of merit. Instead, one is thrown back on one's own devices. One makes a subjective judgement about the work. In appreciation classes this is perhaps more difficult than in creative or participative classes. It is easier to articulate evaluative comments about one's own work than it is about the work of others. There are, after all, no precedents for comments about one's own creative work. But if one makes a derogatory comment about a well known painting one runs the risk of this comment being compared unfavourably to that of an established critic or commentator. It requires no small degree of confidence to comment on the merit of established works of art, especially when one realises that the comments are essentially subjective in nature.

It is important in these situations for the teacher to refrain from telling participants what to think. As a teacher it is easy to slip into the habit of making evaluative comments and inviting the class to agree with them. Many tutors in literature appreciation classes are guilty of uncritically passing on a value system which is essentially their own. Their choice of work to be studied and the reverence with which they treat it encourages students in the belief that the work under consideration embodies a value system which can be explained and demonstrated. This is not the case. Why a work is considered to be good is a function of the tastes of the tutor or critic within a value system that is culturally determined.

Similarly in the creative class it is important for the tutor to refrain from imposing a set of values on the students. In creative work it is the creator, and only the creator, who establishes the value of a work. Within social settings the work may acquire status as a work of art but the processes by which this is done are societal ones. The work may even become valuable. The processes involved here are commercial ones. It is the subjective evaluation of the work which is of prime importance to the members of an adult learning group in the creative arts.

This section has been about the cognitive knowledge required of those involved in education in the arts. The knowledge to be acquired is as much to do with processes as it is to do with facts. The nature of the creative process, of evaluative, cultural and societal processes can all be profitably discussed. It is up to the group to ask the appropriate questions. Why was this painting considered to be better than that? Why is pop music considered to be inferior to classical music? In what way is Shakespeare better than Beckett? The pursuit of answers to these questions can lead to a fuller understanding of the relative nature of cultural values.

Evaluation

Before ending this section on adult learning in the arts it is necessary to spend some time in considering the question of evaluation. I am using the term in the sense of attributing value or worth to an educational activity. The term assessment is used in the sense of attributing value or worth to a student's developing ability. One evaluates courses but assesses students. An assessment of student progress may form part of an evaluation but this is not always the case.

Much has been written about evaluation in adult education and a range of procedures for carrying out evaluations has been put forward. Brookfield (1982:95-100) has given an overview of the thinking on evaluation in adult education which he expanded in his later work (1986:261-82). Here he draws on the work of Scriven (1967 and 1972) and Stufflebeam (1968, 1971 and 1975) amongst others to make the point that evaluation in education is about the attribution or ascertainment of worth or value. It is not simply a question of deciding whether or not previously specified behavioural objectives have been achieved, evaluation is also concerned to make some statement about the value of those objectives and about the value of the learning experience as a whole, including what may be considered as incidental learning.

The Nottingham Andragogy Group make the following statement about evaluation:

> Evaluation is considered to be a form of praxis which, in turn, is a salient feature of andragogy. Evaluation, therefore, must be an integral and continuous activity within each stage of the andragogic process and should involve all participants equally. Evaluation should be concerned with thinking and learning with reference to the subject area, the cognitive and personal development of all group members and the group processes or development as a whole. In any evaluation, equal attention should be given to the thinking and learning within these three aspects. The inter-relationship of these three provides a vehicle for the type of thinking and learning which fosters adult development.
>
> (Nottingham Andragogy Group 1983:45)

Leaving aside for the moment the bias towards intellectual development, what the group is suggesting is that the evaluation should focus not just upon what has been learned in terms of course content, but also on the processes of the

196

group. It is as important to evaluate the way in which learning has taken place as it is to evaluate what has been learned. The difficulties involved in such an evaluation should not be underestimated.

There are questions about when an evaluation should be carried out: the Nottingham group maintain that it should be an integral and continuous activity. It is possible, however, that the results of an educational enterprise are not fully evident until some time after the activity. There are questions about who carries out the evaluation: the Nottingham group feel that all involved in the activity should be consulted. There are times, however, when an external agency has an interest in an educational activity, either because they are providing finance or certifying competence in a particular skill. In either case they, quite reasonably, want to evaluate the learning activity.

The Nottingham Group suggest that there are certain aspects of the andragogical process which may lend themselves to some form of monitoring and evaluation that would be of use to an external evaluator. The examples they quote are:

1. It should be possible to monitor the developing relationships between the participants in the group and to chart the changing nature of these relationships through an examination of the style and content of verbal interchanges.
2. It should be possible to observe and record the manner in which the adult educator hands over the power and responsibility for managing group process and the ways in which this responsibility is taken over and shared by other members of the group.
3. It should be possible to identify the stage at which members of the group begin to take on responsibility for their own learning and begin to explore and push back the boundaries of knowledge and experience in the group, adding to the learning of all.
4. It should be possible for all members of the group to indicate what they have learned from the experience and how, and to identify ways in which the process is helping them to learn, grow and change by recording the process of reflection on the group process. (Nottingham Andragogy Group

197

1983:46)

Much of this is to do, not with evaluating the learning that has gone on in terms of the subject being studied, but with evaluating the learning that has gone on in terms of learning how to learn, learning about andragogy. The assumption seems to be that the subject learning is cognitive in nature and as such can be fairly easily quantified. It is the evaluation of attitude changes to the process of learning itself that is seen to present difficulty.

In the arts, those classes concerned with appreciation would fit most neatly into the Nottingham Group's model. This is a more cognitive sort of exercise concerned with analysis and academic discourse. In a similar way those classes concerned with technical aspects of participation are fairly easy to evaluate. One can readily decide whether or not one can hit the right note on a musical instrument or make the required moves in a ballet. When a student's developing knowledge of a subject can be so readily identified it becomes easier to focus on andragogic process. The problem in the arts lies in the fact that there is a great deal of confusion surrounding the evaluation of creative classes.

What often happens in creative art classes is that the focus of evaluation gets shifted away from the learning that has gone on so that teachers and students end up making evaluative comments about their aesthetic reactions to the works of art produced. Evaluation in such courses is seen as providing an opportunity for making fairly subjective comments about the aesthetic value of the work rather than about the learning. Such evaluations are characterised by the 'criticism'. Here the works produced in the class are gathered together at the end of the lesson and the teacher makes erudite and critical comments about them. The teacher may even invite the students to participate in this activity so that they can develop their own critical faculties. This sharing of the critical function is seen as more andragogic in approach, as involving the students more in decision-making. This, of course, is true. The problem stems from the fact that the whole basis of the evaluation is ill-founded. An evaluation of creative development should focus on the creative process, not the created product. It is necessary to look more closely at the nature of evaluation in creative education.

Apart from evaluating the group and learning processes, as proposed in the Nottingham Group's model, what is being evaluated is the progress made by group members in the four areas of development suggested above. What needs to be discovered is how far the group has become more perceptive, how far they have developed their ability to exploit a medium of expression, how far they are able to become involved in the creative process, and the level of their knowledge about the arts and the processes and value systems involved in creative activity. The works of art produced by a group are only one amongst many sources of evidence on which judgements can be based.

In classes in the creative arts, and this may be true of other areas, there are only three sources of evidence which can be used to decide whether or not a given educational criterion has been met. The work produced provides one source of evidence, watching students at work provides another source, and communicating verbally with students provides a third source. Verbal communication can be either written or oral. It is better if judgements are based on more than a single source of evidence.

If, for instance, one was concerned to find out if levels of perceptual acuity are increasing one can glean some information from watching students doing a drawing exercise which has been agreed upon as a means of developing perception. This is a different sort of exercise from those designed to generate visual metaphors. It is concerned with accuracy of observation rather than with imaginative interpretations. If the object being depicted is accurately drawn, if it is correct in terms of shape and proportion, then one may conclude that it has been accurately perceived. The more normal feedback from students on the subject of their growing perceptual awareness, however, is usually verbal. It consists of their talking about seeing things with new eyes, about noticing colours in the brick wall which they have passed so many times before but never noticed, about being intrigued by the shape of clouds or the colour of trees. It is on usually unsolicited statements like these that evaluations about perceptual acuity can be based. They can be strengthened by reference to drawing exercises and colour work.

Similarly, if one wants to find out if students are able to use a medium in a way which seeks to exploit its potential, then one can look at their works in order to identify any unusual use of the medium, watch them

199

working to ascertain if they seem to be operating at an experimental level and talk to them to find out if they were working beyond their previous experience. Again, it is not enough to look only at the end product. No matter how experimental it may appear, unless one obtains some additional evidence one has no way of knowing whether or not the particular student was simply repeating a well tried approach.

It is in the area of creative development that most difficulty is encountered. Looking at a finished work is of little help here. It will tell us nothing about whether or not its creator was involved in the creative process as we have described it. Watching students work and talking to them is far more helpful. Many teachers say that they can tell when their class is creatively involved. Once they have experienced it, students themselves know when they have been creatively involved. It is possible, from what we know about the creative process, to identify some indicators of creative involvement.

We have already mentioned one of the more common indicators of creative activity in talking about anxiety. Anxiety should be seen as an indicator of success rather than a signal of failure. Further, one can expect students who are working on a primary process level to be so engrossed in their work that they are unaware of what is going on around them. This can also be observed and tested out in conversation with the students. One can also come to some conclusions by watching the way in which they work. Those working on too conscious a level who are unwilling to give up conscious control of the work often appear to be working in an inhibited sort of a way. They hold the brush near to the bristles in order to better control it. They try to pre-conceive the end product and are unwilling to allow the work to develop its own life and existence. I have written elsewhere about these and other indicators of creative involvement (Jones 1975 and 1985) and I do not wish to rehearse them here. Such indicators can be deduced from a study of the literature. The point being made here is that it is the process and not the product that should be evaluated. If one is trying to make value judgements about levels of creative ability then there is no point in substituting aesthetic comments about the works produced and assuming that they are, in some way, saying the same thing.

In adopting an andragogic approach it is clear that these issues will have to be discussed at length with students. Evaluating cognitive development has not been discussed here because it is well covered in the writing on evaluation. The purpose of these paragraphs on evaluation has been to clear up misunderstandings and misconceptions about the focus of the exercise and the evidence to be used. A difficulty arises when students expect a teacher to make aesthetic comments about the work and feel cheated when the teacher refuses. I want to suggest that it is only by talking these issues through in an andragogically oriented group that such misconceptions can be sorted out.

ADULT EDUCATION AND CULTURAL DEVELOPMENT

What I hope has become clear by now is that it is possible for adult education teachers to ask themselves questions about the ways in which they work, the answers to which will help them to decide how their classes are oriented in terms of the prevailing culture. It is possible for them to look at the cultural context in which they are working and decide if they are reinforcing it or trying to change it, or, indeed, reinforcing some aspects of it and trying to change others. They can ask whether or not there are any aspects of cultural life in their locality which are being neglected and whether or not something should be done about this. They can ask themselves whether or not they are encouraging adults to be appreciative, creative or participative, or any combination of these.

I want it to be clear that I am not making value judgements which might suggest that one approach is better than others. It seems important that there should be a broad range of opportunities to engage in different art forms in different ways within different cultural contexts. Should there be a bias towards one particular way of engaging with the arts or towards a set of cultural values which are not those of the community in which the class takes place, then it may be important to consider ways of redressing the balance.

It will be remembered from Chapter 2 that it was suggested that it might be better to consider cultures as being quite small units. To speak of a European Culture poses difficulties. If one asks what the cultural artefacts of a Norwegian fisherman, a young black apprentice from Birmingham and an Italian aristocrat have in common it is difficult to come up with a sensible answer. Cultural

201

development therefore is a matter of influencing the cultural context in which the adult education activity is taking place. This may, in turn, influence a wider culture, as do many styles and fashions arising from the youth culture. But the immediate effect is to influence our perceptions of dominant cultural values.

Whether or not a course contributes towards cultural development depends on more than whether it is a creative, appreciative or participative course. Appreciation courses can simply accept the prevailing value system or they can question it. The way in which the history of European art has been written assumes certain values. Certain works are hailed as great works and others as inferior. The folk tradition is rarely given the status it deserves. A teacher can simply pass on such value systems as accepted or analyse them within their cultural and historical context. Contextualisation provides an opportunity to view such values as being relative and in so doing frees participants to accord equal status to other art forms from other cultural contexts.

This liberation from the constraints of a uni-cultural value system allows a greater opportunity for cultural development. Participants in the learning group can come to see that other forms of cultural expression can also have validity. Our concept of art can be widened to include the activities which were previously thought to be outside a definition of art. This may seem fanciful, but it has already happened in, for example, the case of photography. It is, to a certain degree, the result of photography being taught in colleges and departments of art that it has gained acceptance as an art form to the extent that arts funding bodies now consider it legitimate to grant aid photographic exhibitions. Film and video have also come in from the cold to take their place alongside Renaissance paintings and Classical sculpture as recognised art forms. There seems little doubt that exploring different art forms within an educational framework can influence the ways in which those art forms are perceived. It may take a political campaign to acquire resources for these art forms, but it is clear that educational process can play an important part in influencing attitudes.

What is being suggested, then, is that in appreciation classes the teacher has the option of reinforcing an accepted value system or of questioning this value system and setting it in a global context of a multitude of value systems all arising from particular socio-historic cultural settings. It is accepted that some teachers may feel it important to reinforce a certain value system. There have been times, historically, when it was felt necessary for educationalists to stress the values of what was perceived to be a threatened cultural heritage. The Danish Folk High Schools come to mind as being an expression of an educational movement which consciously focused attention on the prevailing national culture.

I am not suggesting that a uni-cultural approach is wrong. What I am suggesting is that teachers and students should be aware that they have a choice. What is to be deplored is the mindless acceptance of values which may or may not be sympathetic to or appropriate for the cultural context in which an educational activity is taking place, and which have probably been acquired from a source outside the experience of the group participants. The emphasis here is on 'mindless acceptance'. Emphasis of a particular cultural value system should be the result of a considered decision.

It is difficult to see how engaging with the arts in a participative way can affect the cultural context. I am talking here about that sort of participation which is a question of acquiring technical expertise rather than those forms of participation which are concerned with the creative development of participants. I suppose that there are choices about the instruments which musicians can learn to play or the dances which are practised. An awareness of a range of cultural conventions in the performance of works of dance, music and drama can arise from the technical training of participants in these art forms. But it is difficult to see how the second violin learning a particular piece of music is going to make any individual creative contribution to cultural development from involvement in this activity.

It should be remembered that we are concerned with ways of engaging with the arts rather than with individuals. The second violin may indeed make a contribution to cultural development in another context. It is unlikely that this will happen from learning to play the relevant part of a Beethoven symphony.

It is in the area of creative involvement with the arts that most opportunities are lost. One would think that educational courses aimed at the creative development of the individual would be concerned, almost by definition, with cultural development. After all, if participants are learning to operate at a creative level, to work outside their previous experience, then they cannot predict the outcome. The works they produce will, in some way, reflect their own cultural history and the cultural context in which they live and work, but they should move on from this point into unpredictable forms of cultural expression. Unfortunately this rarely happens.

What seems to happen is that many adult classes get stuck in a particular cultural tradition. Many adults want to emulate painters and poets of the past rather than explore their own creative potential. They want to paint landscapes in the European Renaissance tradition or write the great English novel rather than explore their own unconscious processes. It may be possible to explain this preference in terms of their previous educational experience. It seems to be the result of an academic and intellectual approach to the arts. It is not threatening to aim for something that is known, a style, a mode of expression which we have experienced as appreciators. It can be frightening to cast oneself into the unknown depths of primary process thinking.

When creative groups are working on a creative level then they can be said to be extending the range of cultural expression. When their work is constrained within a self-imposed cultural safety net, they are reinforcing the values implicit in that culture. Again, what is being suggested is that the adult group should be made aware that they have a choice. That this activity is the result of a conscious decision rather than a defensive reaction.

There are other areas where current practice precludes cultural or creative development. I want to extend my definition of the arts beyond what some people may find acceptable, but I want to examine the dressmaking class. In higher education this area of activity is known as 'Fashion' or 'Textiles' and involves teaching students to work creatively using fabric and yarns. As with other areas of higher education in the visual arts, emphasis is placed on developing perception and learning to manipulate the medium of expression. Participants are encouraged to become involved in the creative process when designing their garments and to become proficient in the skills involved in making them up.

Now if we look at what happens in much adult education we see a very different picture. Rather than developing the creative abilities of the participants, adult students are encouraged to go along to their local store, to look through a catalogue and to choose a design which they like. They then purchase a paper pattern and look at the instructions to find out what material they need to make the garment. These are then bought, perhaps with some advice from the teacher, and taken along to the class where they learn how to follow the instructions in the packet. They may also learn the skills involved in using a sewing machine. This is, I suggest, very different from the approach taken by those involved in higher education.

It is argued, of course, that these students, usually women, only want to save money by making their own clothes and there is no point in teaching them how to design. They can, I have been told, make some 'creative' decisions by altering the shape of the pocket or collar. It is only important that they gain the confidence to cut out the fabric and use the sewing machine. It is a matter of regret that the women's movement or some other organisation have not taken adult educators to task for this patronising attitude.

In this respect I felt challenged by a statement made by Thomas. He says

What conceivable relationship can there be between the ordinary adult education classes and political structures? The simple answer is that there is indeed such a thing as a non-political dressmaking class ... The reason why, for example, local authorities in Britain mount programmes of activity which are substantially practical and physical now becomes clear. It is because such activities are morally bland and politically neutral.
(Thomas 1982:20)

I am not so sure. If one were to ask about the typical dressmaking class one would have to say that it ensured that participants remained dependent on commercially available paper patterns, that such patterns and designs were aimed at a market that promoted European styles of dress, that the way in which the class was organised denied participants the opportunity of creative and perceptual development and ensured that their learning remained at a technical level, and that this is all usually done without giving participants the choice of approaching the subject in a more creative way. I am not sure that this is 'morally bland and politically neutral', though I am sure that local authorities view it in that way.

There is no reason why teaching Dress in adult education could not be organised on the same basis as in higher education. Part-time courses could be constructed which approached the subject in the same way as the colleges and departments of art approach it. Students on such courses could be offered the choice between simply learning technical skills, satisfying though this may be, and learning to develop their creative ability using fabrics and yarns as the medium. Such a course would give participants greater choice about the way they present themselves to the world and in so doing extend the prevailing cultural norms. The potential contribution of the humble dressmaking class to either cultural stasis or cultural development should not be underestimated. An andragogical approach should ensure that participants have the choice.

This book has attempted to explore the nature of culture and the nature of the arts, it has looked at the different ways in which we engage with the arts and analysed the opportunities available for such engagements. Finally it has explored the contribution that adult education can make to the way in which we relate to the arts and to the cultural context in which we live and work. It has been suggested that there is a case for questioning the value systems implicit in much teaching that goes on in adult education, not necessarily with a view to changing them but with a view to offering students a choice.

I want to suggest that teachers and organisers in adult education ask themselves a number of questions about their programmes and about the way in which their courses are organised. I am not suggesting that everyone should become involved only in cultural development. I, amongst many others, want to retain the opportunity to study Beethoven and Bacon, Schoenberg and Shakespeare. But I also want the opportunity to study Indian and Oriental music, to enjoy and appreciate African and Balinese dance, to listen to the Icelandic sagas and American Indian folk tales, and further, I want the opportunity to explore my own creative potential, to have a choice about the way in which I engage with the arts.

In the United Kingdom school curricula are becoming increasingly prescribed by central government and we are reaching a stage where the only opportunity to broaden the range of cultural activity to which one might be exposed is in the area of adult education. It may be helpful if adult educators were to look at what they are doing and ask:

a. What is the particular cultural context in which I and students who attend classes live and work? Can this be described in the terms suggested in Chapter 2?
b. Do the arts activities engaged in by adult students reflect or contradict this cultural context?
c. Are arts activities from a range of different cultures available?
d. Are participants in adult education activities made aware that value systems in the arts are relative?
e. Are participants in adult education encouraged to question cultural value systems?
f. Are opportunities available for adults to engage with the arts appreciatively, creatively, and participatively?
g. Is attention paid to increasing levels of perception so that participants are better able to perceive art forms from both their own culture and cultural contexts other than their own?

No doubt this list can be extended. Its purpose here is to encourage those responsible for the organisation of adult education activities in what we currently define as the arts to begin to ask themselves questions about how their programme is oriented in relation to the wider cultural context. It is a first step in promoting cultural diversity and cultural development. There will of course be problems. Finding teachers who are knowledgeable about art forms from different cultures can prove difficult outside metropolitan areas. Maybe this is an area where distance learning material might be made available. It should be possible to design resources which would help adult educators over the problems arising from a limited number of people with the required expertise. It may be that a group themselves decide to research a particular form of cultural expression and thus obviate the necessity for specialist knowledge other than about research procedures.

The opportunities here are vast. It is important for those of us involved in adult education to engage in a period of self-examination to find out if we are doing all we can to provide a wide range of opportunities for engaging with the arts. Following this we must devise strategies to give participants in adult learning groups the power to decide for themselves how they wish to engage with the arts. Finally we must take steps to redress the balance in our national cultural life and provide more opportunities for people to become creatively involved in the development of a rich and

Adult Education and Cultural Development

varied cultural environment.

REFERENCES

Arnheim, R., 1969, Visual Thinking, London, University of
    California Press
Bartley, S.H., 1980, Introduction to Visual Perception, New
    York, Harper and Row
Belbin, E. and Belbin, R.M., 1972, Problems in Adult
    Retraining, London, Heinemann Educational
Bion, W.R., 1961, Experiences in Groups, London, Tavistock
Bloom, B.S., 1965, Taxonomy of Educational Objectives,
    London, Longman
Brookfield, S.D., 1986, Understanding and Facilitating Adult
    Learning, Milton Keynes, Open University
Brookfield, S., 1982, 'Evaluation Models and Adult
    Education', Studies in Adult Education, vol. 14,
    September 1982, Leicester, National Institute of Adult
    Education (NIAE)
Department of Education and Science, 1971, Arts in Schools,
    London, Her Majesty's Stationery Office
Ehrenzweig, A., 1968, The Hidden Order of Art, London,
    Weidenfeld and Nicolson
Elsey, B., 1986, Social Theory Perspectives on Adult
    Education, Nottingham, Department of Adult
    Education, University of Nottingham
Freire, P., 1972a, Cultural Action for Freedom,
    Harmondsworth, Penguin
Freire, P., 1972b, Pedagogy of the Oppressed, translated by
    M.B. Ramer, Harmondsworth, Penguin
Freire, P., 1973, 'By Learning They Can Teach',
    Convergence, vol. 6, no. 1
Gagné, R.M., 1975, The Conditions of Learning, New York,
    Holt, Rinehart and Winston
Groombridge, B., 1983, 'Adult Education and the Education
    of Adults' in Tight, M. (ed.), 1983a
Gulbenkian Foundation, 1982, Arts in Schools, London,
    Calouste Gulbenkian Foundation
Herbert, E.L., 1961, 'The Use of Group Techniques in the
    Training of Teachers', Human Relations, xiv, 251-63
Houle, C.O., 1974, The Design of Education, San Francisco,
    Washington, London, Jossey Bass
Hudson, L., 1966, Contrary Imaginations - A Psychological
    Study of the English Schoolboy, London, Methuen

Hutchison, R., 1982, The Politics of the Arts Council, London, Sinclaire Brown
Jarvis, P., 1983, Adult and Continuing Education - Theory and Practice, London, Croom Helm
Jones, D.J., 1975, 'Evaluation and Assessment in Adult Art Classes', Unpublished M.Ed. Thesis, University of Manchester
Jones, D.J., 1985, Creativity, in the series 'Adults: Psychological and Educational Perspectives', Nottingham, Department of Adult Education, University of Nottingham
Keddie, N., 1980, 'Adult Education: An Ideology of Individualism', in Thompson, J.L., 1980, op. cit.
Klein, J., 1956, The Study of Groups, London, Routledge and Kegan Paul
Klein, J., 1961, Working with Groups, London, Hutchinson
Knowles, M.S., 1980, The Modern Practice of Adult Education - From Pedgagogy to Andragogy, Chicago, Follett
Legge, D., 1982, The Education of Adults in Britain, Milton Keynes, Open University
Long, H.B., 1987, New Perspectives on the Education of Adults in the United States, London and Sydney, Croom Helm
Martindale, C., 1976, 'Creativity: It's all in the Head', Psychology Today (U.K.) vol. 2, no. 3, March 1976
Maslow, A.H., 1968, Towards a Psychology of Being, New York, Van Nostrand Reinhold Company
Mee and Wiltshire, 1978, Structure and Performance in Adult Education, London and New York, Longman
Mezirow, J., 1977, 'Perspective Transformation', Studies in Adult Education vol. 9, no. 2, Leicester, NIAE
Mezirow, J., 1981, 'A Critical Theory of Adult Learning and Education' Adult Education vol. 32, no. 1, Washington
Neumark, V., 1986, 'What Have You Got To Be Proud Of?', Arts Express no. 26, April 1986, London
Nottingham Andragogy Group, 1983, Towards a Developmental Theory of Andragogy, Nottingham, Department of Adult Education, University of Nottingham
Ornstein, R., 1975, 'In Two Minds', Psychology Today (U.K.) vol. 1, no. 2, May 1975
Redfern, H.B., 1986, Questions in Aesthetic Education, London, Allen and Unwin
Richardson, E., 1967, Group Study for Teachers, London, Routledge and Kegan Paul

Rogers, A., 1986, Teaching Adults, Milton Keynes and
    Philadelphia, Open University
Ross, M., 1978, The Creative Arts, London, Heinemann
    Educational
Scriven, M., 1967, 'The Methodology of Evaluation' in Gagné,
    R.M., Scriven, M., and Tyler, R.W. (eds) Perspectives in
    Curriculum Evaluation, AERA monograph no. 1, Skokie,
    Illinois, Rand McNally
Scriven, M., 1972, 'Pros and Cons About Goal Free
    Evaluation', Evaluation Comment, vol. 3, no. 4, pp. 1-4
Stufflebeam, D.L., 1968, Evaluation as Enlightenment for
    Decision Making, Columbus, Evaluation Centre, Ohio
    State University
Stufflebeam, D.L., 1975, 'Evaluation as a Community
    Education Process', Community Education Journal
    (USA), vol. 5, no. 2, pp. 7-12
Stufflebeam, D.L. et al., 1971, Educational Evaluation and
    Decision-Making in Education, Itasca, Ill., Peacock
Stumbo, H.W., 1970, 'Three Bases for Research and Teaching
    in the Arts: Subjective, Objective and Projective' in
    Pappas, G. (ed.), Concepts in Art and Education,
    London, Macmillan
Thomas, J.E., 1982, Radical Adult Education: Theory and
    Practice, Nottingham, Department of Adult Education,
    University of Nottingham
Thompson, J.L. (ed), 1980, Adult Education for a Change,
    London, Hutchinson
Tight, M. (ed.), 1983a, Education for Adults; Vol. I, Adult
    Learning and Education, London and Canberra, Croom
    Helm in asssociation with the Open University
Tight, M. (ed.), 1983b, Education for Adults: Vol. II,
    Opportunities for Adult Education, London and
    Canberra, Croom Helm in association with the Open
    University
Tough, A.M., 1968, Why Adults Learn: A Study of the Major
    Reasons for Beginning and Continuing a Learning
    Project, Toronto, Ontario Institute for Studies in
    Education
Tough, A.M., 1978, 'Major Learning Efforts: Recent
    Research and Future Directions', Adult Education (USA)
    1978, vol. 28, no. 4, pp. 250-63
Tough, A.M., 1979, The Adult's Learning Projects: A Fresh
    Approach to Theory and Practice in Adult Learning,
    Toronto, Ontario Institute for Studies in Education
Trist, E.L., and Sofer, C., 1959, Explorations in Group

Relations, Leicester, Leicester University Press
Williams, R., 1986, Culture, London, Fontana

BIBLIOGRAPHY

ACGB, 1949, The Annual Report for 1948-9, London, Arts
    Council of Great Britain
ACGB, 1967, The Charter of Incorporation granted by Her
    Majesty the Queen to The Arts Council of Great
    Britain, London, Arts Council of Great Britain
ACGB, 1983, The Arts Council and Education, A Policy
    Statement, London, Arts Council of Great Britain
ACGB, 1984, The Glory of the Garden - The Development of
    the Arts in England, London, Arts Council of Great
    Britain
Adkins, G., 1981, The Arts and Adult Education, Leicester,
    Advisory Council for Adult Continuing Education
    (ACACE)
Adorno, T.W., 1941, 'On Popular Music', Studies in
    Philosophy and Social Science, 9, New York, Institute of
    Social Research
Adorno, T.W., 1967, Prisms: Cultural Criticism and Society,
    London, Neville Spearman
Adorno, T.W. and Horkheimer, M., 1972, Dialectic of
    Enlightenment, New York, Herder and Herder
Appleyard, B., 1984, The Culture Club, London, Boston,
    Faber and Faber
Arnheim, R., 1969, Visual Thinking, London, University of
    California Press
Ball, M., 1984, 'Small is Confident', Arts Express, no. 10,
    December 1984, London
Barrett, M., 1979, Art Education - A Strategy for Course
    Design, London, Heinemann Educational
Barron, F., 1955, 'The Disposition Towards Originality',
    Journal of Abnormal and Social Psychology, vol. 51,

212

Bibliography

1955
Barron, F., 1958, 'The Psychology of Imagination', in
  Coopersmith, S. (ed.), Frontier of Psychological
  Research - Readings from Scientific American, San
  Francisco, Freeman
Bartley, S.H., 1980, Introduction to Visual Perception, New
  York, Harper and Row
Belbin, E. and Belbin, R.M., 1972 Problems in Adult
  Retraining, London, Heinemann Educational
Bentley, E. (ed.), 1972, The Theory of the Modern Stage: An
  Introduction to Modern Theatre and Drama,
  Harmondsworth, Penguin
Beveridge, W.M., 1935, 'Racial Differences in Phenomenal
  Regression', British Journal of Psychology, 26, pp. 59-62
Beveridge, W.M., 1939, 'Some Racial Differences in
  Perception', British Journal of Psychology, 30, pp. 57-64
Bion, W.R., 1961, Experiences in Groups, London, Tavistock
Bloom, B.S., 1965, Taxonomy of Educational Objectives,
  London, Longman
Bolton, G.M., 1977, 'Psychical Distancing in Acting', The
  British Journal of Aesthetics, vol. 17, no. 1
Bolton, G.M., 1984, Drama as Education: An Argument for
  Placing Drama at the Centre of the Curriculum,
  Harlow, Longman
Bourdieu, P., 1974, 'The School as a Conservative Force', in
  Eggleston, J., Contemporary Research in the Sociology
  of Education, London, Methuen
Bourdieu, P., 1977a, 'Cultural Reproduction and Social
  Reproduction', in Karabel, J., and Halsey, A.H., Power
  and Ideology in Education, New York, Oxford University
  Press, pp. 487-511
Bourdieu, P., 1977b, Outline of a Theory of Practice,
  Cambridge, Cambridge University Press
Braden, S., 1978, Artists and People, London, Henley, etc.,
  Routledge and Kegan Paul
Braun, E., 1982, The Director and the State, From
  Naturalism to Grotowski, London, Methuen
Brinson, P. 1981, 'Adult Education Through Dance', in Jones,
  D.J. and Chadwick, A.F., Adult Education and the Arts,
  Nottingham, University of Nottingham, Department of
  Adult Education
Brookfield, S.D., 1986, Understanding and Facilitating Adult
  Learning, Milton Keynes, Open University
Brookfield, S., 1982, 'Evaluation Models and Adult
  Education', Studies in Adult Education, vol. 14,

213

September 1982, Leicester, (National Institute of Adult Education (NIAE)

Bruce, V. and Green, P., 1985, Visual Perception, Physiology Psychology and Ecology, New Jersey, Lawrence Erlbaum

Calouste Gulbenkian Foundation, 1982, The Arts in Schools - Principles, Practice and Provision, London, Calouste Gulbenkian Foundation

Child, I.L., 1970, 'The Problem of Objectivity in Esthetic Value', in Pappas, G. (ed.), Concepts in Art and Education, New York, Macmillan

Cohen, D., 1977, Creativity, What is it? New York, M. Evans and Co.

Coonan, R., 1985, 'Artists in Residence' Education Bulletin, no. 17, London, ACGB

Council of Europe, 1984, 'Berlin: Ministers adopt Declaration on Cultural Objectives', in Forum 2/84, Strasbourg, Council of Europe

Dennis, W., 1960, 'The Human Figure Drawings of Bedouins', Journal of Social Psychology, 52, pp. 209-19

Department of Education and Science, 1971, Art in Schools, London, Her Majesty's Stationery Office

Ehrenzweig, A., 1968, The Hidden Order of Art, London, Weidenfield and Nicolson

Elsey, B., 1968, Social Theory Perspectives on Adult Education, Nottingham, Department of Adult Education, University of Nottingham

Field, D. and Newick, J., 1973, The Study of Education and Art, London, Routledge and Kegan Paul

Fletcher, J.M., 1982, '"The Glory of the Female Sex", Women Artists c. 1500-1800', in Women's Art Show 1550 - 1970, Nottingham, Nottingham Castle Museum

Freeman, J., Butcher, H.J. and Christie, T. (eds), 1968, Creativity - A Selective Review of Research, London, Society for Research into Higher Education Ltd.

Freire, P., 1972a, Cultural Action for Freedom, Harmondsworth, Penguin

Freire, P., 1972b, Pedagogy of the Oppressed, translated by M.B. Ramer, Harmondsworth, Penguin

Freire, P., 1973, 'By Learning They Can Teach', Convergence, vol. 6, no. 1

Gagne, R.M., 1975, The Conditions of Learning, New York, Holt, Rinehart and Winston

Gibson, J.J., 1966, The Senses Considered as Perceptual Systems, Boston, Houghton Mifflin

Gibson, J.J., 1979, The Ecological Approach to Visual
    Perception, Boston, Houghton Mifflin
Gibson, R., 1986, Critical Theory and Education, London,
    Sydney, etc. Hodder and Stoughton
Gordon, W.J.J., 1961, Synectics - the Development of
    Creative Capacity, New York, Harper and Row
Greer, G., 1979, The Obstacle Race, London, Picador
Gregory, R.L. and Wallace, J.G., 1963, Recovery from Early
    Blindness, Exp. Psychol. Monogra., Cambridge
    (England), Whole No. 2
Gregory, R.L., 1970, The Intelligent Eye, London,
    Weidenfield and Nicolson
Gregory, R.L., 1973, Eye and Brain, the Psychology of
    Seeing, London, Weidenfield and Nicolson
Groombridge, B., 1983, 'Adult Education and the Education
    of Adults' in Tight, M. (ed.), 1983a
Gulbenkian Foundation, 1982, Arts in Schools, London,
    Calouste Gulbenkian Foundation
Habermas, J., 1970, Toward a Rational Society: Student
    Protest, Science and Politics, Boston MA, Beacon Press
Habermas, J., 1974, Theory and Practice, London,
    Heinemann
Hamby, C., 1984, 'Dance and the Dancer', British Journal of
    Aesthetics, vol. 24, no. 1
Harris, J.S., 1970, Government Patronage of the Arts in
    Great Britain, Chicago and London, The University of
    Chicago Press
Heathcote, D., 1984, in Johnson, L. and O'Neill, C. (eds),
    Dorothy Heathcote, Collected Writings on Education
    and Drama, London, Melbourne, etc., Hutchinson
Hebb, D.O., 1949, The Organisation of Behavior, New York,
    Wiley
Hegel, G.W.F., 1979, Introduction to Aesthetics, translated
    by T.M. Knox with an Interpretative Essay by Charles
    Karelis, Oxford, Clarendon Press
Herbert, E.L., 1961, 'The Use of Group Techniques in the
    Training of Teachers', Human Relations, xiv, 251-63
Herskovits, M.J., 1948, Man and His Works, New York,
    Knopf
Herskovits, M.J., 1959, 'Art and Value', in Redfield, R.,
    Herskovits, M.J. and Ekholm, G.F., Aspect of Primitive
    Art, New York, The Museum of Primitive Art, pp. 42-97
Hochberg, J.E., 1978, Perception, New Jersey, Prentice Hall
Hoggart, R., 1985, 'False Populisms, False Elitisms', Arts
    Express, no. 12, February 1985, London

Bibliography

Holmes, A.C., 1964, Health Education in Developing
    Countries, London, Nelson
Horkheimer, M., 1972, Critical Theory; Selected Essays,
    New York, Herder and Herder
Horkheimer, M., 1974, Critique of Instrumental Reason,
    New York, Seabury Press
Horne, D., 1986, The Public Culture - The Triumph of
    Industrialism, London, Sydney, etc., Pluto
Houle, C.O., 1974, The Design of Education, San Francisco,
    Washington, London, Jossey Bass
Hudson, L., 1966, Contrary Imaginations - A Psychological
    Study of the English Schoolboy, London, Methuen
Hudson, W., 1960, 'Pictorial Depth Perception in Sub-
    cultural Groups in Africa, Journal of Social Psychology,
    52, pp. 183-208
Hunt, J., 1982, 'Art with a Capital "A", Woman With a
    Capital "W"', in Women's Art Show 1550 - 1970,
    Nottingham, Nottingham Castle Museum
Hutchison, R., 1982, The Politics of the Arts Council,
    London, Sinclaire Browne
Jarvis, P., 1983, Adult and Continuing Education - Theory
    and Practice, London, Croom Helm
Jones, D.J., 1975, 'Evaluation and Assessment in Adult Art
    Classes', Unpublished M.Ed. Thesis, University of
    Manchester
Jones, D.J., 1978, 'Teaching Art to Adults', Adult Education
    vol. 51, no. 1., Leicester, National Institute of Adult
    Education
Jones, D.J., 1985, Creativity, in the series 'Adults:
    Psychological   and   Educational   Perspectives',
    Nottingham, University of Nottingham, Department of
    Adult Education
Jones, D.J. and Chadwick, A.F. (eds), 1981, Adult Education
    and the Arts, Nottingham, University of Nottingham,
    Department of Adult Education
Jor, F., 1976, The Demystification of Culture, Strasbourg,
    Council of Europe
Jung, C.G., 1964, Man and His Symbols, London, Aldus
Kant, I., 1933, Critique of Pure Reason, 1781, translated by
    N. Kemp Smith, London, Macmillan
Keddie, N., 1980, 'Adult Education: An Ideology of
    Individualism' in Thompson, J.L., 1980, op. cit.
Kelly, O., 1984, Community, Art and the State: Storming
    the Citadels, London, Comedia
Khan, N., 1976, The Arts Britain Ignores - The Arts of

Ethnic Minorities in Britain, London, Community Relations Commission

Klein, J., 1956, The Study of Groups, London, Routledge and Kegan Paul

Klein, J., 1961, Working with Groups, London, Hutchinson

Knott, C.A., 1987, 'I Can't Wait for Wednesday' The Crafts in Adult Education, London, The Crafts Council

Knowles, M.S., 1980, The Modern Practice of Adult Education - From Pedagogy to Andragogy, Chicago, Follett Publishing Company

Latta, R., 1904, 'Notes on a case of successful operation for congenital cataract in an adult', British Journal of Psychology, 1, pp. 135-50

Lawson, K.H., 1982, Analysis and Ideology: Conceptual Essays on the Education of Adults, Nottingham, Department of Adult Education, University of Nottingham

Legge, D., The Education of Adults in Britain, Milton Keynes, The Open University Press

Lewis, J., Morley, D. and Southwood, R., 1986, Art - Who Needs It? The Audience for Community Arts, London, Comedia

London, I.D., 1960, 'A Russian Report on the Post-Operative Newly Seeing', American Journal of Psychology, 73, pp. 478-82

Long, H.B., 1987, New Perspectives on the Education of Adults in the United States, London, Croom Helm

MacKinnon, D.W., 1962a, 'The Personality Correlates of Creativity: A Study of American Architects', in Proceedings of the Fourteenth Congress on Applied Psychology, vol. 2, Munkguard

MacKinnon, D.W., 1962b, 'The Nature and Nurture of Creative Talent', American Psychologist, 17, pp. 484-95

MacKinnon, D.W., 1965, 'Personality and the Realisation of Creative Potential', American Psychologist, 20(4), pp. 273-81

Magarshack, D., 1972, 'Stanislavsky' in Bentley, E. (ed.), The Theory of the Modern Stage, An Introduction to Modern Theatre and Drama, Harmondsworth, Penguin

Marcuse, H., 1956, Eros and Civilisation, London, Routledge and Kegan Paul

Marcuse, H., 1964, One-Dimensional Man, Boston MA, Beacon Press

Martin, B., 1981, A Sociology of Contemporary Cultural Change, Oxford, Basil Blackwell

217

Martindale, C., 1976, 'Creativity: Its all in the head', Psychology Today, March 1976, vol. 2, no. 3, pp. 16-19
Maslow, A.H., 1968, Towards a Psychology of Being, New York, Van Nostrand Reinhold Company
May, R., 1975, The Courage to Create, London, Collins
Mee and Wiltshire, 1978, Structure and Performance in Adult Education, London and New York, Longman
Mennel, S., 1976, Cultural Policy in Towns, Strasbourg, Council of Europe
Mezirow, J., 1977, 'Perspective Transformation' in Studies in Adult Education, vol. 9, no. 2, Leicester, NIAE
Mezirow, J., 1981, 'A Critical Theory of Adult Learning and Education', in Adult Education, vol. 32, no. 1, Washington
Minihan, J., 1977, The Nationalisation of Culture - The Development of State Subsidies to the Arts in Great Britain, London, Hamish Hamilton
Moulin, R., 1976, Public Aid for Creation in the Plastic Arts, Strasbourg, Council of Europe
Munro, T., 1963, 'The Psychology of Art: Past, Present, Future', in Hogg, J. (ed.), 1969, Psychology and the Visual Arts, Harmondsworth, Penguin Books
Nairne, S., 1987, State of the Art, Ideas and Images in the 1980s, London, Chatto and Windus in collaboration with Channel Four Television Company Limited
Neumark, V., 1986, 'What Have You Got To Be Proud Of?', in Arts Express no. 26, April 1986, London
Nissel, M., 1983, Facts about the Arts - A Summary of Available Statistics, London, Policy Studies Institute
Nottingham Andragogy Group, 1983, Towards a Developmental Theory of Andragogy, Nottingham, Department of Adult Education, University of Nottingham
Nunn, P.G., 1982, 'Women Artists in the Nineteenth Century', in Women's Art Show 1550 - 1970, Nottingham, Nottingham Castle Museum
Ornstein, R., 1975, 'In Two Minds', Psychology Today, (UK), vol. 1, no. 2, May 1975
Owusu, K., The Struggle for Black Arts in Britain - What Can we Consider Better than Freedom, London, Comedia
Parker, R. and Pollock, G., 1981, Old Mistresses: Women, Art and Ideology, London, Routledge and Kegan Paul
Pearson, N., 1982, The State and the Visual Arts, Milton Keynes, Open University

Pick, J., Managing The Arts? The British Experience, London, Rhinegold

Read, Sir H., 1968, 'The Problem of Internationalism in Art', The Magazine, Oct. 68, no. 7, London, Institute of Contemporary Arts

Read, H., 1961, Education Through Art, London, Faber and Faber

Redcliffe-Maud, Lord, 1976, Support for the Arts in England and Wales, London, Calouste Gulbenkian Foundation

Redfern, H.B., 1986, Questions in Aesthetic Education, London, Allen and Unwin

Redington, C., 1983, Can Theatre Teach? Oxford, Pergamon

Reid, L.A., 1985, 'Art and Knowledge', in British Journal of Aesthetics, vol. 25, no. 2

Richardson, E., 1967, Group Study for Teachers, London, Routledge and Kegan Paul

Rigby, R., 1982, Community Arts Information Pack, Manchester and London, The Shelton Trust (Manchester) and the Council of Regional Arts Organisations (London)

Robertson, S.M., 1963, Rosegarden and Labyrinth - A Study in Art Education, London, Routledge and Kegan Paul

Rogers, A., 1986, Teaching Adults, Milton Keynes and Philadelphia, Open University Press

Rogers, C.R., 1961, On Becoming a Person, London, Constable and Company

Ross, M., 1978, The Creative Arts, London, Heinemann Educational Books

Rumelhart, D.E., McClelland, J.L. and the P.D.P. Research Group, 1986, Parallel Distributed Processing. Explorations in the Microstructure of Cognition, vol. 1 Foundations, London, M.I.T. Press

Sanford, A.J., 1987, The Mind of Man - Models of Human Understanding, Brighton, The Harvester Press

Scriven, M., 1967, 'The Methodology of Evaluation', in Gagné, R.M., Scriven, M. and Tyler, R.W. (eds), Perspectives in Curriculum Evaluation, AERA Monograph no. 1. Skokie, Illinois, Rand McNally

Scriven, M., 1972, 'Pros and Cons About Goal Free Evaluation', in Evaluation Comment, vol. 3, no. 4, pp. 1-4

Segall, M.H., Campbell, D.T. and Herskovits, M.J., 1966, The Influence of Culture on Visual Perception, Indianapolis, New York, Kansas City, The Bobbs-Merrill Company

Senden, M. von, 1932, Raum und Gestaltauffassung bei
   Operietan Blindgebornen vor und nach der Operation,
   Leipzig, Barth
Shaw, Sir R., 1977, ACGB Annual Report, London, Arts
   Council of Great Britain
Shaw, Sir R., 1987, The Arts and the People, London,
   Jonathan Cape
Simpson, J.A., 1976, Towards Cultural Democracy,
   Strasbourg, Council of Europe
Sparshott, F., 1985, 'Some Dimensions of Dance Meaning', in
   British Journal of Aesthetics, vol. 25, no. 2
Stufflebeam, D.L., 1968, Evaluation as Enlightenment for
   Decision Making, Columbus, Evaluation Centre, Ohio
   State University
Stufflebeam, D.L., 1975, 'Evaluation as a Community
   Education Process', Community Education Journal
   (USA), vol. 5, no. 2, pp.7-12
Stufflebeam, D.L. et al., 1971, Educational Evaluation and
   Decision-Making in Education, Itasca, Ill., Peacock
Stumbo, H.W., 1970, 'Three Bases for Research and Teaching
   in the Arts: Subjective, Objective and Projective' in
   Pappas, G. (ed.), Concepts in Art and Education,
   London, Macmillan
Styan, J.L., 1981, Modern drama in theory and practice, vol.
   3, Expressionism and Epic Theatre, London, New York,
   etc., Cambridge University Press
Symes, C., 1983, 'Creativity: A Divergent Point of View',
   The Journal of Aesthetic Education, vol. 17, no. 2,
   Summer, 1983, pp. 83-96
Thomas, J.E., 1982, Radical Adult Education: Theory and
   Practice, Nottingham, Department of Adult Education,
   University of Nottingham
Thompson, J.L. (ed.), 1980, Adult Education for à Change,
   London, Hutchinson
Thouless, R.H., 1933, 'A Racial Difference in Perception',
   Journal of Social Psychology, 4, pp. 330-9
Tight, M. (ed.), 1983a, Education for Adults: vol. I, Adult
   Learning and Education, London, Croom Helm in
   association with the Open University
Tight, M. (ed.), 1983b, Education for Adults: vol. II,
   Opportunities for Adult Education, London, Croom
   Helm in association with the Open University
Tough, A.M., 1968, Why Adults Learn: A Study of the Major
   Reasons for Beginning and Continuing a Learning
   Project, Toronto, Ontario Institute for Studies in

Education
Tough, A.M., 1978, 'Major Learning Efforts: Recent
    Research and Future Directions', Adult Education (USA)
    1978, vol. 28, no. 4, pp. 250-63
Tough, A.M., 1979, The Adult's Learning Projects: A Fresh
    Approach to Theory and Practice in Adult Learning,
    Toronto, Ontario Institute for Studies in Education
Trist, E.L. and Sofer, C., 1959, Explorations in Group
    Relations, Leicester, Leicester University Press
Underwood, G., 1976, Attention and Memory, Oxford,
    Pergamon
Wilding, J.M., 1982, Perception, From Sense to Object,
    London, Hutchinson and Co.
Williams, R., 1983, Keywords, London, Fontana
Williams, R., 1986, Culture, London, Fontana
Wittgenstein, L., 1953, Philosophical Investigations,
    translated by Anscombe, G.E.M., Oxford, Basil
    Blackwell
Wollheim, R., 1968, Art and Its Objects - An Introduction to
    Aesthetics, New York, Evanston, London, Harper and
    Row

INDEX